Intersex

Intersex

CATHERINE HARPER

Oxford • New York

25.00

English edition
First published in 2007 by
Berg
Editorial offices:
First Floor, Angel Court, 81 St Clements Street, Oxford OX4 1AW, UK
175 Fifth Avenue, New York, NY 10010, USA

Berg is the imprint of Oxford International Publishers Ltd.

Library of Congress Cataloging-in-Publication Data
Harper, Catherine.
    Intersex / Catherine Harper. — English ed.
        p. cm.
    Includes bibliographical references.
    ISBN-13: 978-1-84520-182-1 (cloth)
    ISBN-10: 1-84520-182-5 (cloth)
    ISBN-13: 978-1-84520-183-8 (pbk.)
    ISBN-10: 1-84520-183-3 (pbk.)
    1. Hermaphroditism. 2. Hermaphroditism—Biography. I. Title.

RC883.H37 2007
362.196'69400922—dc22   2007020054

British Library Cataloguing-in-Publication Data
A catalogue record for this book is available from the British Library.

ISBN   978 1 84520 182 1 (Cloth)
           978 1 84520 183 8 (Paper)

Typeset by Avocet Typeset, Chilton, Aylesbury, Bucks
Printed in the United Kingdom by Biddles Ltd, King's Lynn.

www.bergpublishers.com

Contents

This book has been produced with the support of the University College for the Creative Arts, UK, and Arts Council England. Its author is affiliated to the University of Brighton, UK.

Acknowledgements

I would like to thank all those – intersexed and otherwise – who spoke to me, met me and corresponded with me in the course of this research. Almost all subject names used are pseudonyms and the cases are published here with permission. For their candour and generosity – whatever their position and opinion – many thanks.

I am most especially grateful to the University College for the Creative Arts, UK, for generously supporting this project through the Research Fund and the Research Sabbatical Fund. This enabled me to spend valuable writing time at the Tyrone Guthrie Centre at Annaghmakerrig, Ireland, as well as to travel to interview subjects and to contextualize my research.

I would also wish to gratefully acknowledge the Arts Council England's support of my work, with particular thanks to Bob Martin at Arts Council England (South East).

I am grateful to the Visual Arts Department of Goldsmiths College, London, for a Research Bursary, and to both Professor Janis Jefferies and Dr Janet Hand for their research rigour at the genesis of this project in 2001. I am additionally grateful to Central Saint Martins College of Art and Design, London, for financially supporting my stay at Cill Riallaig, Ireland, in 2003, during which I drafted this book's outline.

At Berg Publishers, I wish to thank Kathryn Earle for giving me the chance to publish this work, Hannah Shakespeare for her tremendous guidance during its development, Ken Bruce for his patient work on its design and production, and Julene Knox for her thorough copy-editing. My anonymous peer-reviewer was very helpful and affirming, and I can formalize my thanks to that person here.

Lucy Gundry was invaluable as an assistant to the final edit.

I would also like to sincerely thank Caroline Gallagher-Lavery who encouraged me for years to write a book and who has been such a good friend always.

Amanda Stonham and Tina Cole provided excellent proof-reading as well as detailed suggestions for amendments; Zac Al-Moajil-Cole and Grace Al-Moajil-Cole were very patient and helpful. I'm eternally grateful for the support and encouragement I've received from them.

Special thanks and love always to Amanda.

CHAPTER 1

Introduction

Individuals frequently contact the Intersex Society of North America (ISNA) because they think they may be intersexed. The ISNA indicates that generally those who *are* intersexed do not need to look far for the evidence:

> the evidence is in their own bodies ... women who do not have ovaries, men who don't have testes, women who have no clitoris or inner labia, people who remember multiple genital surgeries during childhood and scars in their genital area and abdomen, people who have ambiguous genitalia ...
>
> Sometimes people tell us that they have fairly typical genitals, but they think that they must have been born intersex and subjected to a sex change as an infant. Surgeons, even today, cannot create 'normal' looking genitals, and surgery was much poorer decades ago. Thus, if you have genitals that look like most women (or men), then you were surely born with these. (www.isna.org/book/print/716, accessed 13 March 2006)

The Uncanny 'Hermaphrodite'

The Observer newspaper's article 'In Ancient Greece, She'd Have Been a God. In Wales, They Spit on Her' (Hugill 1998) detailed some of the life of Linda Roberts, born in London during the Second World War, and then living in a remote part of Wales. The author described Roberts as 'born with a penis and a vagina', and named her a 'hermaphrodite' (ibid.: 7). While the author was sympathetic to his subject, the reference to 'dual genitalia' is inaccurate. Roberts was probably intersexed, and – in all likelihood – exhibited genital ambiguity.

In 1933, Sigmund Freud acknowledged a significant human desire to know with certainty what sex a person is: 'when you meet a human being, the first distinction you make is "male or female?" and you are accustomed to make the distinction with unhesitating certainty' (1933: 113). Freud's text continued by describing sex as a biological fact, with anatomy as stable, binary and indisputable (he subsequently distinguished between *anatomical sex* and the less fixed notion of *gender*). Freud's articulation of cultural investment in the certitude and familiarity of male and female is important, and intersex represents a notable challenge to the 'unhesitating certainty' Freud described as customary.

Earlier, in 1919, Freud had introduced his concept of the uncanny as 'that class of the frightening which leads back to what is known of old and long familiar ...' (1919: 220). Is it the very familiarity and certainty of normative and exclusive male and female sexual anatomy that makes the genital ambiguity of intersex both uneasily familiar and sufficiently different to activate Freud's uncanny? The 'hermaphroditic' body combines both male and female sex signifiers in what might be considered an uncanny merger. Freud further defines his uncanny as that which 'ought to have remained secret and hidden but has come to light' (ibid.: 241), and there is no doubt that this resonates with a cultural appreciation of intersex as taboo, a counter to 'infant purity'. Uncertainty of sex – especially in the newborn – activates parental and cultural shame, guilt and panic. Faced with a 'hermaphrodite' baby, many parents find it intolerable that their child is neither boy nor girl. They fear for their infant's future, and they fear for themselves. The drive to surgically 'normalize' the genitalia of those infant intersexuals whose genitals diverge from a familiar norm is arguably connected to a desire to dispel the force of uncanniness, with its associations of superstition, deathliness and negation.

'Hermaphrodites' and Intersexuals

> [U]ntil recently no-one wanted to know about us; except for the quaint bit of mythology but certainly not as the living reality ...
>
> Chris, correspondence 21 May 2004

The word 'hermaphrodite' arguably carries mythological and fetishistic associations that serve to dehumanize and stigmatize the living and real individual to whom the word is applied. If an intersexed newborn is considered uncanny, freakish, mythic or monstrous, as may be implied by the word, and labelled as and by 'its' genitals, then perhaps it becomes easier to advocate what is considered by some as 'sexually mutilating' (Chase 1998a) surgery on those genitals. Alice Domurat Dreger (1998b), for example, notes that the conventions of medical ethics become vulnerable in instances of 'hermaphrodite' births where infant genitals are ambiguous, and non-consensual, non-urgent treatment can rapidly be normalized. The secrecy and stigma surrounding intersex perpetuates the perception of monstrosity, indicating to intersexed people that their 'defect' is so monstrous it should be erased.

While 'intersexual' is now often preferred to 'hermaphrodite', the latter is adopted ironically in, for example, the Intersex Society of North America newsletter *Hermaphrodites with Attitude*: 'it is time for us to counter physicians' assertion that a life as a hermaphrodite would be worthless, by embracing the word and asserting our identity as hermaphrodite. This is the way to break the vicious cycle in which shame produces silence, silence condones surgery, and surgery produces more shame' (Anon 1994: 6).

Interviewee Anja proudly wears a T-shirt proclaiming *Schon mal mit nem Zwitter gesprochen? Hier ist die Gelegenheit (Ever talked to a hermaphrodite? Here is your chance)*. Anja reclaims the previously pejorative 'Zwitter' (German for 'hermaphrodite') to re-value herself as intersexed. And one of Roz Mortimer's subjects, quoted on the Wonderdog website in relation to her film *Gender Trouble* (2002), finds 'hermaphrodite' 'rather poetic', using it particularly to dispel its traditional 'hint of freakishness' (Mortimer 2002). 'Hermaphrodite' continues to be used widely in medical literature, although 'intersexed' more accurately describes those with conditions and configurations neither wholly male nor wholly female. Unlike mythological 'hermaphrodites', intersexuals are present in this world. Variations in genetic formulation, hormonal effects before and after birth, and developmental atypicalities with unknown causes result daily and globally in the birth of 'boys' with tiny or absent penises and/or undescended testicles, 'girls' with enlarged clitorises or no vaginas, or infants whose chromosomes, organs and hormones are mixtures of those typical for girls or boys. In the face of intersexual evidence, however, medical science continues to insist on perpetuation of a two-sex system, determining that those babies who vary from easy definition still need to be defined within that system.

Just as developments in medical science in the nineteenth and early twentieth centuries resulted in a surge of reported 'hermaphrodite' cases, the development of intersex advocacy in the later twentieth and early twenty-first centuries has seen much wider exposure of intersex and the variety of its presentations. Estimations of intersex frequency vary in quality and exactitude (Blackless *et al.* 2000): firm guidelines for the definition and diagnosis of some intersex conditions do not exist; definitions of a typical male and female vary somewhat; and the frequency of some intersex conditions differs for different populations. These factors reinforce the elusive nature of the apparently mythical 'hermaphrodite'.

Chase asserts that at least 1 in 2,000 births is sufficiently sex ambiguous 'that professionals cannot easily determine what sex to label the baby' (1998a: unpaginated). Blackless (Blackless *et al.* 2000) proposes deviation from the 'ideal' dimorphic body in the United States may be 1 in 50 of live births, of whom 1–2 in every 1,000 subsequently receive 'corrective' genital surgery, while Professor Milton Diamond of the John A. Burns School of Medicine, University of Hawaii, and the Pacific Center for Sex and Society, Hawaii, asserts that 'the best stats on intersex conditions … are those in the work of

Dr. Anne Fausto-Sterling' (correspondence 2 April 2002), specifically refer-encing Table 3.2 in Fausto-Sterling (2000: 53). Fausto-Sterling (in Blackless *et al.* 2000) is also the source for statistics posted on the website of the Intersex Society of North America, and the ISNA synopsis simplifies what are complex and condition-specific figures:

> If you ask experts at medical centers how often a child is born so noticeably atypical in terms of genitalia that a specialist in sex differentiation is called in, the number comes out to about 1 in 1500 to 1 in 2000 births. But a lot more people than that are born with subtler forms of sex anatomy variations, some of which won't show up until later in life. (www.isna.org/faq/frequency, accessed 13 June 2004)

If 1 in 2,000 infants exhibit noticeable genital atypicality, then around 320 such babies would have been born in England and Wales in 2004 alone (since there were 639,700 live births in that year). Sarah Creighton, Consultant Obstetrician and Gynaecologist at Elizabeth Garrett Anderson Hospital, University College London Hospitals, UK, is somewhat sceptical of these figures, but indicates that current statistical monitoring for intersex is in disarray, and there is an urgent need for formal collection of data before it is possible to say with any accuracy how frequent intersex is (interview 9 February 2006).

Orientation of the Subject

Dreger's book *Hermaphrodites and the Medical Invention of Sex* (1998a) charts how scientists and medical practitioners historically encountered intersexuals in the nineteenth and early twentieth centuries. Dreger indicates how those encounters both informed the evolution of scientific understanding of human sex development and contributed to the development of surgical capabilities by which to define and shape sex 'normality'. Tony Briffa, President of the AIS Support Group Australia, suggests that around 25 per cent of intersexed infants have visibly ambiguous genitalia (correspondence 3 April 2002). Since the 1950s, many of these infants born within Western medical culture have been subjected to early genital surgery, frequently reinforced by hormone treatment. Surgeries include: the removal of clitoral tissue perceived as over-large; the reconfiguration of penises with openings other than at their tip; removal of ovarian or testicular tissue deemed inappropriate to the sex assigned; etc. These procedures sound like the reassuring correction of wrongs, but there have been many associated problems. A medical convention developed, for example, of non-disclosure of the details of their conditions and treatments to intersexuals as they matured. Some intersexed people discover only in adulthood that they are intersexed, that they were operated on in infancy, that their sex was *determined* surgically, and that there may have been other treatment options that are now no longer available to them as adults. Their own bodies become uncanny signifiers, at once familiar and unfamiliar. This 'stigma of the self', coupled with social-cultural stigmatizing, has led many to suffer psychiatric difficulties and sexual dysfunction. Others mourn the permanent loss of either an intersex identity or a sex identification opposite to that assigned to them.

Until recently, follow-up research to determine the long-term effects of such surgeries has been poor. More current research indicates that cosmetic (rather than life-saving) genital surgery in infancy is frequently not wholly successful (Creighton *et al.* 2001a), and the secrecy surrounding many such diagnoses has been described as damaging and destructive to the subject's sexual, erotic and emotional health (Hendricks 2000 referencing Chase). While those who are dissatisfied are probably most vocal, and while those commenting on their own surgeries are describing procedures carried out years before (Ransley, interview 6 September 2005), there are significant numbers of adults who express rage and despair at their non-consensual loss of erotic sensation and self-determination: 'having been one of the folks who got mangled (relatively lightly) in childhood – I can generally control my anger these days, but at times in the past (before I worked through it all), it could reduce me to a wreck if I dared think about it too much … it's a wicked business …' (Claire, correspondence 29 March 2002).

Sex of Rearing

An intersexed person is holistically defined as one 'whose biology includes an identifiable mixture of male and female characteristics, regardless of the appearance of the genitalia at birth' (Diamond 2004a: v). Professor Milton Diamond has long advocated a non-surgical route in the medical management and care of intersexed infants. He perceives recent significant changes in the US in respect of surgical treatment of intersexed infants: 'about 75% of the pediatric surgeons would no longer follow the protocols they followed [in the 1990s] … Currently they would be more in keeping with our recommendations' (correspondence 2 December 2005).

Diamond acknowledges a 'marked step forward' (2004a: iv) in critical and ethical examination of this subject, and cites a range of shifts – including the formation in 2000 of the (now disbanded) North American Task Force on Intersex to collect data on long-term outcomes of intersex treatment and management – as evidencing growing concerns for reflection on progress to date. The recommendations of the late 1990s to which Diamond refers above are detailed in Chapter 4, but broadly he (1999) and colleagues Kipnis (Kipnis and Diamond 1998) and Sigmundson (Diamond and Sigmundson 1997a) advocated:

- holistic examination of the infant rather than solely visual examination of the genitalia which tends towards precipitous appearance-based diagnosis;
- expert multi-disciplinary team diagnosis rather than an individual professional deciding on sex assignment and treatment;
- honest disclosure of intersex diagnosis as opposed to obfuscation or denial with resultant secrecy, stigma and shame;
- clear information and specialist counselling for parents to help them come to terms with diagnosis and to prepare them to best support their child;
- total patient and family confidentiality, respecting patient privacy, and enabling parents to process information privately and disclose it as they deem appropriate;
- decisive and informed determination of *sex of rearing*, with a moratorium on infant genital surgery (except in instances of unavoidable hazard to the child).

While Diamond emphasizes the third recommendation regarding honesty (correspondence 13 January 2007), the last – *sex of rearing* – is also key to *this* author's interest in his recommendations. Diamond held that, rather than permanently assigning sex to an intersexed infant via cosmetic surgery on its genitalia and associated hormone treatment, the child should be assigned sex without lasting changes to its body. The *sex of rearing* should be decided on the basis of a range of complex signifiers rather than solely on genital appearance:

- genetic sex (if that is straightforward);
- *in utero* and post-natal endocrine (hormone-related) events that will most likely affect development at puberty;
- genital configuration;
- the child's potential for sexual and social development through and after puberty.

When these are all considered, Diamond argues, a reconciled decision informs which sex – male or female – the intersexed child should be raised as. Diamond recommends that cosmetic genital surgery and major prolonged hormone treatment (except, for example, for the essential management of Congenital Adrenal Hyperplasia, an intersex condition with some potentially life-threatening complications detailed later) should be avoided until after puberty. Following the substantial changes puberty delivers, the patient can make informed consensual choices about any treatment to be undertaken, and take responsibility for its consequences. Diamond indicates that his recommendations are beginning to be adopted by a significant number of paediatric surgeons in the United States (correspondence 2 December 2005). This signals the initiation of a potentially different culture of intersex management where some surgeons who previously advocated surgery and hormonal prescription to 'correct' the ambiguous sex of intersexed infants are rethinking their practices.

The Sex Binary

There continues to be strong adherence to the sex binary (male and female), and only marginal interest in more radical approaches to sex – as more than two; or as a male-to-female continuum with intersex somewhere in the middle. Anne Fausto-Sterling, for example, in *Sexing the Body: Gender Politics and the Construction of Sexuality* (2000), argues for allowance of significant variation in human sex and sex-behaviours. She synthesizes material from discourses within social science, feminism, biology to form a position tolerant of flexibility and evolution in relation to a person's sex. Sharon E. Preves, in *Intersex and Identity: The Contested Self* (2003), examines the personal narratives of intersexed adults weighing up 'sexual deviance' against sexual conformity in their personal construction of sex identity, while Suzanne Kessler, in *Lessons from the Intersexed* (1998), concludes that it is unlikely that the exclusive sexual binary will be undone in the mainstream in the foreseeable future.

Kessler does, however, detect a gradual relaxation about genital variation (she prefers this term to genital ambiguity), and she welcomes this as potentially, eventually, unhooking genitals from signification of sex and therefore gender. Her thesis is that as long as a genital dichotomy is idealized, and surgery used to reinforce it, then '*genitals mean gender* [Kessler's emphasis]' (1998: 132). If variation – in the wide range of genitals understood as male, as female, *as well as those that are ambiguous or intersexed* – is accepted and normalized, then Kessler argues that we can let go of the 'responsibility and [the] burden' of gender (ibid.). She presses that we 'must use whatever means we have to give up on gender' (ibid.), insisting that to do so would be to understand bodies as *idiosyncratic* in their biology (sex), allowing *individuals* to operate *subjectively* in social-culture in terms of how they *act, look, evolve* (gender), and how they *sexually relate* (sexuality). In Kessler's scenario, heterosexist agendas, the need to 'normalize' bodies that do not conform to strict formulation, and the desire to *determine* sex, are contested.

The concept of a sexless utopia where gender is acted out rather than fixed (Butler 1990) and is therefore always a work-in-progress (Kessler 1998), and where the simple dichotomies of sex and gender, and the essentialisms of biological determinism, are destabilized within a biology increasingly understood as medically invented (Dreger 1998a), remains peripheral to mainstream thought. Separation of sex from gender, so that, for example, a female (sex term) can operate as a boy or man (gender terms), and a male (sex term) can operate as a girl or woman (gender term) continues to present a cultural challenge in actuality (Diamond and Beh 2006). Sarah Creighton at Elizabeth Garrett Anderson Hospital, London, highlights the 'innate conservatism of little children' in social-cultural environments where 'sex normality' (for which read sex dualism) is upheld (interview 9 February 2006). Without a change in social-cultural acceptance of intersex, she urges, raising an intersexed child openly and comfortably is problematic. Yet without this public presence it is difficult to appreciate intersex in actual rather than abstract terms. To Creighton, discourses currently developing between clinicians, academics and theorists in the field of sex and gender are potentially where these issues can begin to be addressed.

Kayla's Story

William Reiner, once a urologist at Johns Hopkins Medical Institutions, Baltimore, and subsequently trained as a psychiatrist, is one of those who surgically assigned sex to intersexed newborns in the 1970s and 1980s. Reiner's change of practice came when he provided psychiatric support for a troubled 7-year-old patient called Kayla (pseudonym), a genetic male born without a penis, whose testicles had been removed in infancy, and who had been raised as a girl. Reiner's psychological tests indicated that Kayla exhibited 'male' gender-typical behaviours and self-conception. Reiner and Kayla's parents concluded that she ought to know of her genetic sex, her original genital anomaly and her treatment. In Hendricks' report of Reiner's conversation with Kayla (2000: unpaginated), Kayla is referred to using male pronouns:

'His eyes opened about as wide as eyes could open,' recalls Reiner. 'He climbed into my lap and wrapped his arms around me and stayed like that'.

As Reiner cradled the child in his arms, he felt as though an enormous weight had been lifted, and he himself was overcome with emotion. The child remained in his arms without moving for half an hour.

Reiner now believes children are born either boys or girls, and that no matter what happens to them, be it surgery or rearing, they remain that way.

'The sense of who one is ... is a crucial existential aspect of humanity. It is powerful and inborn'. The absence or presence of a penis is incidental. 'The most important sex organ is the brain'.

Reiner now says that surgeons ought to hold off on surgically castrating patients like Kayla ... 'if it's not life threatening, I would favor prudence'.

Absence of penis, castration in infancy and nurture as a girl were not enough to undermine Kayla's sense of self as closer to 'maleness' than to 'femaleness'. While still upholding sex as binary, Reiner here radically unbridles 'being a boy' from 'having a penis', seemingly activating something of the separation of genitals and gender proposed by Kessler (1998). And, lest Kayla's case study becomes an argument for pursuit of genetics as the determinant of sex, there are many instances of children developing gender identities at odds with their genetic patterning as much as at odds with their anatomical and/or hormonal formation. As much as Reiner's reconsideration of Kayla illuminated a dislocation of gender and genitals, there are arguments too for a dislocation between gender and chromosomes, gender and hormones, and gender and internal as well as external anatomy.

While Reiner exemplifies the conceptual shifts Diamond detects in current US thinking, Creighton is less certain of such shifts in the UK. She concludes that because of the lack of long-term reliable follow-up of infant genital surgeries the 'evidence base for and against surgical sex assignment is in stalemate' (Creighton and Liao 2004a: 659). Her feeling, however, is that there is a tendency among colleagues to discuss cases more both with their peers and with parents, and that – certainly in clitoral surgery – there 'is a lot more effort to do as little as possible, to damage the nerve as little as possible' (interview 9 February 2006). Creighton also reports movement in parental attitudes towards later surgery and growing acceptance of slight genital variation (Creighton reported in Ahuja 2004).

Sex Development

Intersex occurs when sexual development and differentiation *in utero* is atypical, and a baby is born, for example, with 'a blend of both male and female internal and/or external genitalia' (Creighton and Liao 2004a: 659). This may be obviously signified in ambiguous genitalia or it may manifest in a range of internal and external configurations. For example, the infant may have apparently female external genitalia, but have one ovary and one testis, with that singular testis being hidden inside. Alternatively, there may be internalized gonads that contain both ovarian and testicular tissue mixed together. Similarly, or in addition, genetic configurations and hormonal balances may be atypical for a regular male or female.

The sexed body's development is fascinating and complex, and there are many references in the literature to divisions and misalignments between genetic sex, gonadal sex, hormonal sex, internal reproductive morphology and/or external genitalia. In a *typical* newborn these components are in agreement, and the infant is announced as male or female. In the intersexed subject, the result of these divisions and misalignments can be extremely diverse.

Alvarez-Nava (Alvarez-Nava *et al.* 2004), for example, references the overexposure of a genetically female foetus to androgens during gestation. Androgen is a masculinizing hormone that in males is responsible for penis growth, facial and body hair development, muscles and skeleton growth, and voice deepening. In males androgen comes from the testes and the adrenal glands, whereas in females nearly all androgen comes from the adrenal glands, with only a small contribution from the ovaries. For Alvarez-Nava's subject, adrenal over-production of androgen on the part of the pregnant mother resulted in foetal virilization (a condition that used to be called 'female pseudohermaphroditism'). A penis-like phallus developed where the clitoris would typically be, though obviously no testicles emerged. Genetic sex was of course unaffected by these developments, and the child remained an unambiguous genetic female. The question for parents and paediatricians was whether this infant should be permitted to grow up without genital surgery (raised either as a boy without testicles or a girl with an atypically large clitoris), or whether surgeons should excise and bury the penis-like phallus, and have the child raised as a girl with an absent or reduced clitoris. Currently the most likely outcome is the latter, even though there is evidence that sexual sensation is compromised by such treatment.

Genetic sex itself may be complicated, and is no guarantee of how a child will look or feel. Chromosomal mosaics occur where the infant is not exclusively genetically male or female, or where cells contain different combinations of sex chromosomes. Zucker (Zucker *et al.* 1987) describes a 'genetically intersexed' infant with anomalous penile genitalia and no external testes (therefore not dissimilar in appearance to the genetic female above). This baby was assigned male at birth (without genital surgery), and then re-assigned female at two months (with genital surgery carried out at nine months). In surgery, the infant's 2.5 cm phallus – which had been named as a penis for the first two months of life while the child was considered male, but then was renamed as a clitoris when the child was re-presented as female – was almost entirely removed. That renamed tissue, first a small penis, then an 'oversized' clitoris, symbolizes the arguable irrationality of trying to make an intersexed infant conform to a two-sex system. It is apparent how 'appropriate' external genitalia are surgically formed to support the named sex: a shift from male assignment to female assignment required exactly the same tissue to be no longer named a penis, and required that it be physically reduced and renamed as a clitoris. Furthermore, the internal gonads discovered subsequently, and removed at thirteen months old, were found to be one hormone-productive (undescended) testis and one ovotestis (a gonad formed of a mixture of testicular and ovarian tissue). A uterus with incomplete Fallopian tubes was also detected. So, the internal genitalia/gonadal formations gave no decisive clue as to a 'definite sex'.

Surely such an individual is essentially intersexed, that is, fundamentally *between the sexes*? Surely the insistence on assigning that child as a boy or a girl is to force a mixed-sex child into an ill-fitting system designed to erase that child's representation of difference? Zucker's paper (Zucker *et al.* 1987) is concerned with the child's subsequent psychosexual development, which in synopsis variously included gender disturbance, gender dysphoria and gender ambivalence. In contrast to Alvarez-Nava's subject, genetic sex was as ambiguous as the appearance of the external genitalia. Moreover, because the gonadal sex was also muddled (ovotestis on one side, testis on the other), and these organs were not removed until thirteen months of age, the subject's exposure to male hormones *in utero* and in the first year of life also resulted in hormonal sex ambiguity.

Opinions divide among clinicians, paediatricians and other medical professionals over the relative influence of the various components that form sex. Some view hormonal exposure in the womb as especially significant in determining the sex assignment or sex of rearing best suited to an ambiguously sexed individual. Others adhere more closely to genetic sex as the indicator of how an intersexed infant should be 'sexed', and seek to decipher ambiguous genetics accordingly. Others again are most swayed by the appearance of external and internal sex organs, gonadal and associated structures (penis, clitoris, testes, labia, uterus, ducts and ovaries) and the likely manifestation of secondary sex characteristics post-puberty (breasts, hair, muscle, voice).

As well as physical sex an individual's full sexual identity includes psychological sex, gender identification and sexual orientation. There are, for example, intersexed people who are transsexuals, just as there are non-intersexed persons who are transsexuals. A transsexual is defined as a person whose 'psychological sex does not match his or her anatomical sex' (Noble 1996: unpaginated) or 'whose gender identity is not congruent with their apparent physical gender' (Press for Change Mission Statement). Transsexuals operate within the male–female binary, with body and psyche being sexually opposite, and with their alignment being a goal. Intersex blends male and female characteristics at genital, organ, tissue, hormonal and/or genetic levels. Many intersexuals, however, are surgically assigned as male or female, and for some that assignment causes such disharmony between body and psyche that the subject then transsexes in adulthood. Interviewee Jacob, for example, described himself as undergoing a 'sex change from intersex female to male' (correspondence 4 April 2004).

There are arguments that transsexuals are 'psychological intersexuals' blending the *psyche* of one sex with the *body* of the other. Consultant Psychiatrist Dr Russell Reid, for example, argues that the psyche is as much a part of the person as the physical body, and that misalignment of the two in transsexuals – arguably resulting from differing effects of *in utero* hormone exposure on foetal brain and foetal body – is comparable to the misalignment of genitalia with chromosomes in some intersexuals (correspondence 24 January 2007; interview 2 May 2004). There is still much to know in relation to 'brain sex' (Zhou *et al.* 1995), and in the absence of comprehensive data on this, this book confines examination of intersex to those conditions signalled by ambiguous infant genitalia and/or discretely hidden internally, at tissue, hormonal, cellular and chromosomal levels.

CHAPTER 2

The 'Mythological Hermaphrodite'

Michel Foucault touched a nerve when he called those of us of the present day 'other Victorians'. In terms of sex, we have much in common with the Victorians. We still worry a great deal about sex and about order, and about ordering sex. We still insist there be no hermaphrodites, lest they grow and multiply. (Dreger 1998a: 198)

Dreger's words are significant. First, Western culture collectively tends to value sexual conservatism. Secondly, intersexed bodies threaten chaos, disrupt order, and trouble our collective cultural 'norms'. Thirdly, by insistence, intersex can be erased. But intersex is *not* erased: even when surgery, shame and silence combine to write intersexuals out of cultural history, they remain.

'True and Pseudohermaphrodites'

The least frequent manifestation of intersex is that sometimes termed the 'true hermaphrodite'. Statistics are hard to find and verify, but Fausto-Sterling (1993) suggests that perhaps 12 persons in every million exhibit 'true hermaphroditism', while Blackless (Blackless *et al.* 2000) similarly proposes a frequency of 1 in every 100,000, noting higher rates in certain regions such as southern Africa, and within particular families. A 'true hermaphrodite' is typically defined as having both ovarian and testicular tissue (Jha undated; Kim *et al.* 2002; Kipnis and Diamond 1998), either presented separately as one testis and one ovary; or mixed as an ovary and an ovotestis; two ovotestes; a testis and an ovotestis; or one single ovotestis only. Those with a single ovary and a single testis form about 30 per cent of the 'true hermaphrodite' population (Jha undated). It is therefore not mythologizing 'dual genitalia' that defines the 'true hermaphrodite', but rather the signs of 'gonadal intersex' (Dreger 1998a).

Approximately 60–70 per cent of 'true hermaphrodites' are genetic females with an XX karyotype (chromosomal complement) (Jha undated; Duckett and Baskin 1993). Occasionally an additional Y chromosome is present (XXY karyotype) or a chromosomal mosaic occurs. Potential variations between a 'true hermaphrodite's' gonadal formation, karyotype and genital configuration suggest that determination of any 'true sex' becomes impossible and redundant. The typical formation of the phallic tissue of the 'true hermaphrodite', for example, is tantalizingly described as 'not completely virilised' (Hatch 2003: unpaginated). The 'true hermaphrodite' will most likely also have some kind of uterus, typically hypoplastic (underdeveloped) or unicornuate (single-horned, banana-shaped, rather than being almost triangular, with two horns connected to two Fallopian tubes, one on each side). There are also likely to be oviducts and a vagina, but external genitalia will vary from female-appearing with clitoromegaly (enlarged clitoris) to – more commonly – male-appearing with hypospadias (urethral opening for urine exit is at the phallus base or on its shaft, and the phallus may also be twisted, hooked or hooded) and a bifid (split) scrotum (Jha undated; Duckett and Baskin 1993). On assignment of sex, the phallus will be named as either a penis or a clitoris. 'Male pseudohermaphrodite' and 'female pseudohermaphrodite' variants of 'true hermaphroditism' also occur.

'Male pseudohermaphroditism' manifests variously, but individuals are always genetically male and have testes or a testis exclusively (although these tend to be softer than is typical). Poor virilization results in variable degrees of feminization, with genitals ranging from those appearing male to those appearing female and with a range of ambiguities in between (including microphallus, varied scrotal or labial fusion, and perineoscrotal hypospadias). Causes include *in utero* errors of testosterone biosynthesis, 5-alpha reductase deficiency (discussed in Chapter 10) and underdevelopment or complete lack of development of Leydig cells (cells involved in the production of testosterone in the testes). At puberty, in these conditions, there is usually some virilization. Other causes include Androgen Insensitivity Syndrome (discussed in Chapter 9) where the developing genetically male foetus resists the effects of its own androgens resulting in what has been known as 'testicular feminization'. In these cases, the external genitalia in the newborn will be ambiguous or apparently female, but the vagina will be blind-ended with no uterus. For those, puberty will bring some breast development, scanty or no pubic or axillary hair, no menstruation and possible discovery of undescended testis as inguinal hernia (Jha undated). In some instances of 'male pseudohermaphroditism' there is potential male fertility (ibid.).

'Female pseudohermaphrodites' are genetic females, with almost completely female internal genitalia (that is, they most often have ovaries, uterus and other internal female structures). Their external genitalia usually appear as male through clitoral enlargement (Kipnis and Diamond 1998) but can range from minimal clitoromegaly to apparently complete virilization of the genitalia (Jha undated). Causes include exposure *in utero* to foetal androgens or, more rarely, transplacental androgen effects where, for example, the mother has a virilizing ovarian or adrenal tumour during pregnancy, or where the mother was treated with progestational agents with virilizing side effects in order to prevent miscarriage (no longer used). 'Female pseudohermaphrodites' most often 'pass' socially as female, and are capable of sexual activity and potentially of reproduction (ibid.).

When is a clitoris not a clitoris though? Remember Zucker's case (Zucker *et al.* 1987) from the Introduction where the same phallic tissue was called a penis when the intersexed infant was defined as a boy, and a clitoris when the child was re-defined as a girl. The location of the urethral opening – at the tip or base of the protruding tissue – is no sure signifier of what that tissue is. And the presence or absence of other typical sex-defining signs – a vaginal opening, ovaries or testes, XX or XY karyotype – muddles rather than clarifies definition of sex in 'true hermaphrodites'. If indeed there are various contributors to biological sex (Zucker *et al.* 1987), and these are not aligned in 'true or pseudohermaphrodites', then these individuals challenge culture's assumption that sex is an exclusive binary.

Antiquity, History, Pornography

There is ready access to so-called 'hermaphrodite porn' on the Internet. The 'chicks with dicks' fetish feeds pop-culture's imagined sense of the 'hermaphrodite' as a composite woman with a penis. Interviewee Sarah-Jane identifies herself (interview 9 June 2004) as a 'hermaphrodite', later qualifying her self-identification: 'I am an Intersex Woman. There are other terms/names for "my species" such as Hermaphrodite ... or derogatory names like Freak or Goddess ... we are amazingly enough Human Beings' (correspondence 17 January 2007). Sarah-Jane works as pole-dancer and escort. She rejects web-based 'hermaphrodite' pornography as fake (interview 9 June 2004), asserting that she is possibly the only *genuine* 'hermaphrodite' working in the UK sex industry. She claims never to have encountered another person like herself, and believes she would have been introduced with a view to a 'double-act' should another person like her have been on the UK porn circuit. She also asserts that her 'Unique Gender' has resulted in her rejection by some porn acting agencies in the UK, concluding that she 'must be really weird to be rejected by people like this' (correspondence 17 January 2007). The volume of web-based material, and Sarah-Jane's specialist popularity, testifies to some salacious cultural interest in 'hermaphroditism', but this arguably mythologizes and exoticizes intersex rather than normalizing it.

In Greek antiquity, two versions of the 'hermaphrodite' myth exist. In one, Hermaphroditos, child of Hermes and Aphrodite, combines both their bodily characteristics in one body. Alternatively, a water nymph falls in love with the beautiful son of Hermes and Aphrodite, entwining her body with his until they become co-joined (Fausto-Sterling 2000). These gave language the word 'hermaphrodite', but provide no biological accuracy. The mythic notion of 'hermaphroditism' being similar to the uncanny co-joining of twins persists (Roberts in Hugill 1998). And the self-impregnating, dual-genitalled and mythological 'hermaphrodite' feeds cultural revulsion since 'it' suggests an uncannily sexual and reproductive body, simultaneously 'other' to both the 'true heterosexual' *and* 'normative' sex binarism.

Dreger (1998a) intimates that the development of medicalized culture through the nineteenth and early twentieth centuries exposed those 'hermaphrodites' who had previously resided unrevealed. Dreger references Michel Foucault's publication of the diary of French nineteenth-century 'hermaphrodite' Herculine Barbin (Foucault 1980), designated female at birth, but remaining physiologically intact as a 'hermaphrodite' because s/he was born before now typical surgical or hormonal intervention. Barbin's affair with a woman resulted in 'her' re-classification as male at age twenty-two, again without physiological interference, but nevertheless in reinforcement of heterosexual assumptions that arguably underpin some of the requirements for the intersexed to be re-sexed (Lee 1994 in Dreger 1998b). The physician attending Barbin's suicide at age thirty discovered his/her intersexed genitalia, and Dreger paraphrases the report of the scene (Goujon 1869: 607–8):

> Régnier discovered not signs of syphilis, but a strange mélange of sexual anatomy: a short imperforate penis, curved slightly backward and pointed toward what Régnier could only call a vulva – labia minora and majora, and a vagina large enough to admit an index finger. (Dreger 1998a: 16–17)

Note the paraphrasing of Régnier's struggle for language, and reference to both penis and vagina again in one person. Labelled drawings made by Régnier show the complex configuration of a bulging right testicle, a large urethral opening below a phallus or clitoris emergent like the head of a penis from a shaft of skin running through the middle of the genitalia, a small vaginal opening with several tiny glands and excretory orifices, and another orifice apparently for the excretion of sperm (Dreger 1998a: 19–20). Barbin's memoirs were hidden in the French Department of Public Hygiene until their discovery and presentation by Foucault in 1980. That combination of state secrecy and state preservation testifies to both public horror and cultural curiosity towards the sexual 'abnormality' Barbin's story illustrated. Dreger contextualizes Barbin's case in relation to narratives of other 'hermaphrodites' of that time, and she concludes that the historical examples cited indicate 'just how messy and unpredictable sex could be' (ibid.: 57).

'Normalizing' genital surgery for intersexed infants with ambiguous genitalia has been practised since the 1950s. Older anatomical textbooks define many genital structure variations among intersexed individuals, and these went unaltered prior to the development of advanced specialist surgical techniques during and post-Second World War (Hampton Young 1937; Latou Dickinson 1949). Mayer, for example, wrote in *The Lancet* (1836) of an individual born in 1780 and raised as a female (changing to the male role at age forty). Doctors disagreed as to whether this person was male, female or – in the opinion of several eminent anatomists – whether s/he 'did not belong exclusively to either sex' (1836: 140). Of course, there was no surgical intervention, and the detailed autopsy description confirms the subject's complex intersexed anatomy. Having spent forty years as a girl/woman, and another fifteen as a man, this individual lived and died with divergence between sex and gender that presents a modern conundrum but in the mid-1800s was reconciled: his/her *sex* was that of a 'hermaphrodite', his/her *gender* was in turn that of a female, then a male.

If sex is more variable than the male–female binary allows – and intersex suggests that it is – might intersex conditions define a range of sexes? There is arguably sufficient variation in male, female and intersexed bodies to warrant reconsideration of how advances in medical science have allowed bodies to be shaped to fit the perceived norm of the sex binary. Prior to those advances, intersexed bodies (for better or worse) stayed as they were. Contemporary medical and surgical practitioners can advocate the construction of apparently 'normal' binary genitalia precisely because surgical processes and understanding of sexual anatomy and endocrinology have refined continually over the last sixty years to allow the delicacy of procedure required for this 'normalizing' and 'corrective' line of treatment. Such treatment, however, confirms cultural assumptions that 'lurking inside the mixed-sex child is a real male or female body', a body that surgery can 'find' (Fausto-Sterling 2000: 76).

An alternative perspective insists that intersexuality is a life-long condition irrespective of whether the individual undergoes surgical 'correction' of their 'deviant', 'erroneous' anatomy or not (Dreger 1999; Holmes 1994a). If this is the case, why not permit its evidence, in ambiguous genitalia and in other physiological signs, to stay unaltered (except where medical intervention is necessary for preservation of life)? To disallow or negate intersex is surely to arrogantly overlook the possibility for meaningful critique of the sex bipolarity insisted on by science and culture, but routinely transgressed by intersex.

Normal and Natural

Jeffrey Eugenides' novel *Middlesex* introduced a 'male pseudohermaphrodite' as its contemporary protagonist. A genetic male with ambiguous genitalia, Eugenides' character was raised as a girl until age fourteen, and then lived as a male:

I was born twice: first, as a baby girl ... and then again, as a teenage boy ...

Specialised readers may have come across me in Dr. Peter Luce's study, 'Gender Identity in 5-Alpha-Reductase Pseudohermaphrodites' published in the *Journal of Pediatric Endocrinology* in 1975. Or maybe you've seen my photograph in chapter sixteen of the now sadly outdated Genetics and Heredity. That's me on page 578, standing naked beside a height chart with a black box over my eyes. (Eugenides 2002: 3)

Eugenides' novel matches a series of alienations and non-conformities – of sex, ethnicity, class – to explore the essence of 'normality' in US contemporary culture. Eugenides' use of the term 'hermaphrodite', however, is challenged by the AIS Support Group UK (Media Guidelines 2005). They note that intersex conditions such as Androgen Insensitivity Syndrome and 5-alpha reductase deficiency have previously been referred to as 'male pseudohermaphroditism', and assert that while a subject is defined by such an historicizing umbrella term, then trauma, offence and obfuscation rather than meaningful illumination results.

The terms 'normal' and 'natural' are used repeatedly with authority and conviction in discussions of sexual anatomy. Frequently, they are used interchangeably to uphold social, cultural and scientific understanding of 'body normality' within a harmoniously balanced 'natural world'. This 'norm' is constructed as a sex binary of absolute male (with penis, external testosterone-productive testes, hard musculature, flat chest and exclusive XY karyotype) and absolute female (with vagina, uterus, oestrogen-productive ovaries, breasts and exclusive XX karyotype). Advocates of surgical intervention argue that it is possible, or *preferable*, to achieve 'normality' where infants are born with ambiguous genitalia, reproductive organs, gonadal configuration and so on via surgery and hormone treatment. It is, of course, impossible to alter karyotype. Such 'normality' is arguably as much a cultural construct as is biology, and the social-cultural consequences of such intervention have, until recently, been neglected in the wider discourses of medical, biological and anatomical theory.

Jorge Daaboul, then Director of Pediatric Endocrinology at the Children's Hospital of Oakland, noted in 2000 that a naturalized system has become current in which bodies are considered either 'normal' or 'deviant' based on the unexamined assumption that there is no precedent for intersex in the binary system enforced by culture and medical practice. In spite of historical examples of 'hermaphroditism' and contemporary testimonies from intersexed individuals, it appears that a concealment practice has been activated, which reconciles the 'deviant anatomy' of intersex to cultural expectations of binarism (Kipnis and Diamond 1998: 405). That practice arguably empowers the cultural implementation of 'normality' as it simultaneously 'diminishes the value of difference' (ibid.).

Diamond and Sigmundson advocate use of the terms 'atypical', 'unusual' or 'less frequent' rather than 'abnormal', maintaining that it is possible – at least symbolically – to include all bodies, intersexed or otherwise, in the expanded language of 'normality'. They argue for intersex conditions to be considered 'biological varieties' (1997a: 1,046), anticipated products of natural biodiversity, and therefore part of biological and anatomical science. Their argument relates to that of Harry Benjamin who, as early as 1925, proposed that the sexual binary had 'no accurate scientific meaning', and urged the cultural ingestion of the idea of a sex continuum with 'many "in between"' (1966: 44).

At conception, embryonic sex differentiation may be atypical. Blackless (Blackless *et al.* 2000) suggests that approximately 1 in 1,700 newborns have karyotypes other than XX (female) or (XY) male. For the first six weeks of embryonic development, the genital ridge is undifferentiated, and internal/external genital structures (such as they are at that stage) are sex ambiguous. *Where genetic sex is male or female*, foetal development is then as follows:

- *'Genetic male' foetal development:*
  A portion of the genetic male's Y chromosome is responsible for development of testes from undifferentiated primitive gonads. These testes manufacture the principal male sex hormone testosterone, which causes the internal male reproductive structures to form. Formation of internal female reproductive structures is simultaneously inhibited. At around week seven of gestation, this testosterone also initiates development of male external genitalia – penis and scrotum. By birth, penis size has typically increased ten-fold, testes have descended (Jha undated) and development of the male phenotype – the observable outward physique – has begun.

  In genetic male foetuses where testosterone is absent or severely reduced because, for example, testes do not develop fully or are mixed ovotestes (as in Complete or Partial Gonadal Dysgenesis), combined male and female genital structures result. Similarly, a genetic male foetus' inability to respond typically to its own hormones (as in Partial or Complete Androgen Insensitivity Syndrome) also results in ambiguous genitalia. An *undervirilized genetic male* may have, for example, hypospadias; extremely underdeveloped penis (micropenis or microphallus); and/or a split scrotum with a cleft between the two testes inside causing it to resemble plump labia.
- *'Genetic female' foetal development:*
  For genetic female foetuses, absence of a Y chromosome causes previously undifferentiated gonads to develop into ovaries at week eleven to thirteen of gestation. Absence of testosterone means the foetus follows the 'default' pathway, with clitoris, lower vagina and labia forming from tissue that until then was physically indistinguishable as male or female. Female phenotype

development depends on uninterrupted formation of the Fallopian tubes, uterus, cervix and upper vagina rather than on the effects of ovarian hormones.

Where a genetic female foetus is over-exposed *in utero* to male hormones – either by its own adrenal over-production (as in Congenital Adrenal Hyperplasia), or from its mother – some virilization of the developing structures takes place. The clitoris may be enlarged, labia partially fused resembling a part-formed scrotum, and vagina or uterus may be absent or semi-formed.

Foetal sex-development is complex, with atypical progression resulting in production of foetal intersex characteristics. In some instances, diagnosis of the intersex condition(s) is relatively straightforward. In others, the form of intersex is complex, unique and impossible to name:

I was brought up as a boy, with very small male organs visible. Testes didn't fully drop and were tiny and hard (description of abnormal by a surgeon later), and penis never sufficiently developed for normal intercourse.

I had severe hormonal imbalances at various times from childhood on, with both extremely high levels of female hormones, and extremely high levels of male hormones. I never had a proper puberty. I developed female breasts. Body shape, looks, and body hair distribution have always been bizarre and ambiguous.

Underarm hair fairly sparse like with many girls. Pubic hairs sparse, fine and soft, pattern ambiguous, though leaning towards the male pattern. Facial hair a bit of a problem (as a woman) though not sufficient to grow a proper beard. Mostly these facial hairs are fine. I pluck them out when they come through. Hair on torso is extremely short fine soft female pattern, with the following exceptions. I have five hairs which grow on my left breast, which I very occasionally shave off because they grow long, though soft and fine. I also occasionally grow a ring of pubic hairs around each nipple. These hairs around the nipple seem to appear and stay for a few months, and then must just drop out because they vanish. Legs are mostly strangely hairless, but with odd small patches and tiny tufts of soft fine hair.

Facial features are acceptable as reasonably attractive female. No 'Adam's apple'.

From waist down I am within normal acceptable female shape with gently female hips though not like the really exaggerated hips some women have. Shoulders and arms well within normal female proportions with narrow shoulders … Elbow locking angle only slightly tending towards female – in truth more towards the male pattern but with a slight 'female type' reversal in locking … Hands small, slightly stubby but normal female shape. Feet small …

Ribcage has always been large … The pinching into the waist is not very pronounced …

Nipples are really bizarre. I have five! There are two tiny vestigial nipples under my left armpit. The nipples on my breasts are of female size, but weirdly indistinct …

In childhood I found it very difficult being accepted as a boy because I was always much more like a girl … Even before corrective surgery, I was able to pass for female when naked. This caused me some big problems in childhood, being once dubbed

'Miss Body Beautiful' by a cruel teacher, and banned from ever letting any other children see me when changing.

In my teens and twenties I lived as both male and female because all my documentation made me male, but many friends found it easier to relate to me as female, and I had some considerable peer pressure ... to switch to being entirely female. In my late twenties I did this. I didn't get surgery though until I was in my thirties. I had corrective surgery in 1992, after living many years as a woman. There was insufficient material to construct more than a tiny vagina. I only had that one operation which left me looking normal for a woman 'below'. My breasts have always been mine, un-enhanced by medical intervention.

Trying to live as a man was extremely difficult, and I was often taken for being a woman pretending to be a man. I was never properly accepted as male by anyone. But I am accepted properly as a woman now.

I suspect I might have some small ovaries still inside me, because I don't take hormone replacement or anything, but my skin condition, muscles and bones etc have stayed young, and I still pass for thirty something despite being in my fifties. I still have 'hormonal type' swings, though less exaggerated now, and something must be keeping the facial hair growing ... I am aging extremely slowly. I think I actually have more sex drive now than before corrective surgery, so something must be creating that.

As far as sexuality goes, I have only fancied other women ... I am happy as a woman and as a lesbian. I am open about being intersex. I do not know any name for my condition, which goes somewhat further than just the intersex elements. Twenty years ago my doctor of that time stated that there wouldn't be a name for my condition unless someone decided to do some research on it ... (Laura, correspondence 22 March 2003; interview 3 August 2004)

Typical and Atypical

Although atypical sex differentiation happens, Diamond and Sigmundson (1997a) still adhere to the *concept* of sex bipolarity in their 'sex of rearing' approach to intersex management and treatment. They prefer to encourage *gender role assignment* as a kind of mimicry of male or female rather than either advocating irreversible surgical/hormonal treatment or dismissal of a sex binary altogether. Their acknowledgement of this mimicry, however, evidences acceptance of intersex as actual, even as it is 'normalized' into an expanded sex morphology. That is, 'normal' is expanded to fit 'manifesting'. To 'rear as male' or 'rear as female' an infant in accordance with the sex whose genitalia theirs most resembles is much less emphatic and permanent than the surgical/hormonal interventionist alternative. It is both provisional and expedient.

Hugh was born in 1949 in South Dakota with what his family doctor described as 'hermaphrodite genitals' (correspondence 17 January 2003). He was assigned as female in early infancy and raised as a girl, but without the feminizing surgery that would subsequently be usual. Hugh's small protruding phallus was not amputated, and he remembers being cautioned by his sister never to be seen naked. He recalls his parents' lack of concern for or acknowledgement of his atypical intersexed genitals, and he describes stoically 'being a girl' in spite of progressive virilization through childhood and adolescence. He was conscious, however, from an early stage of 'acting' as a girl rather than feeling he was a girl. Hugh developed a phallus that was about an inch long when erect and sexually sensitive, although he never ejaculated and his urine opening was on the lower side of the phallus. At puberty, he developed significant facial hair, but did not menstruate or grow breasts. At this time, he experienced severe emotional confusion, and considered suicide. Hugh's parents and sister ignored his difficulties through puberty, and he describes his teenage self as 'an odd lonesome terrified girl', with a flat chest, atypical genitals, no periods and needing to shave regularly to keep a beard at bay. He even recalls that he 'smelled like a man not like a girl' (correspondence 17 January 2003).

When Hugh reached eighteen, a teacher counselled him to seek help, and through a local doctor he learned about oestrogen therapy (oestrogen is produced in the ovaries in women, and small amounts are produced in fat tissue in men). So ingrained was the message of his upbringing that he was female, he embarked on twelve years of female hormone ingestion to support the sex assignment decided upon at birth. Although some scant breast tissue formed, when Hugh was thirty-two he was unable to continue to fight his essentially male feelings. He moved away from his family locale, ceased hormone therapy, allowed his facial hair to grow and self-assigned to male. He refused to consider surgical enhancement of his phallus, which he began to call a penis, feeling that his body had been 'messed up enough', and that he 'just wanted to sit still for a bit' (correspondence 17 January 2003). Hugh's birth certificate names him as Linda and as female, since that was the sex to which he was assigned. He is unaware of his genetic sex, but is unconcerned about this, indicating that the most important issue, in spite of struggling for many years with a sex assignment that 'didn't fit', was that he had not received surgical intervention in infancy on his genitals. While Hugh cannot think of himself as a 'normal' 'full man', he acknowledges that he is 'as near as [he]'ll get' (correspondence 17 January 2003).

Had Hugh been born a few years later, his sex assignment would probably have been enforced surgically. The small penis which signals Hugh's maleness would have been lost, and his adult choice to live as male would have meant living without a penis, or seeking prosthetic assistance. Counter-arguments insist that the removal of Hugh's phallic protrusion in infancy would have aesthetically reinforced the original female sex assignment and enhanced its likelihood of success, but without holistic (genetic, internal and external) and multi-disciplinary examination of the infant as advocated by Diamond and Sigmundson (1997a) and Kipnis and Diamond (1998) it is impossible to provisionally forecast sexual and social changes that may occur before and through puberty.

Genetic males with testes but no penis occur only once in a million births, while genetic females without vaginas are possibly as common as 1 case in 6,000 (Blackless *et al.* 2000). Just as Hugh operates as a man, albeit with a smaller than average and atypically formed penis, interviewee Rachel is a genetic female without a vagina. Her condition is Mayer-Rokitansky-Küster-Hauser Syndrome, characterized by congenital absence of vagina, rudimentary uterus, and typical ovaries and Fallopian tubes. Ovulation, breast development, body form and body hair are typical for a female, but menstruation does not occur. MRKH Syndrome is caused by atypical development of the Müllerian ducts, the structures from which the vagina, cervix, uterus and oviducts derive during foetal growth. Rachel was diagnosed only when she failed to menstruate at puberty. Medical examination revealed what she calls her 'absence' (correspondence 17 July 2003), and she writes of being 'utterly overwhelmed' by the treatment undertaken when she was aged fourteen to sixteen (she is now forty-four). This consisted of surgery to fashion the entrance to a vagina, dilation with plastic dilators of increasing size, and she resents the focus at that sensitive age on her inability to 'receive a penis'. She is thankful, however, that she was diagnosed at puberty, avoiding invasive scrutiny as a smaller child. Rachel has experienced periodic semi-closure and vaginal infections, but is reasonably satisfactorily hetero-sexually active as an adult. She does not consider herself to be intersexed, insisting that she is 'a woman if not a "whole" woman' (correspondence 17 July 2003). For some others with MRKH Syndrome, they live as women: that is, their gender is female, but their sex is not 'female enough' to go 'uncorrected' so they may feel more intersexed. Esther, for example, was diagnosed as having MRKH Syndrome in adolesence and describes a highly emotional reaction related to not feeling like a 'normal teenage girl', being isolated by her condition, and having to accept that she would be unable to have biological children. She expressed this as 'paralysing to some extent' and indicates how she 'went from thirteen at the age of discovery to an instant adult', having to consider sex issues beyond her years and being 'medicalised out of puberty' (interview 19 August 2004). Interestingly, Esther notes that while vaginal agenesis tends to get overlooked, those intersexed children with, for example, perceived over-sized clitorises are subjected to clitorectomies that she finds 'really appalling' (interview 19 August 2004). When challenged about the generosity of deflecting sympathy onto other intersexed individuals, Esther concedes that she is both concerned about the welfare of those others and thankful that her condition, which tends to be unseen until puberty brings no menstruation, avoids the extreme intervention experienced by others. Unlike those subjected to infant clitoral surgery, Esther's diagnosis allows her to 'still have [her]

sexuality' (interview 19 August 2004). Nevertheless, Esther has found it difficult to make contact with MRKH women who consider themselves as intersexed. Finally, she argues that there is an errant presumption that sex for a
woman absolutely requires a vagina, and suggests that 'women are found to
have vaginal agenesis in their teens – usually before they are sexually active –
and there is something very wrong that society has convinced them that they
have to have these surgeries or treatments before they get the chance to
examine their sexuality' (interview 19 August 2004).

From personal experience of 'clitoral recession' (shaving down the clitoral
shaft) of what was in infancy described as her 'over-large' clitoris, Holmes
(1995) contends that attempts to surgically construct 'normality' are essentially cosmetic, homophobic, and designed to satisfy cultural requirements of
sex binarism rather than to acknowledge the diversity of intersex. Blackless
too asserts that 'absolute dimorphism is a Platonic ideal not actually achieved
in the natural world' (Blackless *et al.* 2000: 151), and maintains that while
this *is* recognized by scientists and biologists, the normalizing drive of medical
science displaces that recognition and 'abnormalizes' that which deviates
from a binary genital distribution or sex chromosomal composition. Fausto-
Sterling appreciates the threat to culture of bodies that 'blur and bridge the
great divide' of binary sex (1993: 24), but she contends that there is in operation a kind of 'averaging' reductive bias, or alternatively an 'idealising exclusivity', for genitals and therefore for sex. Fausto-Sterling urges another
perspective:

> complete maleness and complete femaleness represent the extreme ends of a spectrum
> of possible body types. That these extreme ends are most frequent has lent credence to
> the idea that they are not only natural (that is, produced by nature) but normal (that is,
> they represent both a statistical and social ideal). Knowledge of biological variation,
> however, allows us to *conceptualise the less frequent middle spaces as natural although sta-
> tistically more unusual* [this author's emphasis]. (Fausto-Sterling 2000: 76)

Suzanne Kessler, Professor of Psychology and Dean of the School of
Natural and Social Sciences, Purchase SUNY, also notes that clinicians are
'aware that concordance and dimorphism do not always exist' (1990: 25).
That is, she maintains, clinicians understand that two mutually distinctive
sexual anatomies are not the only sex options. Kessler believes, however, that
understanding biological complexity does not necessarily inform clinical
response to it. The 'natural', which, she asserts, is the *full* range of bodies in
human natural history, and which would be *immutable* were it not for medical
interference, is considered 'unnatural' where it strays from 'typical' binary
morphology. Kessler argues that medical intervention is *constructed* as 'natural'
since it seeks to alter the 'unnatural' body to what it 'ought to have been'.
Hence, a 'normative' and 'naturalized' situation is *constructed* around what

Kessler terms a 'culturally indisputable, *gender* [this author's emphasis] dichotomy' (ibid.: 24). By using the word *gender* to name the dichotomy, Kessler significantly refuses to name *sex* as binary.

Fiction and Myth

The television drama series *Footballers' Wives* (2002) was a camp fantasy featuring a 'hermaphrodite' baby born to two protagonists. Writers Ann McManus and Maureen Chadwick believe that popular representation of the subject is helpful to public understanding of intersex:

> People ought to be concerned about this ... More babies are born with intersex conditions than are born with Down's syndrome. When the storyline was leaked to the press, it was a typical, predictable tabloid reaction of laughing and mocking. But through storylines like this we are able to explore society's attitudes and prejudices to a 'less than perfect child' ...
>
> A lot of people will now know ... what intersex is, that it exists, that it's not funny. (Lee 2002: 8)

However awkwardly intersex is exposed in this programme, and one might argue that this context served to enhance perception of intersex as 'freakish', McManus and Chadwick make an important point. Intersex is more common than another well-known genetic difference, but much more taboo and misunderstood. Laughter and mockery are symptoms of unease, and there is great cultural unease about 'aberrant' bodies that challenge the certainty of male and female as mutually exclusive, complementary (some would argue preferably heterosexual) and thereby 'wholesomely' reproductive. *If this is the case,* then can one empathize with those who assert that the medically sanctioned destruction of tissue and organs – with life-long implications for gender identity, erotic sensation and possibly reproductive potential – that is infant sex assignment doubles as a culturally sanctioned construction of a favoured biology and anatomy?

In the BBC drama *Ted and Alice* (2002), Ted was a single-sex alien from a planet entirely inhabited by 'hermaphrodites'. He was doubly alien – to his culture and ours – as he travelled to Earth in search of an 'opposite sex' romance. While Ted flipped the normative concept of 'hermaphrodites' as unusual, even 'freakish', the programme was not focused on the issues this proposed, and arguably the 'hermaphrodite' references were peripheral rather than central. Nevertheless, again this drama raises issues key to understanding culture's predominant attitude towards intersex. Holmes (1995) uses the word 'queer' – most usually employed to denote homosexuality either in pejorative or reclaiming terms – in reference to intersex. Intersex, with its possibility of 'eccentric' genital configuration, and its 'peculiar' mixing of sex signifiers throughout the body's structure, *is* in many ways 'queer'. It therefore readily becomes mythologized and fictionalized, and *Footballers' Wives* and *Ted and Alice*, however much they highlight or forefront intersex, serve nevertheless to distance the actuality of that word from the understanding of their audience. 'Hermaphrodites' become historical and romantic, fictional and epic, camp exotic, or – literally – alien. The lived reality of intersexuals like Linda Roberts, Hugh or Esther is more complicated. Roberts' intellectually primitive neighbours read 'hermaphrodite' as a potent emblem of dysfunction, horror, even death, and acted accordingly: 'She has been spat at and stoned; her windows smashed ... She was forced to the ground, kicked and stamped on, her bones broken ... She was a "filthy queer" ...' (Hugill 1998: 7).

Monstrous and Abject

Just as Freud's *The Uncanny* (1919) is activated by cultural consideration of a mythic 'hermaphrodite', two other authoritative voices are also pertinent. Barbara Creed's articulation of the 'monstrous-feminine' (1993) was developed especially in relation to depiction of women in the horror film genre, but it has relevance to this discourse. Creed notes that: 'The horror film is populated by female monsters, many of which seem to have evolved from images that haunted the dreams, myths and artistic practices of our forebears many centuries ago' (ibid.: 1).

Creed defines the specifically female 'monster' variously: primeval mother, vampire, monstrous womb, bleeding wound, possessed body, castrator, killer beauty, aged psychopath, non-human animal, woman as life-in-death, and, significantly, 'monstrous boy-girl' (ibid.). This last is the 'monstrosity' of the archetypal 'phallic female', the virilized girl-child, and arguably – although this is not Creed's territory – this is the cultural (mis)understanding of the 'hermaphrodite'. Creed's thesis indirectly locates the *intersexed body* as monstrous, and her contribution corresponds with that of Julia Kristeva whose articulation of the abject seems also apt to discourses on intersex in social-culture: 'It is thus not lack of cleanliness or health that causes abjection but what disturbs identity, system, order. What does not respect borders, positions, rules' (Kristeva 1982: 4).

In 1834, *The Lancet* referenced 'one of these monsters', a 'disgusting spectacle', a 'freak of nature', examined live at age thirty-four in Liverpool, England (Anon 1834: 558). The long and detailed description of the genital configuration makes clear the complexity of the ambiguity, and activates Kristeva's 'disturbance' of the order and identification of 'normal' genitalia. Notably, the subject's 'pretty strong sexual desires', preference to '*jouer le role de la femme*', and capability for

> ... nocturnal emissions, and emissions also on libidinous ideas being excited with regard to *either* sex, the semen flowing from the small orifices below the clitoris or glans penis ... (ibid.)

seems designed to shock, terrify and dismay in that era particularly. Creed notes Kristeva's separation of 'the human from the non-human and the fully constituted subject from the partially formed subject' (Creed 1993: 8). The 'hermaphrodite' is here constructed through reportage as 'incomplete' or 'sub-human', operating with a bastardized body and base carnal desires (Holt 1861).

Kristeva's text finds the abject 'where meaning collapses' (1982: 2), Creed's in 'the place where "I" am not' (1993: 9). Arguably, the 'hermaphrodite' is as incomprehensible to the greater numbers of those who are culture's sex-differentiated 'norm' *now* as it was in 1834. The binary of sex is so rigidly constructed and perpetuated in culture and medical science that 'meaning collapses' (Kristeva 1982: 2) at the appearance of bodies whose morphology differs from the 'norm'. Here, fundamentally, is the threat of the chaotic, the destructive, the meaningless that intersex – irrationally considered – poses. However civilized is the 'management' of intersex, and however powerful are the promises to 'fix' aberrant genitalia, reconfigure errant organs, relocate doubtful sex, the implication remains that the consequences of inaction are fearful. Creed's words point us to a critical issue in the discourses of intersex: the 'I' is the person who is not intersexed. That is, intersex resides in the place of 'the other', for which read the peripheral, the discounted and the objectionable. The threat of the 'abject intersexual' is a perceived threat to life itself, and all that life stands for. The abjection – in this discourse – of intersex is then to be 'radically excluded' (Kristeva 1982: 2). Permission is granted for surgical/hormonal intervention where intersex is detected in newborns because culture perceives an enormous threat from the 'hermaphroditic' body. That body – as abject – 'crosses or threatens to cross the "border"' (Creed 1993: 11) of reason, acceptability, appropriateness and the 'normal'. Kristeva's allusion to a 'clean and proper body' (1982: 71) makes such a body distinct from what Creed calls 'the abject body, or the body which has lost its form and integrity' (1993: 11), here activated as intersexed. Kristeva is clear in her account of what causes the bodily defilements or pollutions to which she refers. For her, both the excremental and the menstrual activate abjection. Arguably there is a third: the perceived 'malformation' of the 'hermaphrodite' operates in the same way ...

CHAPTER 3

Louise's Story and Others

Perhaps sexual dimorphism seems so natural that our culture and – therefore – Western science have scarcely considered the absolutism that this piece of common sense exercises over sex research.

Gilbert Herdt, *Mistaken Sex: Culture, Biology and Third Sex in New Guinea*

Louise

Louise is a 29-year-old woman who appeared on the UK Channel 4 *Secret Intersex* programme in 2004, and subsequently agreed to contribute her story to this book. Her karyotype is 46,XY (male), and she was born with part of one testis, an internal ovary and a rudimentary vagina. Absence of a uterus indicates that there was probably some testosterone-producing activity in the testicular tissue during foetal development (Ogilvy-Stuart *et al.* 2004). Louise's external genitalia were undeveloped at birth, with sexually sensitive phallic tissue being ambiguous and dispersed, unrecognizable as either male or female. Her diagnosis following investigation reads 'intersex penile agenesis and ectopic urethral orifices in anorectum' (*Secret Intersex* 2004). This means that she is intersexed, genetically male, with congenital absence of a penis, and with plural urethral (urine-carrying) openings situated out of place in her anal and rectal regions.

Is this the 'heretical' body referenced by Fausto-Sterling (2000: 8)?

Is this Freud's 'uncanny body', Creed's 'monstrous body', and Kristeva's 'abject body'?

Given that her body is so profoundly sex ambiguous, Louise's labelling as male or female in infancy arguably became a 'social decision' rather than a medically meaningful one. As in many cases of ambiguous genitalia in newborns, the attending physician encouraged parental consent for genital surgery. Although Louise's physiological problems included severe urinary difficulties needing attention quickly after birth, her ambiguous genitalia were not essentially life-threatening. It is important to note here that there are some significant instances where an aspect of an intersex condition might be life-threatening: in Congenital Adrenal Hyperplasia (discussed in Chapter 8) infants can suffer a 'salt-wasting' adrenal crisis which if not treated urgently is fatal (although it should be noted that salt-wasting is not relieved by genital surgery); in Cloacal Exstrophy, genital ambiguity is accompanied by 'a devastating pelvic field defect' where surgical reconstruction of the pelvic organs is medically essential (Reiner 2004b); and there are also some concerns about elevated risk of gonadal tumour in certain genetic intersex instances. Nevertheless, with those exceptions, some would contend that the speed with which consent is sought and surgery occurs indicates the cultural rather than medical 'problem' presented by the infant with genital ambiguity. There is arguably an urgent desire to 'fix' intersex physiology rather than to reflect on what it might mean for the patient to have this configuration and for society to have to cope with the difference. Fausto-Sterling criticises what she indicates is an arrogant medical profession: 'Physicians believe that their expertise enables them to "hear" nature telling them the truth about what sex such patients ought to be. Alas, their truths come from the social arena and are reinforced, in part, by the medical tradition of rendering intersexual births invisible' (2000: 27–28).

Fausto-Sterling's assertion is important, but Louise's testimony is a reminder to beware dogma and simplicity in considering the treatment, management and care of diverse individuals some of whom do not want to be 'queer', different or exceptional, but who deeply desire to be what they believe is 'normal'.

Louise's ovary and partial testis – respectively the source of oestrogen for typical females and testosterone for typical males – were removed at some point in infancy. In interview (27 September 2005), Louise described how she found her childhood genital surgeries difficult to remember with accuracy since some were concerned with cosmetic results, while others were aimed at controlling the incontinence resultant from her unusual urinary construction. These early surgeries tended to be unsuccessful: no satisfactory vagina or urinary control was achieved, and artificial drainage of urine continued to be necessary. Later, at around age twenty, Louise recalls repeatedly asking for a mirror to see her genitalia following another surgery, and being refused. A flap of skin from her shoulder and a leg vein had been employed in a then pioneering procedure, but to no avail, and when Louise was permitted to look the result resembled a severely swollen and bruised testicle and took four months to reduce.

Louise has experienced numerous surgeries since infancy, but her email of 28 November 2005, following her final vaginoplasty, indicated some form of conclusion: 'there is nothing else for them to do ... it went well'. Louise's consultant, Mr Christopher Woodhouse at Middlesex Hospital noted in *Secret Intersex* (2004) that Louise has a 'unique physiology', a narrow pelvis, and a mass of scar tissue resulting from earlier surgeries. These make complete vaginoplasty and pelvic widening extraordinarily difficult. Nevertheless, Louise was insistent beforehand that the surgeries would 'make me feel whole as a person – if I get married, basically I can't have sex at the moment ... I want to go the full distance and make myself complete as a woman' (*Secret Intersex* 2004).

Louise reported that by 2004 she had a vagina that could be penetrated, but further cosmetic surgery was completed in late 2005. Louise has taken twenty-nine years to reach this point. Her articulate statement of desire for 'whole wifely womanliness' is touching given her complex intersexed body, her genetic maleness and her testosterone exposure *in utero* (as indicated by her absent womb and some phenotypic evidence of virilization).

Woodhouse, however, is more circumspect than optimistic about surgery's potential to allow Louise the female 'authenticity' she says she wants: 'Genital surgery does not create either a normal female appearance or normal female sexual function' (correspondence 10 January 2007). Woodhouse indicates that he strives to make it as close as possible, but 'objective tests of sexual function in long-term follow-up have shown that sexuality is far from normal. Broadly speaking the more removed from normal female gender is the patient the less good is the outcome' (correspondence 10 January 2007). Furthermore, he suggests that 'the best defence of such surgery is that it may be better than no surgery at all ... in creating an "artificial" vagina that allows penetration it could be said that some is better than none at all' (correspondence 10 January 2007). Significantly, he 'emphasises the importance of fully informed patient consent' (correspondence 10 January 2007). In *Secret Intersex* (2004) Woodhouse acknowledges that Louise might well have been assigned male if she had been born today, but indicates how new, rare and individually tailored this kind of surgery is. Surgeons, he reveals, in some instances 'make it up as [they] go along' (*Secret Intersex* 2004).

Althaea Yronwode (1999) quotes Cheryl Chase's criticism of surgeons' faith in new techniques and technology:

> I don't think doctors who are doing this are setting out to hurt their patients. They are confronted with parents who are upset ... They are trained to 'fix' things. When people like me grow up and say 'this hurt me', they don't want to hear it, because they would have to see how they had hurt patients, and they would have to admit their impotence in addressing this by surgery. (ibid.: unpaginated)

Woodhouse's humility, even as he attempted these repeated surgeries, indicates the difficulties also experienced by surgeons. This is developmental, evolving surgery, carried out with a genuine desire for improvement, but in painful cognizance of gaps in knowledge. Surgeons, paediatricians, endocrinologists involved in intersex care are much criticized, and undoubtedly there is need for close scrutiny of medical practice, especially as anecdotal evidence amasses from those who are both intersexed and unhappy with their earlier treatment. Interviewee Mr Philip Ransley, Consultant Paediatric Urologist at Great Portland Street, London, responds to the repeated criticism by noting cultural insistence on two exclusive sexes, and sees his role as delivering what society has requested:

> it doesn't seem so bad if society's going to continue to require us to make decisions as to whether you're male or female, and at the moment it does ...
>
> it doesn't seem such a terrible crime for a surgeon or a team of caring physicians to make that decision as best they can on the information available.
>
> And I think we take too much stick frankly ... (interview 6 September 2005)

It's a Boy, It's a Girl

Louise's parents were initially told their baby was a boy, and they made their announcement in their local newspaper. They were then told that they had a girl-child, and then finally that their child was intersexed. Louise's mother's awkwardness when she recounts this (*Secret Intersex* 2004) illuminates the 'social emergency' of an intersexed birth (Dreger 1998b: unpaginated). Paediatric haste to nominate the child as boy or girl, coupled with severe genital confusion, resulted in misdiagnosis, misinformation and mistake.

Ransley is certain that there is no intrinsic problem with female assignment against genetic sex as in Louise's second diagnosis. Indeed he speaks generally of 'the terrible error of this dreadful emphasis on chromosomes' (interview 6 September 2005) where, in actuality, 'the only job of the Y chromosome is to tell the gonad to become a testis' (in Louise's case, her gonads developed as a partial testis and an ovary). Ransley recounts a case of a 'true hermaphrodite' with internal ovotestes, no uterus, a 'not bad' 6 cm infant vagina, a 'moderate-sized' phallus, and XX (female) karyotype. He maintains that this individual could either operate as a sexually functional but infertile female (assignment with karyotype) or as an infertile male without 'natural' testes (assignment against karyotype). If assigned female, the phallic tissue would typically be surgically reduced to make the external genitalia appear closer to that of a regular female. If assigned male, the vagina would be concealed by the introduction of prosthetic testes. In both cases, the ovotestes would most likely be removed because, it is argued, there may be a risk of cancerous development in these tissues (Jha undated). Ransley argues that sex assignment must be undertaken most promptly because the testicular element of the ovotestes may expose the infant to the virilising effects of testosterone. There is typically a testosterone surge at around day ten and day sixty after birth, and Ransley insists that 'it is imperative you make that decision and act on it ... in the first two weeks of life' (interview 6 September 2005) to avoid the effect of post-natal testosterone exposure if sex of assignment is female.

In Louise's case, the timescale for her original assignment, the reversal of that decision, and when exactly in infancy her gonads (a partial testis and ovary) were removed is not known in detail. There is a good chance there was some delay in her gonadectomy, and Ransley (speaking generally) argues that such delay – in the presence of even a partial testis – may 'prejudice the outcome' of a female sex assignment:

> I think that post-natal testosterone exposure is extremely important ... if you are faced with a male, or possible male, who has been exposed to some testosterone pre-natally, if you are going to successfully raise that person as a female then it is absolutely im-perative that their testosterone is switched off at birth ...
>
> Many of the disasters which occur in intersex states ... [happen to infants exposed to] ... some testosterone before birth, and in whom the decision to raise female is delayed too long in the post-natal period so that they get post-natal testosterone expo-sure ... (interview 6 September 2005)

Ransley is referring not to cosmetic surgery on ambiguous genitals, which may well be uppermost in parents' minds, but rather to the crucial decision to remove or not remove physiology-affecting testosterone-producing gonads. In cases of internalized indeterminate gonads, without biopsy or removal it is dif-ficult to determine whether they are testicular (and therefore testosterone emitting) or ovarian (and – in a culture of enhanced reproductive technology – possibly fertile). Once removed, they cannot be reinstated. Nevertheless, Ransley urges careful, speedy and decisive action informed by immediate endocrine investigation. Hormone stimulation of the gonads and assessment of their capability for testosterone production are examined, but Ransley acknowledges that ease of decision as to sex of assignment varies. He also admits that in some cases the phallus size is the ultimate biological marker sig-nalling how much testosterone has already been produced and how well the body has responded to it. Ransley acknowledges the responsibility the surgeon and supporting team must shoulder in assigning sex: 'you can't get back to square one again ever' (interview 6 September 2005). But, he urges that doing nothing, thus allowing the child to decide later, is a 'cop-out': 'by doing nothing ... you are allowing testosterone to work its "evil" work on the brain ... it's not nothing. Doing nothing is just walking away from the issue' (inter-view 6 September 2005).

Ransley further insists that parents are much more intimately involved and informed than they used to be in these vitally significant first few weeks. But he reasons that it is 'ludicrous and unrealistic' to expect the vast majority of parents within two weeks 'to assemble the concept of intersex, work their way through it, and come to the rational decision of what is correct for their child' (interview 6 September 2005). He stresses the lengthy process of his training and the confusing nature of the subject matter (interview 6 September 2005). Ogilvy-Stuart (Ogilvy-Stuart *et al.* 2004) also stresses the range of experiences – those of urologists, endocrinologists, geneticists, clinical psychologists and parents – that must combine to determine the sex of rearing or the sex of surgical assignment, and she acknowledges how extremely difficult this decision can be particularly given the paucity of data on long-term outcomes.

Secrets and Lies

As with many others, Louise's parents were told to raise their baby as a girl, to keep her intersex status 'hush-hush' from their community and most importantly to keep it secret from Louise. The secrecy and taboo surrounding an intersex birth persists: Linda Roberts' father beat her 'black and blue' in the 1940s when she raised the issue as a child (Hugill 1998: 7), while more enlightened parents mourn the loss of joy engendered by this secrecy:

> [we were] ... confused and concerned by it all. I felt very lonely and frightened by what I didn't understand. My husband felt so angry at the doctors. I just felt that they wanted to say Joe wasn't natural and to tidy him away. Our happiness at becoming a mum and dad was totally ruined, we nearly fell apart, and yet thankfully we still managed to keep loving our baby ... (Alison, correspondence 6 August 2003)

Louise is now in adulthood making her own decisions about her continued surgical attempts towards 'normality', and indeed her management of being intersexed. She is conventional in her desires to operate 'normally' in the world as a woman: 'I'd like the right man to come along – like most people would ...' (*Secret Intersex* 2004), but her childhood experiences of growing up as a girl are not straightforward. Louise's adult choices are irreversibly coloured by medical decisions in infancy to remove her gonads, and thereby to close her off to much post-natal testosterone exposure, to try multiple genital surgeries and to prescribe female hormones during her teens to produce breast development. The consent given was, in the first instance, that of Louise's parents, and was painfully uninformed: 'I couldn't talk to her [Louise] because I didn't know anything ...' (Louise's mother, *Secret Intersex* 2004).

There is also likely to have been a rational argument put to Louise's parents that perhaps their child should not know about her intersexed status in order to psychologically preserve the sex assignment made and to spare her the social awfulness of discovery. Louise grew up looking different to other girls, tending to play with 'boy's toys', being mysteriously and frequently hospitalized, and exhibiting aggressive and disruptive behaviour. She describes herself as a sad, lonely child, confused about her gender role and associated expectations. Intersex was never discussed or explained to her, or indeed to her parents.

Discovery came around age thirteen when Louise was staying at a residential care school because of behavioural difficulties. She dreamt about her marriage and motherhood, and announced to the matron that she intended to 'settle down with a lovely man and have a couple of kids' (interview 27 September 2005). According to Louise, the matron's face dropped, she closed the door and told Louise that she would never have children. Louise remembers feeling that her 'world ended'. While the matron offered further details and discussion, Louise simply closed down. She didn't want to discuss the detail of the subject either in school or at home, and she entered a period of despair during which she contemplated suicide. Old enough to question her medical treatment, it was too late to reverse decisions made about sex assignment. Louise's reaction to revelation in adolescence that she was intersexed was contained in a painful and angry letter to her mother: 'you lied to me ... why did you keep me alive to go through all this?' (*Secret Intersex* 2004).

Louise experienced shock, horror, anger, fear and bitterness. This pain is what Beh and Diamond call the 'last cost of secrecy' (2000: unpaginated), that is, the devastating shame and despair experienced by those individuals who find out (long after it is known by clinicians and parents) that they are intersexed and were surgically assigned sex in infancy. Holmes (1998), for example, writes, 'knowledge of myself and where I fit in is what was stolen from me by being medicalised and by having my body altered against my will' (ibid.: 224). Moreover, Holmes maintains that 'Having my genitals mutilated has made me no less intersexual; it has merely made me a mutilated intersexual' (ibid.: 225). Holmes subsequently notes that

> I do not believe in an essential intersex body, or a reified sense of intersex identity. I do not walk through the world without a recognizable gender, nor do I feel that I am inappropriately gendered in a very typical "femmey" body type. MY refusal to accept the surgery as the necessary suturing of the gender identity is really the point of that statement [above] and it is because I thought it might be most useful, at the time when I authored it, to indicate to surgeons that their efforts were fruitless ... (Morgan Holmes, correspondence 2 Feburary 2007)

Holmes insists that this is not to advocate a eugenicist erasure of intersex, but reports a hope that the 'your surgical interventions are ineffective' message would encourage a move away from intervention, finally stating

> I remain more than hurt and annoyed and insecure about my 'appearance' precisely because of what they did to me ... but having been in one relationship for 19 years, I'm not worried that I am a repulsive partner. (Morgan Holmes, correspondence 2 Feburary 2007)

Others describe various expressions of rage, emotional numbness and suicidal despair at discovery of their 'hermaphrodite' diagnosis at birth, their naming as male or female, and their surgical alteration in infancy or young childhood to better resemble their selected sex: 'Non-consensual surgery cannot erase intersexuality and produce whole males and females; it produces emotionally abused and sexually dysfunctional intersexuals' (Chase 1998b: 214).

Louise's adolescent rage was directed towards her mother. During her teenage years, she hit her, threatened her with knives, was 'the evil-est you could get' (interview 27 September 2005). She recognizes now that she was desperately trying to get her anger out of herself before she completely imploded. At the same time, she was placed on oestrogen treatment, gained 22 kilos in weight in six weeks and developed some feminine body curves, breasts and pubic hair. The hormone treatment was so distressing, coupled as it was with the enormous emotional burden of coping with revelation of her intersexuality, that Louise refused any more oestrogen therapy after one year.

Louise explains that while she thinks it was the right decision to assign her female in infancy, she is 'not fully' sure when she thinks about what it would have been like to be a boy. It transpires, however, that she and her mother have considered relocating in order to allow Louise to live as a man. Louise's hesitancy here undermines her assertions above about wanting to be 'complete as a woman'. She talks about her mother being 'robbed of a son' and of the subject 'screwing her mind up' so that she didn't know 'what I was, who I was' (interview 27 September 2005). Arguably, Louise is making the most culturally acceptable, self-acceptable, sex-normative 'best' of the reconstructed, surgically amended, scar-tissued, hormone-enhanced intersexed body she has. While her mother is now convinced that the assignment decision was not right, Louise makes more abstract statements: 'it would be a bit unfair to say whether it was right or wrong ... but it shouldn't be done ... children should be given the choice when they get older whether they should be brought up as a boy or a girl ...' (interview 27 September 2005).

Louise's birth presents a challenge to the 'norm' of binary sex distinction, and her subsequent surgeries have been both concerned with correcting her problems of incontinence, as well as trying to align her body as closely as possible to that of a female, her assigned sex. But many questions persist:

What would have happened if Louise had not been subjected to sex assignment?

Would her single testis, if left intact, have continued to produce some virilizing testosterone?

Might any subsequent decision by Louise to live as a female have been rendered more difficult as a result of post-natal testosterone exposure?

Might a phalloplasty have been successful in adulthood?

What would have happened if Louise's intersex status had not been kept a secret from her?

What would have happened if Louise's birth-notice in her local paper had read 'intersexed child' rather than boy, and subsequently girl?

The Primacy of the Penis

William Reiner is Associate Professor at the University of Oklahoma Health Sciences Center in the Department of Urology and of Psychiatry. His paper, 'A 7-year Experience of Genetic Males with Severe Phallic Inadequacy Assigned Female' (Reiner and Kropp 2004a), concerns eighteen genetic male subjects diagnosed with a range of conditions causing 'severe phallic inadequacy':

- Cloacal Exstrophy (where severe pelvic anatomical disarray manifests, testes fail to descend into the scrotum, and the urinary opening is above the phallus);
- partial androgen resistance (where testosterone has not completed the virilization of the foetus);
- Gonadal Dysgenesis (where the gonads do not form testes, but rather gonadal tissue that will not produce male or female sex hormones, and which lies in undeveloped streak gonadal formation in the abdomen);
- penile agenesis (where the penis fails to form).

Of these eighteen individuals (aged 3–30 years), fifteen were assigned female and three were assigned male. Although not called 'hermaphrodites', the fifteen case histories echo Louise's experience of being genetically male, but being surgically assigned female. Written after his experience with Kayla (discussed in the Introduction), Reiner examines the rationale for these assignments by considering the physical, social, psychological and sexual identity development of the subjects. Significantly, in all eighteen cases typically male behaviours and interests were observed, even though fifteen of these had been assigned female in infancy (Reiner and Kropp 2004a). And of the adults in the whole group only those living as male were living independently or had had personal relationships. Reiner's conclusions of this longitudinal study are clear:

> … males with severe phallic inadequacy reared male and those reared female but converting to male can have functional psychosocial developmental trajectories.
>
> Those reared female have a realistic likelihood of recognizing male sexual identity and converting to male.

Those not converting to male appear to have less successful psychosocial developmental trajectories ... (Reiner and Kropp 2004a: 2,395)

These conclusions imply that sex assignment for cosmetic rather than for
clear medical reasons where infant life may be compromised presents a poor
choice. These subjects, having been raised in most cases against karyotype (as
female, since they are genetic males), and without the penis that culturally
typifies males, have nevertheless tended to self-assign to male as adults, and
where they have done so have tended to be more independent and to have
more successful sexual relationships (even in spite of their anatomical incom-
pleteness). So, in these cases, sex assignment as female was not an especially
successful course.

Ransley also recalls his experience with genetic males, with testosterone-
productive testes, typical scrotums and satisfactory *in utero* hormone exposure,
but who have penile agenesis – complete absence of the penis in an otherwise
typical male anatomy. Traditionally, these individuals would have been raised
as female (as were the majority of Reiner's group above, and as was Kayla),
having their testes removed in infancy to cut off their testosterone, and with
oestrogen administered at puberty (Kayla had begun to live as a male prior to
puberty, and therefore avoided oestrogen therapy). Ransley defines his subjects as 'the most unsuccessful male-to-female XY conversions', indicating
'most of us now have changed our view for that population, that should be
raised male' (interview 6 September 2005). Ransley goes on to explain that
this is problematic since there continues to be a cultural equation of maleness
with a penis. Surgical construction of a 'cosmetically acceptable', physically
and sexually functional penis cannot be undertaken until adulthood, and
success is not guaranteed. Ransley notes that phalloplasty can be a 'highly
unsatisfactory procedure' (interview 6 September 2005) often producing an
unrealistic penis, with little sensitivity, no erotic sensation, no erectile function, and needing artificial stiffeners that often migrate outwards. Ransley contends that aphallic subjects assigned male must go through childhood with
either no penis or a 'little "digi-thing" made out of skin', and he addresses
those advocating this course: 'the non-surgical counsellor will say "we'll make
you a penis in adult life – don't worry you can go through school, you can go
and play rugby without your penis, you can go and have a communal shower
without your penis, get in the rugby bath without your penis ..."' (interview 6
September 2005).

Ransley argues that male assignment in absence of a penis presents a stark
prospect: a culturally unsatisfactory – and sexually challenging – male body,
with poor prospects for phalloplasty. Alternatively, a decision to surgically
assign a genetic male without a penis as female runs the risk of the subject
rejecting the assignment in adulthood. Ransley urges that, if the latter course

is selected and the infant assigned as female, then critically the testicles must be removed within a fortnight of birth or the female assignment decision will be adversely affected by testosterone exposure. And Ransley argues vigorously that such female-assigned subjects, who subsequently report dissatisfaction with their assignment, have, most likely, experienced delayed orchidectomy (removal of the testes) and have therefore been subjected to the post-natal testosterone wash that genetic male infants with intact testes experience.

Ransley describes his small group of genetic males with Cloacal Exstrophy. These all had very early orchidectomies and were assigned female. Their current assessment by clinical psychologist Polly Carmichael at Great Ormond Street Hospital, London, has, to date, given Ransley no reason to doubt the original assignment (although he accepts that the group is small and the oldest is only aged twenty-four). Ransley again stresses the importance of early removal of testes in these cases, and also how 'gender-appropriate cosmesis' is crucial to good psychological development. He notes that there is no existing lifetime study of the poorly virilized or non-phallic 'failed male' (interview 6 September 2005), and he suggests that teenage suicide claims some such individuals, raised as male, but with tiny or absent penises. Ransley concludes that if males cannot function satisfactorily without an appropriate penis, then decisions made early in the lives of those without such must reflect that.

Dr John Money's 'Optimal Gender Policy'

To consider the questions raised above, it is important to examine the so-called 'optimal gender policy' (Creighton and Liao 2004a, referencing Money *et al.* 1955) still influencing paediatric urologists, endocrinologists and gynaecologists, and based on guidelines for the management of intersexed infants proposed in 1955 by John Money of the Johns Hopkins Medical Institutions, Baltimore. A prolific publisher, Money's near monopoly of this area of research has resulted in a kind of essentialist methodology for treatment of intersex in infants which has only relatively recently been critiqued by a number of key clinicians and commentators on sex, gender and sexuality. Money became the central proponent of surgical intervention in cases of infant genital ambiguity. Yet, his original senior dissertation (1952) from Harvard University, USA, stated clearly that the 250 'hermaphrodites' he studied were, for the most part, able to live comfortably and contentedly without surgical intervention: 'the majority of patients rose above their genital handicap and not only made an "adequate adjustment" to life, but lived in a way virtually indistinguishable from people without genital difference' (Money 1952, referenced in Footnote 100 of Beh and Diamond 2000: unpaginated). Money did not publish these findings subsequently in the professional literature.

Broadly, Money argued that infants are 'psychosexually neutral' at birth (Diamond and Sigmundson 1997b: 298), and remain so until around age two, when language development becomes ascendant. Money and Ehrhardt (1972) presented a case history to support their position. They described two infants, both genetic females and anatomically identical, both with Congenital Adrenal Hyperplasia (discussed in Chapter 8) resulting in virilized clitorises at birth. Money and Ehrhardt claimed that these infants were raised to function perfectly adequately, one as a female in a female role, and the other as a male in a male role. The infant assigned as female had her enlarged clitoris surgically reduced, while the other child's enlarged clitoris was renamed as sex-neutral phallic tissue, and then as a penis in keeping with the male assignment. This case study was used as a prime illustration of the 'optimal gender policy', which asserted that during that first eighteen to twenty-four months of life the infant's sex is malleable and can be influenced by rearing. The infant's sex, according to the 'optimal gender policy' is connected to the appearance of the genitalia, but not fixed by that. Money and Ehrhardt's proposition was that an infant can be raised in contradiction of sex at birth, provided that the child is surgically assigned and hormonally treated in accordance with that decision, that the decision is made sufficiently early and that it is positively reinforced by nurture. Money asserted that the sex of rearing of an intersex child could be insisted upon by assignment over and above the sex indicators of karyotype, gonads, *in utero* hormone exposure, internal or external genitalia (Money *et al.* 1957, referenced in Zucker 2002a). This continues to inform treatment of intersexed children today.

No long-term follow-up was presented for Money and Ehrhardt's 1972 case study, but subsequent case studies in which long-term effects of these kinds of decisions are more clearly articulated prove less definitive in relation to infant-to-adult sex identification. One can see, however, how Money's thinking informed the infant Louise's treatment. Presenting physically at birth as sex ambiguous, she was initially pronounced male (supporting evidence being her one testis and her genetic sex), and subsequently renamed female (supporting evidence being her one ovary, her rudimentary vaginal opening and possibly the easier route towards aesthetic achievement in genital surgery). In these decisions, it is apparent how Louise's psychosexual identity was presumed to be unformed, a neutral sheet upon which to inscribe a decided sex, and around which the physical manifestation of sex could then be assembled.

At around twenty-four months, Money contended, the effect of the socio-cultural environment exerts a stronger influence on the formation of gender identity, but by this stage the infant Louise had been named, socialized and surgically worked on to support the clinical decision that she should be a girl. The increasing influence of the wider social and cultural environment she was in would serve only to reinforce her presentation as a girl and censure any tendencies – which in fact she exhibited in childhood – to act out as masculine. The secrecy surrounding Louise's intersex status upheld and strengthened the social, cultural, medical and parental signalling of sex conformity.

Money insisted that for gender identity to form psychosocially boys primarily require an 'adequate' penis with no vagina, and girls primarily require a vagina with no easily noticeable phallus. For Money's strategy to work the intersexed child's genitalia must be made to match the gender identity being decided upon. Consequently, he advocated 'corrective' surgery and hormone therapy in accordance with the sex the child most apparently represents, or, where that was impossible to determine – as in Louise's case – in support of the gender identity decision made (Money and Ehrhardt 1972). It is apparent that as soon as it was decided that Louise would be a girl, all the systems of surgical intervention, parental nurturing, naming and supporting fell into place in corroboration of that decision, with secrecy disallowing discussion or reflection.

The 'optimal gender policy' advised parents to hide diagnostic details from their children so that this would not interfere with the gender signal of assignment (Creighton and Liao 2004a, referencing Fausto-Sterling 2000). And for some parents, for whom their child might be a reflection of the 'health' of their own sexuality, there is arguably relief in the secrecy being offered through medical authority. The huge flaw in Money's belief that infants assigned a gender before they reached twenty-four months could be successfully raised, nurtured and fixed in that gender was that the gender decision required surgical and hormonal enforcement, which was permanent. Moreover, long-term follow-up was significantly overlooked. Kessler and Creighton are particularly critical of this omission in the majority of Money's subsequent case histories (Kessler 1990; Creighton and Liao 2004a).

Louise's story is in keeping with Money's system. Her scarred genitals signal a lifetime of feminizing surgery, and her socialization means that she seeks 'wholeness' through being a 'complete' woman who can marry a man (in spite of being genetically 'male') and have penetrative sex. Louise was kept in the dark for her childhood about being intersexed, and was reinforced persistently as female by parents, clinicians and the wider community. Long-term follow-up has not acknowledged Louise's continued gender identity struggles, or recognized that she has considered, but rejected, the massive step of repositioning herself – after all she has been through – by living as a male.

CHAPTER 4

David's Story and Diamond's Recommendations

The presuppositions that we make about sexed bodies, about them being one or the other, about the meanings that are said to inhere in them or to follow from being sexed in such a way are suddenly and significantly upset by those examples that fail to comply with the categories that naturalise and stabilise that field of bodies for us within the terms of cultural conventions.

Judith Butler, *Gender Trouble*

David Reimer committed suicide aged thirty-eight on 4 May 2004. In 2000, David stated in the BBC2 *Horizon* documentary *The Boy Who Was Turned into a Girl*:

I was never happy as Brenda, never. I'd slit my throat before I'd go back to that ... It didn't work because that's life, because you're human and you're not stupid and eventually you wind up being who you are.

David Reimer

David Reimer was *not intersexed*, but his experiences have had a major impact on how intersexed individuals have been treated, as well as being used to illustrate what Diamond refers to as the 'so-called power of nurture to overcome nature' (Diamond in May 2005: 76). After David Reimer's death, Betsy Driver of US advocacy and support group Bodies Like Ours wrote: 'David was admired by so many within the intersex movement for his strength to speak out publicly about the injustice that was done to him. Many survivors of similar medical treatment are overwhelmed by intense shame and David rose above that ...' (Driver 2004).

David Reimer's treatment – the so-called John/Joan 'classic' case – became a template for the medical treatment of intersexed infants (Colapinto 2000). A non-intersexed genetic male (then called Bruce), one of male twins born in Winnipeg, Canada, in 1965, David had his penis accidentally destroyed during a routine circumcision at the age of about eight months. At twenty-two months, long after the two weeks testosterone-exposure threshold referenced by Ransley above, David had surgery to remove his testes, and his remaining genitalia were surgically re-fashioned from his scrotal tissue to resemble a vulva. Diamond's words are chillingly illustrative of the massive nature of this decision: 'It was recommended that the traumatised child be castrated, have a vulva and a vagina fashioned and be reared as a girl' (Diamond 2004a: i).

David was then named as a girl, raised as a girl, treated as a girl and encouraged to behave as a girl. That girl – Brenda – was provided with psychological support, further surgical treatment in childhood and female hormones were administered prior to puberty to produce breast development. The person who masterminded this 'entirely experimental' (Beh and Diamond 2005: 12) course of action was Dr John Money, then a psychologist at the Johns Hopkins Medical Institutions, Baltimore. David's twin brother acted as the 'control' of Money's experiment since he was genetically identical to the subject, and had been born anatomically identical to his (then) brother. Both children were subjected to the same medical scrutiny during childhood.

By the time David Reimer, having been raised as Brenda, had reached age seven, Money claimed great success. He used the case to support his hypothesis that where cosmetic genital alteration is performed early and the genital appearance is then considered unambiguous, it is possible to assign sex to the 'psychosexually neutral' infant (Diamond and Sigmundson 1997b: 298), and for that infant to grow up successfully and happily in that gender (Money and Ehrhardt 1972). In fact, Brenda did not accept the assigned sex, experiencing cognitive dissonance as a child, as well as body image and behavioural problems in childhood and at puberty (Colapinto 2004). In the *Horizon* documentary (2000), Brenda's mother reported:

> I could see that Brenda wasn't happy as a girl, no matter what I tried to do for her, no matter how I tried to instruct her, she was very rebellious, she was very masculine and I could not persuade her to do anything feminine. Brenda had almost no friends ... Everybody ... called her cave woman. She was a very lonely, lonely girl.

At puberty, Brenda's family stopped contact with Money, and when Brenda was aged fourteen told her of her birth as a boy, of the circumcision accident and of her surgical/hormonal sex assignment. Nothing was heard about Brenda's subsequent developments for the next fifteen years, during which Money continued to promote the success of the case and the hypothesis that gender identity could be changed by nurture. Brenda in fact reverted to living as a male (now called David Reimer), later telling his biographer John Colapinto (2004) that the revelation made sense of much of what he had felt as a child. David underwent a mastectomy to remove the breasts that had developed as a result of oestrogen treatment at puberty. He also elected to have four more genital surgeries to try to convert the surgically feminized genitalia he had grown up with to something more 'male-looking'. These were, of course, problematic procedures since his infant penile structure had been damaged in the circumcision accident even before his sex assignment surgery. David's penis reconstruction was not especially satisfactory: tissue was without sensation, and he urinated through a fistula (a hole in the repaired urethra) at the base. He did have prosthetic testicles created to replace those removed in infancy, and testosterone injections were used to increase his musculature. Diamond (Diamond and Sigmundson 1997b) reports that David became capable of ejaculation as a result of male hormone treatment, although earlier removal of his testes rendered him infertile.

David married a woman and, via adoption, became father to her three children. The marriage was long-lasting – another testimony to the lack of imagination that insists that men can only ever fully function with intact penises – but it did eventually fail. David Reimer and his wife enjoyed occasional orgasmic coitus, and Diamond notes that they 'mostly pleasure[d] each other with a great deal of physical affection and mutual masturbation' (Diamond and Sigmundson 1997b: 301). Money's original decision to assign this injured genetic male infant as female was based on an assumption of psychosexual neutrality at birth, and on a belief that the infant would satisfactorily develop a sexual identity in conjunction with the fashioned presentation of the genitalia. Like Kayla, David did not. In his own description of his development as a girl, there is a terrible painful self-awareness:

> I was so pitifully lonely and I tried to put make-up on, but I looked like Bozo the Clown. You ever can imagine a guy trying to put make-up on himself. After a while trying I just gave up, says what's the sense of trying. No matter how much I, I put out in effort it's never going to work.
>
> There's, there's no way of, of knowing whether you're a boy or girl 'cos nobody tells you. You don't waken up one morning and say oh I'm, I'm, I'm a boy today, you know. You know. It's, it's, it's in your, you know, it's in your genetics, it's in your brain ... nobody has to tell you who you are ... (*Horizon* 2000)

David's twin brother, who had been subjected to 'control' examinations by Money throughout his childhood died in 2002 from an overdose of antidepressants. After David's suicide in 2004, Bodies Like Ours produced a detailed email stating the following:

> [David's mother] Janet Reimer was widely quoted in Canadian media today saying that she believes her son would still be here if he had not been subjected to the gender experiment. She said she also still harbors anger towards Dr. Money for convincing her and David's father Ron to allow the gender experiment and blames Money in part for David's suicide. Dr. John Money has not commented publicly as of early this morning on the death of his most famous experiment. (Driver 2004)

In 1994, Money seemed to indicate a softening of his position when he acknowledged that the causes of gender identity disorder lay in any combination of the subject's genes, *in utero* hormonal experience, post-natal socialization and post-pubertal hormonal determinants. In short, Money indicated 'there is no one cause of a gender role ... Nature alone is not responsible, nor is nurture, alone' (Money 1994: 166). This shift in position came long after his powerful messages about gender malleability had informed the strong conventions of current day treatment for intersexed infants with ambiguous genitalia.

Money's 'Theory of Neutrality'

Emi Koyama, Director of the Intersex Initiative (USA), criticizes Money's established and 'unreliable' theory, his 'wrong assumption about David's gender development', and the 'sexually and physically invasive examinations and tests' carried out on David and his twin brother (quoted in Driver 2004). A range of physicians and commentators on intersex support Koyama's opinion. Diamond and Sigmundson (1997a) maintain that most intersex conditions manifesting as genital ambiguity need not require surgical intervention. Philip A. Gruppuso, MD, Paediatric Endocrinologist at Brown University, Providence, RI, advocated a moratorium on infant genital surgery until long-term research is carried out into its effectiveness to date (1999), and other clinicians, such as Schober (1998b, 1999), have also questioned the need for cosmetic genital surgery. Dreger (1998b) and others (Kessler 1990; Fausto-Sterling 2000) noted that while contemporary microsurgical techniques for infant genital surgery allow for often-excellent cosmetic effect, long-term follow-up of patients whose sex was surgically assigned in infancy is still significantly lacking.

Anecdotal and clinical evidence is amassing that indicates substantial risk with such surgery of loss of erotic sensation and orgasmic function, infertility (in instances where fertility might have been retained), life-long urinary pain and dysfunction, pelvic infection and endocrine malfunction, and psychological trauma (Schober 1998a).

Related to this, Dreger reminds us that intersex is permanent, a life-long condition, which cannot be erased by surgery (1999). There are growing numbers of voices from medical practice and from those who were subjected to genital surgery in infancy that surgical/hormonal intervention for children whose genitalia are neither typically male nor typically female should not be permitted (except in certain specific instances where the infant's life is endangered). Rather, such children should be raised in their most likely gender, with the understanding that this may not be correct, and with the clear idea that children will indicate to their parents what their gender is as and when they can. This approach would be reinforced via counselling and peer support for child and family to eliminate the 'medical trauma' of the 'current conceal-ment-centered protocol' (Driver 2004).

For many years, as a result particularly of Money's experiment with David Reimer's sexual and gender identity, science has asserted that it is possible to turn a boy into a girl, and to make that boy look, think, feel like a girl. In essence, the supposition has been that science – using nurture as a tool, and surgery/hormonal therapy as a method – could overturn genetic blueprints, complex endocrine constructions and the physical and hormonal evidencing of sex, even when these are atypical. This was, in 1965, a radical viewpoint. It sought to overthrow the prior belief that male and female behaviour was fixed within the womb, and that sex identification was determined prior to birth. For Money and his team

> ... the main key to how we developed our gender identity was not genetic or hormonal. It was how we were raised.
>
> A child might be born with some innate sense of its gender but this could be over-ridden by upbringing ... nurture could override nature.
>
> A child taught to behave in a masculine way would grow up thinking and feeling like a boy. Raising a child like a girl – for instance giving it dolls to play with – would encourage it to develop a maternal instinct and a feminine way of behaving.
>
> If this theory was true, it could be used as the basis for raising [David] successfully as a girl. (*Horizon* 2000)

Although David Reimer was not intersexed, Money transposed his findings from David's case onto theories he had been developing from the 1950s about the treatment of intersexed infants. He proposed, for example, that a genetic female, with ovaries and uterus intact, but who had virilized external genitalia due to an overdose of testosterone in the womb, could be raised as a boy in keeping with the outward appearance of genitalia that looked more like a penis. Similarly, a genetic male, who received too little testosterone in the womb, and whose penis was therefore underdeveloped, could be raised as a girl in keeping with the outward appearance of what looked more like a clitoris. Money believed that for the first two years of life humans have such a neutral and unformed gender identity that our brains are malleable. That is, a baby could be 'trained' to believe itself male *or* female. If started early enough, with sufficient psychological support for parents and with genital surgery to more closely mimic the genitals of the designated sex, Money believed that sex could be decided upon and fixed. After two years, that malleability would end and the child's gender identity would be formed. Money's 'Theory of Neutrality' became widely embraced by the medical community and shaped – continues to shape – the lives of thousands of intersexed children: '[Money] advised doctors to pick whichever gender seemed most suitable and assign the baby accordingly, importantly before it was two years old. This decision would often mean performing surgery to alter the genitals of the child' (*Horizon* 2000).

This theory was a comfortable one in many ways for the medical community to embrace. It allowed paediatricians to deal with shocked and upset parents who desperately wanted a boy- or a girl-child, but whose infant was intersexed and had ambiguous genitalia. A surgeon could offer a surgical solution to 'fix the problem', and could support that solution with a psychological theory of infant sex neutrality. The surgeon could cosmetically enhance the appearance of the infant's external genitalia, and propose a way forwards in terms of naming and rearing the child, assuring the parents that this solution was workable and would guarantee a happy child and a successful outcome. Understandably the majority of parents chose – continue to choose – an apparently immediate and medically sanctioned 'solution' over an unknowable possible future problem.

Surgical Sex Assignment

Money's work is still valued in the field. Philip Ransley was interviewed by Dilly Barlow in the BBC2 documentary *The Boy Who Was Turned into a Girl* (*Horizon* 2000). Discussing the case of a genetic male infant born with a tiny penis, undeveloped testicles and some mixed ovarian and testicular tissue inside, Ransley was insistent that the incomplete virilization of this male child would have resulted in an enormous psychological burden: 'There was no difficulty in this case in everyone agreeing that the appropriate sex of rearing was female and she was gender assigned female ... I think the stage is set for this child to have an extremely successful life as a female' (Ransley, *Horizon* 2000).

As was discussed in Chapter 3, that incomplete virilization is likely to cause a boy and an adult male grave psychological difficulty, especially in a culture fixated by penile dimension. David Reimer's life was never going to be easy after his accident in infancy, but men do cope with damaged, small or even absent penises. Justine Reilly and Christopher Woodhouse, then of the Institute of Urology at St Peter's Hospitals and The Hospital for Sick Children, London, asserted in 1989 that they could draw two conclusions from their study of twenty patients primarily diagnosed with micropenises in infancy: 'a small penis does not preclude normal male role and a micropenis or microphallus alone should not dictate a female gender reassignment in infancy' (1989: 571).

In the Reilly and Woodhouse study, of the twelve subjects of ages seventeen to forty-three, all had erections, nine were sexually active and reported vaginal penetration, seven were married or cohabiting and one had fathered a child. Nevertheless, Ransley indicated that surgical assignment as female where virilization is poor seems to be in the best interests of the child, contending that 'we would not undertake surgical intervention if we were not convinced completely that this was the correct course of action' (*Horizon* 2000). Ransley was incorrect, however, when he stated that *everyone* was in agreement about the course of action described, which would have included irreversible surgery in infancy and hormone replacement therapy in adolescence. The child, the subject of these actions, was too small to voice an opinion – either way.

The David Reimer case suggests that sex and gender cannot be imposed. Rather they seem to be essential to the subject, possibly regardless of how that subject appears physically or manifests internally. Moreover, they are highly complex, affected both by biology, environment before and after birth, and learning. Diamond, commenting just after David Reimer's death, notes that 'Even though [David] didn't have a penis, he still knew he was male' (Diamond quoted in Black 2004: A.03).

'Acceptable' penis size, penetrative potential and the ability to eventually urinate while standing are of 'paramount importance' in the deliberations required for an intersexed child with ambiguous genitalia to be designated male (American Academy of Pediatrics Policy Statement 2000). Kessler critiques Money's assertion that a much smaller than average penis may compromise the sex – the 'essential maleness' – of the infant and the gender – the 'male's manliness' – of the adult (1990: 12), and she quotes Money: 'The primary deficit (of not having a sufficient penis) – and destroyer of morale – lies in being unable to satisfy the partner' (Money 1974: 217 in Kessler 1990: 20). Kessler's empirical studies of clinicians' anxieties regarding sex assignment surgery bear this out (1990), as does Phornphutkul *et al.*'s articulation of the principles governing management of patients with ambiguous genitalia: 'Current pediatric endocrinology textbooks continue to include phallus size among the most important considerations in assigning gender in the newborn with ambiguous genitalia' (2000: 135).

Ransley is concerned about the 'very unsatisfactory male body' that has a 'penis like a Swan Vesta matchstick', and his practice over a lifetime has been to tend to assign infants exhibiting these as female (interview 6 September 2005). 'Concern' is the appropriate word here – it is apparent that the vast majority of those involved in the management of intersex genital ambiguity are *concerned* with seeking the best outcome *in their opinion*. There are no evil paediatricians, monstrous surgeons or sadistic endocrinologists here – just differences of strategic approach to complex, often unsolvable, problems. Interviewee Belinda, for example, insists that doctors and surgeons are not the 'ogres' that they are sometimes described as and acknowledges the difficulty of decisions they are called to make (correspondence 26 April 2003). Creighton too acknowledges that the situation regarding sex assignment in intersex is confusing for those within the medical profession as well as their patients and subjects: 'Many clinicians are puzzled by the intense criticism of their well-meaning and skilful work. Some experts advocate the same policies but with improved techniques, whilst others urge a thorough re-examination of every aspect of infant sex assignment' (Creighton and Liao 2004a: 659).

Ransley acknowledges female assignment of genetic males with phallic 'inadequacy' is not nearly as acceptable as it used to be, and he notes that parents are now much more challenging on questions of sex, sexual function and gratification than previously when 'oh, it's horrible, chop it off ... would have been the reaction' (interview 6 September 2005). Nevertheless, Ransley remains concerned about how outcomes are measured, and he maintains that ultimately quality of life for the subject will determine how successful a line of treatment has been, and – as he says – that is much less easily measured than the length of a penis, the number of sexual partners a subject has or their fertility.

The 'Good Enough' Penis

As Ransley confirms, there has been a historic tendency, still prevalent, for genetic male intersexed infants, often with functional testes and with reaction to injected testosterone, to be assigned female. Both Schober (1998a) and Chase (1998b) suggest that 90 per cent of intersexed infants who are assigned sex in infancy are assigned female. This decision requires a combination of interventions, depending on the nature of the genital ambiguity, to maintain the female sex assignment: removal of frequently healthy testes; fashioning labia from a scrotal sac if one is present; clitoridectomy or clitoral recession to reduce the phallus to a socially suitable clitoral dimension; surgical creation of a vagina and opening of the vaginal introitus. Just before the onset of puberty, oestrogen replacement therapy will be necessary to prompt the development of breasts, and the subject will be infertile (as a woman).

As regards vaginal and clitoral surgery, Creighton (Creighton and Liao 2004a, referencing Wilson and Reiner 1998) notes that the creation of a 'functional' vagina in a newborn can only really have the purpose of reassuring parents since that child will not require a vagina until puberty. Ransley too asserts that he is 'not sure it's possible to do an operation on a six-month old baby that can take on the sexual rampages of a seventeen year old female without some additional modification', and he believes that additional vaginal surgery at puberty should be expected (interview 6 September 2005). Moreover, Ransley states, the vagina constructed in infancy really requires good endocrine control in childhood to avoid the subtle virilization that may close it by stenosis (narrowing). Creighton (Creighton and Liao 2004a, referencing Alizai et al. 1999) notes that vaginal stenosis is a common problem, with 36–100 per cent of subjects experiencing this after infant surgery. Repeat surgery in adolescence is frequent, and sexual function scores are poor, with those who have had clitoral surgery 'significantly less likely to report experience of orgasm than those who had not had surgery' (Creighton and Liao 2004a: 660). Consequently, Creighton asserts, 'past confidence among pediatric surgeons in unimpaired sexual function after clitoral surgery seems no longer tenable' (ibid.).

And remember, this is *cosmetic* surgery, not surgery to preserve life. That is not to underestimate the 'awfulness' for a male of not having a penis of 'acceptable' dimension – but David Reimer coped, married and lived as a functional male. He did this not without difficulty, and arguably with the added 'awfulness' of being raised in conflict with his gender identity, having to reconcile gender dysphoria in adolescence/adult life, and having a body that did not 'support' his gender identification. If David Reimer could have a micropenis, enjoy alternative sexual pleasure to penetrative sex and urinate sitting down, might it not be preferable to allow such subjects to develop to puberty and self-determine whether phalloplasty and testosterone treatment would be an acceptable augmentation of genetic sex, whether transition to female would be a better course of action or whether a 'middle path' could be tailored for that individual? Diamond and Sigmundson (1997a) notably contend that individuals with a micropenis may not only be fertile, but also capable of mutually satisfactory, if unconventional, sexual relations. In these cases, it seems, the ambiguity is not whether the genetic male infant's phallic tissue is a penis but whether 'it is "good enough" to remain one' (Kessler 1990: 13).

What size of neo-natal penis is 'acceptable' for a male infant? Some sources indicate that less than 2.5 cm is considered 'problematic' (Meyers-Seifer and Charest 1992, referenced in Dreger 1998b). The American Academy of Pediatrics (2000) recommended a *stretched penile length* of at least 2.0 cm as 'adequate', and Kessler reports an anonymized paediatric endocrinologist's claim that 'if the phallus is less than 2 centimeters long at birth and won't respond to androgen treatments, then it's made into a female' (1990: 18). Maximum size for a socially 'acceptable' clitoris is also confusing. Diamond (2004a) indicates that over the past forty years an arbitrary maximum of 0.9 cm in length for the clitoris became the most accepted treatment benchmark, while McGillivray (1991) in Dreger suggests 'clitorises – meaning simply phalluses in children labelled female – are frequently considered too big if they exceed one centimetre in length' (Dreger 1998b: unpaginated).

Dr David Ralph of University College London's Institute of Urology is involved in current refinement of phalloplasty and penis enlargement procedures for patients whose micropenis has some sexual sensitivity. In his study the erotic tissue present is incorporated into the surface of transplanted skin from the patient's forearm, a urethra is constructed to enable urination, and an inflatable prosthesis is inserted to allow erection and penetrative sexual intercourse. Nine subjects – including three 'hermaphrodites' – were treated, and while all patients were reported as aesthetically satisfied, only four can urinate when standing and four can have regular intercourse. In several cases infections and prosthetic shifts required revision surgeries, and there was a high risk of complication. Again, cosmetic phallic appearance is privileged in the attainment of 'satisfactory maleness', followed by penetrative capability, then upright urinary function. The successful preservation of erotic sensation, which could be discussed in a qualitative way since these surgeries are being done to adult men, is not reported. Nevertheless, Ralph is enthusiastic: 'This operation can change the life of young men, improving their self-esteem and quality of life and allowing many of them to have sexual intercourse, sometimes for the first time in their life' (Ralph 2004: unpaginated).

Dreger (1998b) contends that there are different standards for vaginoplasty and phalloplasty in infant sex assignment. She believes that more is *culturally demanded* of the fully functioning penis, which is required to be of adequate size, recognizable shape and colour, capable of appropriate erection and flaccidity, able to conduct urine and semen separately, competent at upright urination, and with the urethral opening at the tip (Coventry 1998; Creighton and Liao 2004a). *Less than this* is not considered 'adequate'. By contrast, Dreger asserts, the vagina is *culturally required* only to be a 'receptive hole' that is 'big enough to fit a typical-sized penis' (1998b: unpaginated). Erotic sensitivity, ability to change shape with sexual stimulus and self-lubricate, correct position and dimensions have been overlooked or considered of secondary importance to penetrative possibility and external appearance (see variously Gearhart in Bailez *et al.* 1992, referenced in Dreger 1998b; Kessler 1990; Duckett and Baskin 1993). With such exacting cultural standards for penile acceptability, it is suggested that there is cultural asymmetry operating in decisions regarding infant sex assignment (Holmes 2002). Arguably, a 'phallic culture' is preserved in which only 'penises of perfection' are acceptable, with standards remaining high.

Good Housekeeping

The accurate accumulation of knowledge and understanding of the treatment – surgical or otherwise – of intersexed infants is vital to progress. Much current discussion of intersex management is based on infant case studies and surgical procedures from at least twenty-five years ago. Ransley indicates that even subjects of age twenty-five may still be too young to fully assess the success of their sexual function (interview 6 September 2005). Schober (1998a) provides a 'time-line' from 1939 to 1993 detailing the evolution of clitoral surgery, and indicating the various forms of excision, incision, burial and amputation employed for female assignments where the clitoris was 'enlarged'. Ransley acknowledges that such practices gave unsatisfactory long-term results with loss of erotic sensation, pain and discomfort being typical. Various forms of selective reconstructive clitoral reduction evolved from those procedures over the last fifteen years, and those who have experienced more recent surgeries in infancy need to reach adult sexuality to be able to comment on the results.

Ransley also notes that surgeons have limited lifespans of practical expertise, and 'one surgeon's experience in a lifetime can never be enough to properly gauge what's going to happen' (interview 6 September 2005). All this, coupled with generally poor record-keeping and written communication between obstetrics (where foetal care notes stay with the mother's notes), paediatrics (where post-natal care is documented) and adolescent/adult medical carers, has made overview and evaluation problematic. Ransley advocates 'continuous feedback and analysis within an interested group, and good record-keeping' (interview 6 September 2005), particularly where electronic records also document the opinions, predictions and projections of the infant care team and monitor their ongoing discussions. He believes that in twenty-five years this practice will reflect well on intersex care and on the practices surrounding the assignment of sex in infancy.

Professor Milton Diamond's Recommendations

Professor Milton Diamond also took part in the *Horizon* documentary (2000). His position is somewhat different to that of Money and Ransley. As a biologist, he saw that animals had instinctive behaviours to act like males or females, and while he could also see that learning and social conventions were highly influential in shaping the behaviour of human beings, he was convinced that 'our basic framework or predispositions ... come from biology' (*Horizon* 2000). Two key scientific developments were underway in parallel to Money's proclamations of infant psychosexual neutrality and malleability and in support of Diamond's position. First, Diamond was able to show in animal tests that testosterone overdose or underdose *in utero* affected not only the physical virilization or non-virilization of the developing foetus, but also the kinds of sexual behaviour of the animal after birth. This indicated that the theory of psychosexual neutrality at birth was untenable and that antenatal endocrinological development was vitally important in both the sex differentiation and gender identity development of the foetus.

Secondly, Dr Roger Gorski of the University of California, Los Angeles, discovered a significant difference in the size of an area of the hypothalamus of the brain between female and male rats (*Horizon* 2000). While it was unclear what this part of the brain did, Gorski's discovery provided evidence of sex differentiation in the brain before birth. Further experimentation showed that the development of this part of the brain was linked to testosterone dosage in the womb, and that genetically female rats could develop 'male brains' *in utero* as a result of testosterone exposure. This then affected their sexual activity. Dick Swaab of the Netherlands Institute for Brain Research verified these findings in *post mortem* human brain examinations over five years: 'I think if we look at the entire set of data it's clear that we are not born neutral, that our sex difference is present already very early in developments' (Swaab, *Horizon* 2000).

Diamond's, Swaab's and Gorski's findings separately challenged Money's claims of infant psychosexual neutrality. In relation to their assertions, and as a counter to Money's treatment protocols that had dominated the field for so long, Professor Milton Diamond and Keith Sigmundson MD offered alternative recommendations for the treatment of intersexed infants acknowledging that some of these 'are contrary to today's common management procedures' but asserting that 'many of those procedures should be modified' (1997a: 1,046). A synopsis of Diamond and Sigmundson's recommendations is presented below:

1. In cases of infant ambiguous genitalia, a specialist clinical team should carry out a rapid, but not rushed, complete patient history (immediate and extended family) and physical examination (evaluation of gonads and genitals; internal and external genital structures; genetic and endocrine configuration).

Final determination of sex of rearing should be made only when doubt has been – as much as is possible – resolved. Where prediction of future outcome remains doubtful, sex-neutral names may be used.

2. Parents should be informed that their child is intersexed immediately, told that intersex is uncommon but not unheard of and informed that they are not to blame and that their child can have a full, productive and happy life. They should receive full, honest information and specialist counselling.

3. The child's condition is not shameful, but child and family confidentiality must be respected. Genital inspection should be minimized, and permission should always be asked of the child. Lack of respect for patient privacy is unnecessary and traumatizing.

4. Where an intersex diagnosis evidently points to a sex of assignment – as with hypospadias (male) and Congenital Adrenal Hyperplasia (female) – sex of rearing can be determined rapidly. Where the diagnosis is less clear, sex of rearing should be based on the most likely outcome for the child.

Diamond and Sigmundson (1997a) believe that most children adapt and accept their assignment and that it will coincide with their sexual identity.

Where there is disharmony, their non-surgical approach leaves room for re-evaluation of sex of rearing if necessary.

5. Sex of rearing should *not* be based on size or functionality of the phallus alone, but should equally consider that 'the nervous system involved in adult sexuality has been influenced by genetic and endocrine events that will most likely become manifest with or after puberty' (1997a: 1,047).

In the majority of cases – but not all – sex of rearing will indeed be in concord with broad genital appearance. However, Diamond and Sigmundson are less concerned with matching genitalia to sex of rearing in infancy, and more concerned with how an individual 'will develop and prefer to live post-puberty when he or she becomes most sexually active' (1997a: 1,047).

6. Surgery should not be performed for cosmetic reasons alone, and childhood appearance (however difficult for parents and child) may prove less important than long-term genital function and post-pubertal erotic sensitivity. Diamond and Sigmundson (1997a) warn that genital surgery in infancy can impair sexual and erotic function, and recommend waiting until puberty or when the patient may give informed consent if surgery is required.

They also contend that prolonged hormone administration (other than for the essential management of Congenital Adrenal Hyperplasia, as discussed in Chapter 8) should require informed consent. Where gonads *must be* removed for health reasons, this should be explained as much as is possible to the subject and consent achieved if possible. Generally, however, Diamond and Sigmundson argue that gonads should remain intact so that 'any genetic-endocrine predisposition imposed prenatally can be activated with puberty' (1997a: 1,049).

7. Parents must support sex of rearing, and not consider their child neuter. Intersex is not yet accepted as a social designation although some individuals now choose to identify as intersexed. Diamond and Sigmundson (1997a) suggest that when the child is old enough to make informed choices, intersex should be offered as an optional identity along with male and female.

8. Intersexed children should be allowed free expression and choices in toy selection, game preference, friend association, future aspirations and so forth.

9. Counselling, advice and contact with an appropriate support group are extremely important for both parents and child. Children should receive age-appropriate biological, medical, psychological, social and sexual counselling, and as the child matures there must be opportunity for private counselling sessions.

10. The intersexed child is unique. Before or after puberty, she or he might accept life as a 'tomboy' or a 'sissy', or even switch gender altogether. The child may develop sexual orientation towards males, females, both or none at all (1997a: 1,048).

11. As puberty approaches, endocrine, surgical and life options should be openly and honestly discussed so that decisions made by the intersexed individual are fully informed.

Diamond and Sigmundson contend that most individuals have formed a sense of sexual self by age ten to fifteen, but they encourage that individuals have some experience upon which to base any irreversible decisions they may wish to take. For example, a sexually inexperienced adolescent female with a large clitoris 'may not realize the loss in genital sensitivity and responsivity that can accompany cosmetic clitoral reduction' (1997a: 1,049).

12. Diamond and Sigmundson are convinced that most intersex conditions do not require surgical intervention:

> A woman with a phallus can enjoy her hypertrophied clitoris and so can her partner …
>
> Women with androgen insensitivity syndrome or virilizing congenital adrenal hyperplasia who have smaller than usual vaginas can be advised to use pressure dilation to fashion one to facilitate coitus …
>
> A woman with partial Androgen Insensitivity Syndrome likewise can enjoy a large clitoris …
>
> A male with hypospadias might have to sit to urinate without mishap but can function sexually without surgery.
>
> An individual with a micropenis can satisfy a partner and father children. (1997a: 1,049)

Finally, Diamond and Sigmundson (1997a) provide a series of broad guidelines for sex of rearing:

Rear as male
- XY individuals with Androgen Insensitivity Syndrome (Grades 1–3 ranging from typical virilization *in utero* through to male phenotype with severe 'defect' in foetal virilization, small penis, perineoscrotal hypospadias, bifid scrotum or undescended testes);
- XX individuals with Congenital Adrenal Hyperplasia with extensively fused labia and a penile clitoris;
- XY individuals with hypospadias;
- those with Klinefelter's Syndrome;
- XY individuals with micropenis;
- XY individuals with 5-alpha or 17-beta reductase deficiency.

Rear as female

- XY individuals with Androgen Insensitivity Syndrome (Grades 4–7 ranging from severe genital ambiguity with clitoral-like phallus, labioscrotal folds, single perineal orifice through to apparently typical female phenotype);
- XX individuals with Congenital Adrenal Hyperplasia with hypertrophied clitoris;
- XX or XY individuals with Gonadal Dysgenesis;
- those with Turner's Syndrome.

They advocate that individuals with Mixed Gonadal Dysgenesis and 'true hermaphrodites' be assigned male or female depending on the size of the phallus and extent of the labia/scrotum fusion, while if there is a micropenis then assignment should be male. They acknowledge that in some instances clear diagnosis is impossible as the genital appearance is so ambiguous and prediction of future development and gender preference is difficult. In such 'difficult cases', nevertheless, a non-surgical approach allows for subsequent re-assignment should the original decision prove incorrect for the individual concerned. They note that there is 'little evidence a poorly functioning clitoris and vagina is any better than a poorly functioning penis and there is no higher reason to save the reproductive capacity of ovaries over testes' (1997a: 1,047).

Diamond and Sigmundson's recommendations were not published in 1987 when Oluyemi, the subject of the next chapter, was born.

CHAPTER 5

Oluyemi's Story

There is no question therefore, of any intellectual uncertainty here: we know now that we are not supposed to be looking on at the products of a madman's imagination, behind which we, with the superiority of rational minds, are able to detect the sober truth; and yet this knowledge does not lessen the impression of uncanniness in the least degree.

Sigmund Freud, *The Uncanny*

Oluyemi is twenty, and lives in his country of birth, Nigeria. He describes himself as an 'intersex individual' with 'some outward features of both male and female' (correspondence 7 May 2004). He currently has large breasts, no facial hair, a very small penis, and what he believes is one undescended testis.

Diagnosis and Infant Treatment for Hypospadias

Oluyemi's genetic sex is unknown. While chromosomal configuration is only one contributor to the sexed body, Diamond and Sigmundson's guidelines indicate that it should nevertheless be part of the investigations carried out at the birth of a recognizably intersexed child (1997a). They recommend that complete patient history in relation to family medical history, plus evaluation of gonads, genitals, internal and external genital structures, and endocrine details should also contribute to initial and early evaluation. Oluyemi's mother, a nurse, indicated how Oluyemi was diagnosed as intersexed at birth by a urologist who noted that he appeared to have undescended right and left testes, hypospadic location of his urethral opening at the base of his small hooked penis, and a split scrotum which looked like female labia.

The causes of hypospadias are unknown, but are likely to include alteration of testosterone metabolism and/or external oestrogen effect on the foetus during gestation (Fausto-Sterling 2000). In typical foetal development of genetic males the hitherto sexually undifferentiated genital folds fuse together to form the penis shaft encasing the urethra entirely. Typically, the urethra – the tube that conducts urine and semen through the penis – forms running through the length of the penis and exiting at its tip. In instances of hypospadias and epispadias this development is atypical. The genital folds fail to fuse properly, and the penis is left open in part with an incompletely formed urethra exiting either on the underside of the penis (hypospadias) or on the upper side of the penis (epispadias). In the mildest cases, the urethra opens just before the tip of the penis. In more severe cases, the opening may develop closer to the scrotum on the penis, on the perineum (the area between the scrotum and anus) or form as a large slit up the length of the penis. Severe curvature (chordee) or twisting (torsion) of the penis may also be experienced, and in most cases foreskin formation is incomplete.

Frequency statistics vary: Hatch (2003) indicates that approximately 0.8 per cent of penises are hypospadic, while other sources suggest frequencies of 0.4 per cent (Centers for Disease Control and Prevention, USA), up to 0.3 per cent (Dolk *et al.* 2004), or 0.0125 per cent (Coventry 1998). Fausto-Sterling (2000) reports that severe hypospadias affects about 1 in 2,000 genetic males (0.05 per cent), while instances where the urethra opens between the corona (the ridge of flesh demarcating where the head of the penis and the shaft join) and tip of the glans of the penis occur in around 1 in 770 genetic males (0.14 per cent).

Severity also varies: descriptions include Derek's 'one-inch slit underneath beginning from the top, and then another hole underneath' (correspondence 3 March 2005) and Guy's 'tear along the side with holes near the base where sperm oozes out if I ejaculate and some "dead" skin where my only surgery failed to work' (correspondence 13 November 2004). Most commonly, hypospadias or epispadias causes problems with urination while standing, and severe curvature of the penis can cause painful erections. The shortened urethra may also create susceptibility to urinary tract infection and the location of the urethral opening may make ejaculation into a vagina difficult (although fertility levels are typically unaffected).

While traditional treatment of hypospadias has been to surgically assign subjects as female, Diamond and Sigmundson (1997a) recommend male *sex of rearing* for genetic males with hypospadias. Oluyemi's karyotype is unknown, yet the phallic tissue that protruded above his urethra was named as a (small, hooked, imperforate) penis based on visual examination of his infant genitalia and on unproven diagnosis of internal gonads of the male type. Oluyemi's mother described his genitalia at birth thus: 'his genitalia looked like a frenulum of a penis seen and felt at birth without penal gland, also two-scrotal sac without testicle. Eight days after birth, I could feel the small penal gland erect occasionally and the testicle in bilateral inguinal region ...' (correspondence 8 June 2004).

The frenulum of the penis is the membrane under the foreskin, but could here equally be the prepuce surrounding a clitoris. The 'two-scrotal sac' without testes inside might surely also resemble the doubleness of labia and the 'small penal gland' might surely be possibly clitoral. Karyotype was untested, and the internal 'testicle' was strictly an unknown gonad. The endocrinology of Oluyemi's pre-natal life was not clear, and his phallus was particularly small. Yet Oluyemi was named and reared as a boy, with no further deliberation. Diamond and Sigmundson (1997a) specifically assert that sex of rearing should not be based on the size or functionality of the phallus alone, yet in this instance the presence of protruding phallic tissue appears to have been the key determinant.

Treatment in Early Childhood

Treatment was not carried out immediately. At thirty months, some unspecified surgery was carried out on Oluyemi's internal gonads. It is likely that only one was removed since Oluyemi and his mother believe he still has one 'undescended testis' left inside (Oluyemi's mother, correspondence 8 June 2004). There is no note of the findings of that gonadectomy: was the tissue removed ovarian, testicular or mixed?

Oluyemi's hypospadias was also 'repaired by Dr B, a visiting philanthropist surgeon from America' (Oluyemi's mother, correspondence 8 June 2004). In what seems to be a classic case of lack of even short-term follow-up, adequate record-keeping, or indeed personal responsibility, this surgeon left for the US two days after the surgery, his voluntary assignment accomplished. The following is quoted directly from Oluyemi's mother's correspondence (7 May 2004):

> After some days complication of urethral blockage and repair breakdown was observed. All efforts to correct these complications proved abortive. Eventually [Oluyemi] was referred to a consultant paediatric urologist at Lagos ... with catheter in-situ.
>
> ... by God's grace the surgeon opened the blocked urethra and the hypospadias was repaired partially at three years old.

In spite of these horrific difficulties experienced by Oluyemi between thirty and thirty-six months, his mother reserves great respect for Dr B who, she writes, 'annually comes ... with his equipment to save souls of those who need help' (correspondence 8 June 2004). There were, however, no subsequent treatments or check-ups for Oluyemi, and it seems that Dr B's focus was on the 'corrective immediacy' of his surgical practice rather than on the more banal practice of recording of aftercare and findings.

Problems encountered in surgical intervention in cases of severe hypospadias include scarring, fistulation and formation of strictures, and loss of sensation. Yet the articulated success rates for such surgery are often unrealistically optimistic. There is typically no substantial long-term methodological follow-up of these surgeries, especially post-adolescence, so it is impossible to gauge whether these interventions *generally* permit satisfactory sexual function. Interviewee Ray indicates that he has fathered two children with his hypospadias untreated by surgery, and his only continuing issue is that he needs to be careful with urinating to ensure that he aims correctly (correspondence 27 March 2003). Another interviewee – Eoin – did have his hypospadic penis reconstructed at age nine, and he now experiences urinary problems, discharge and pain that he did not have prior to surgery (correspondence 3 September 2004). Again, it seems that the culturally important cosmetic appearance of the penis tends to be forefronted over urinary function, eventual sexual efficacy or erotic pleasure. While microsurgical techniques are improving constantly, there are still many individuals who find the promised genital 'normality' eludes them. Hester (undated) notes in particular how the cultural importance ascribed to the penis brings great embarrassment, despair and anxiety to those whose penises are hypospadic, and references urinary difficulty, fear of intimacy, disgust of penis and depression as the extreme consequences.

Yronwode reports Laurence Baskin, Associate Professor of Urology and Pediatrics at the University College of San Francisco in 1999, as stating that he 'honestly feel[s] sorry for those people who feel mutilated by their surgeries' but arguing that the surgery carried out some years ago was done by well-intentioned physicians who did not fully understand the genital nerve supply (Baskin quoted in Yronwode 1999: unpaginated). Baskin indicates that surgeons collectively began to comprehend the intricate phallo-clitoral nerve supply around the end of the 1980s (Yronwode 1999), and Diamond has suggested that there may be a growing number of US surgeons who are now considering avoidance of genital surgery if possible (correspondence 2 December 2005). Nevertheless there are many who remain deeply distressed by being contributors to an improved understanding rather than its beneficiaries: 'There is a principle in medicine – do no harm. They [surgeons] don't know what effect their drastic, invasive, irreversible interventions are having. Given that they don't have knowledge about the effect of their interventions, it's unethical to do them on unconsenting infants' (Chase quoted in Yronwode 1999: unpaginated).

Oluyemi suffered urethral blockage and accompanying psychological trauma as a small child *as a result* of genital surgery. The surgery on his phallus was for aesthetic improvement rather than to avoid threat to life: 'the hypospadias was repaired partially, which partially enables him to pass out urine without much wetting of his trouser ... if Oluyemi had not received surgery, he would be stooling down to pass urine like a female ...' (Oluyemi's mother, correspondence 8 June 2004).

Again, Diamond and Sigmundson's guidelines (1997a) insist that such cosmetic surgery should not be done, in spite of how socially difficult that treatment path can be for parents and for the developing child. They warn that such surgery is potentially damaging to long-term sexual, erotic and urinary function.

The Endocrine Effect

As noted earlier, it is probable that one of Oluyemi's internal gonads was removed at age thirty months, some time after an infant with a functional testicular gonad would have experienced a testosterone surge around day ten and day sixty of life. The outcome of the gonadectomy is not recorded, so there is no confirmation of the removal of a testis, ovary or ovotestis. Diamond and Sigmundson (1997a) argue for maintenance of gonads if possible so that prenatal endocrine disposition can materialize at puberty. If there were undescended testes (or testis) present in an individual, then some virilizing testosterone would typically be released before birth, after birth and again at puberty. Removal of one internal testis (presuming that this was testicular rather than ovarian or an ovotestis) means that Oluyemi's (theoretical) ability to secrete his own testosterone at puberty was compromised, if not completely destroyed (depending on the nature of the remaining gonad).

Oluyemi's incomplete phallic development in infancy and through to adulthood would suggest that his testosterone effect is either compromised if Oluyemi is genetically male, or heightened if he is genetically female. Whichever, there is reason to believe there was some introduction of virilizing hormone *in utero* and after birth but before gonadectomy. Oluyemi has not been given any hormonal treatment at any point in his life to augment or supplement his body's endocrine development and his male assignment, although records of his entire medical history are scant and unhelpful in this regard. In adulthood, his feminized appearance post-puberty is out of alignment with his male assignment in infancy. To support that assignment long-term, Oluyemi should have received testosterone treatment post-puberty for the rest of his life. What was begun medically in infancy has not been followed through medically in adulthood, and the results are difficult for this person.

Breast Development

Oluyemi's mother describes him post-puberty thus: 'without vagina but with penal gland of 1.5 inches in length at present, and with undescended testis plus 2 large breast tissues each which is half a football in size' (correspondence 8 June 2004). Some oestrogen activity, testosterone compromise and/or genetic intersex are indicated by Oluyemi's development at puberty of large breasts. His breasts are more visible than his ambiguous, surgically altered genitalia, and they are 'regularly fastened to flat level with a firm elastic band to avoid any embarrassment' (Oluyemi's mother, correspondence 7 May 2004). It seems that embarrassment would be suffered as much by social-culture in general as it would be by Oluyemi and his family should his breast tissue be revealed.

Oluyemi, an excellent scholar at his college, leads a difficult and lonely life. He recounts that those people who know of his condition 'treat me badly' (correspondence 9 June 2004), and he now tries to avoid making new friends or having social contact:

> Some of them do refer to me as an hermaphrodite ... This always makes me to feel sad. I do try to tell them that I'm not a hermaphrodite but there was no evidence to show ...
> I try not to make any friend ...
> Although I do use a girdle, if you touch my chest you feel some strange there. I do try as much as possible not to allow anyone to touch my chest.
> The girdle makes me uncomfortable because it is too tight. I must put it on 24/7 ...
> (Oluyemi, correspondence 9 June 2004)

Oluyemi's breast development at puberty is an example of why, unless the infant's life is in danger, it seems sensible not to make permanent surgical alterations to the genitalia in infancy. Puberty brings a whole new phase, with the typical development of secondary sex characteristics (breasts, menstruation and body fat depositing for typical girls, and facial hair, voice deepening, muscular development for typical boys). These changes are triggered by surges in oestrogen and testosterone respectively. In some instances it is only at puberty that, for example, karyotype difference becomes apparent (Klinefelter's Syndrome); irregular menstruation and unwanted hair growth alert clinicians to Late-Onset Congenital Adrenal Hyperplasia (see Chapter 8); or failure to menstruate and develop body hair results in diagnosis of Complete Androgen Insensitivity Syndrome (see Chapter 9). Puberty brought Oluyemi a new dimension to his already stark, but nevertheless readily hidden, difference. And with that came new dangers as Oluyemi was exposed to his society and its potential for superstitious aggression: 'Oluyemi is at risk here, and stigmatized, hence at puberty he has to press down the mammary gland with elastic band to hide it from lookers and ritual killers ...' (Oluyemi's mother, correspondence 8 June 2004).

This recalls Linda Roberts' experience in Wales (see Introduction), and the small-minded abuse and bitter prejudice she suffered from neighbours who would have felt justified in kicking her, spitting at her, stamping on her, forcing her to the ground and generally terrorizing her for being a 'filthy queer' (Hugill 1998: 7). Universally, there is a kind of special terror activated by the taboo of intersex that sparks a particular violence fuelled by fear and ignorance. And, arguably, an alternative violence? By dehumanizing and/or mythologizing intersexed individuals, by maintaining intersex as 'the last great taboo' (Chris, correspondence 21 May 2004), an allowance is made for strategies of continued surgical intervention on the genitals of those individuals which in other circumstances would be considered highly abusive.

Hindsight and Desire

Both Oluyemi and his mother are currently less enthusiastic about the infant treatment he received. Oluyemi acknowledges the benefit in his male assignment of being able to stand erect while urinating (correspondence 9 June 2004), although Diamond and Sigmundson noted 'a male with hypospadias might have to sit to urinate without mishap but can function sexually without surgery' (1997a: 1,049). Arguably 'unfinished', Oluyemi would like to have breast reduction surgery, testosterone therapy, penis enlargement and some treatment (which he cannot explain) to help with his testes. He experiences his intersex status as 'abnormal', a 'mutation' and 'shameful because of how people treat you' (correspondence 9 June 2004). He is 'defiantly not' comfortable with being called intersexed, and neither – in spite of her obvious love for her child – is his mother. Oluyemi's self-loathing is fuelled by exactly the social-cultural lack of acceptance that arguably drove David Reimer to take his own life. Here is the real-life face of statistics that propose genital ambiguity as manifesting in at least 1 in 2,000. There's nothing fetishistic, mythological or fictional about this 20-year-old's experiences, but Oluyemi provides the same challenge to another society/culture that cannot cope with the perceived dysfunction and purported monstrosity of intersex as did Linda in Wales, Louise in England and David in Canada.

We do not know whether Oluyemi's genital ambiguity and subsequent breast development are related to genetic atypicality. There is some uncertainty from both Oluyemi and his mother about the nature of his remaining internal gonad, and while there is no evidence that there may be ovarian tissue present, Oluyemi's medical investigations seem perfunctory and over-determined that his assignment should have been male.

Oluyemi's adult phallus is not completely virilized, and he has never ejaculated. The 'small penal gland erect occasionally' (Oluyemi's mother, correspondence 8 June 2004) of his infancy is arguably as potentially clitoral as it is penile, and in the mixed and complex realm of intersex it need not be solely either one or the other. There is no outwardly discernible vagina, no evidence of uterus or functional ovaries and therefore no menstruation. We have no way of understanding Oluyemi's internal anatomy without ultrasound scanning. No medical follow-up by the 'visiting philanthropist' Dr B has meant that there is no explanation as to why Oluyemi developed breast tissue and did not develop masculine facial hair at puberty. If we go back to Louise's single partial testes, no penis, single ovary, rudimentary internal vagina and unrecognizably male or female external genitalia we can just begin to get a sense of the complexity and individuality of intersex manifestation. As with Louise, there is an encultured sense in Oluyemi's testimony that further medical and surgical treatment in adulthood can bring 'wholeness' by 'completing' what nature – and infant surgical intervention – has failed to finish. And there is resistance to the possibility of intersex as a – less frequent – natural condition of humans.

As for Louise, Oluyemi's initial treatment was given parental rather than personal consent, was irreversible and was arguably at least partly cosmetic. Unlike Louise, however, Oluyemi has not received any medical care after his second set of corrective surgeries, which dealt in part with problems arising from the first, and he is aware that the tangible result from that surgery has addressed one social-cultural demand (that males urinate while standing) but ignored another (that males do not have breasts).

Oluyemi expresses no desire that his assignment was female. He does not wish that his phallic tissue had been excised, that his labia-like scrotum had been rendered closer to labial construction or that a vagina had been surgically constructed. He believes himself to be a man, albeit – reluctantly – an intersexed man. His issue is that his body lets him down in terms of male typicality. But what would have happened to Oluyemi if he had grown up without infant surgery, with ambiguous genitalia which might with effort be hidden, 'stooling down to pass urine like a female' (Oluyemi's mother, correspondence 8 June 2004) but in private, and with his eventual pubescent breast development? His body would still have signalled to him that he was intersexed, and indeed his external genitalia might be thought of as resembling more closely those of a female with a larger than average clitoris, and no known internal vagina, than a male. Oluyemi could have 'passed' as female, safeguarding his privacy in a hostile environment, and allowing him time to reach puberty and come to terms with his intersexuality prior to any decisions about self-identification and sex assignment. This does not discount the potential trauma of post-pubescent sex change, or the personal stigma of intersex in a culture violently hostile to sex atypicality, but it would have bought time for careful consideration. Now, Oluyemi's only option is to find a way to have the breast reduction and penis enlargement surgery, the life-long testosterone treatment and the testicular implants necessary to 'complete' his male assignment. This, as his mother indicates, is virtually impossible for them in Nigeria and beyond their means financially elsewhere.

Money's 'optimal gender policy' would presume Oluyemi was 'psychosexually neutral' (Diamond and Sigmundson 1997b: 298) until around age two, and contend that satisfactory formation of his gender identity would depend on 'corrected' genitalia matching that identity. In fact, Oluyemi's first surgery was when he was thirty months old, so by Money's reckoning his gender identity would have been fixed already. Even with his genital ambiguity, Oluyemi would have been 'trained' without question that he was a little boy, but his genitals would not have matched. Professor Milton Diamond, by contrast, argues that individuals are psychosexually biased at birth, with psychosexual development related to, but not dependent on, genital appearance (Diamond and Sigmundson 1997b). Diamond's proposal for the management of intersex infants, while still operating within the sex binary, is that infants should be *reared as* the sex they most resemble (or, if genitalia are very ambiguous and karyotype straightforward, they should be *raised* with karyotype). This allows dormant psychosexual bias to surface, and continued sexual development to puberty to take place before any surgical action is taken. Diamond's approach operates in opposition to strong social-cultural desire to align intersexed bodies permanently to the normative medically upheld binary of mutually exclusive male and female.

In a potent text titled 'David Reimer's Legacy: Limiting Parental Discretion', Beh and Diamond press for a reconsideration of parental authority in intersex management, and argue that for parents to be permitted to determine whether their intersex child should have irreversible 'normalizing' surgery on ambiguous genitalia exceeds their authority because it 'unnecessarily forecloses the child's right to an open future' (2005: 5). They contend that parents in these circumstances may not be unbiased or fully rational in their choices, and may well be 'conflicted by their own anxieties, guilt, shame or repugnance' (ibid.). Finally, they maintain that the chaos of long-term data collection in intersex management means that parents will most likely have poor and incomplete information upon which to base their judgement. They conclude that, for these three reasons parents should be encouraged to 'love, cherish and nurture the child that is' (ibid.: 9) rather than succumb to fear of their condition.

CHAPTER 6

Sarah-Jane's Story and Others

During the research for *Gender Trouble* I interviewed many intersex women around the UK. All spoke with an openness and candour that stemmed from their desire to change the way intersex was medically managed and to also change the culture of secrecy that surrounds their conditions. However, all but four people were genuinely afraid to speak out publicly. They were afraid of losing their jobs, attracting unwanted media attention and being ostracised by neighbours.

Roz Mortimer, *Director's statement*

Neither Fully Male nor Fully Female

In interview (9 June 2004), Sarah-Jane asked if this author was curious about 'what was between her legs' either as illustration or proof of intersex. As noted earlier, Briffa suggests that possibly only 25 per cent of intersexuals are born with genital ambiguity (correspondence 3 April 2002), and intersex is a condition of the whole person not just the genitalia. Nevertheless, Sarah-Jane's question reflects how intersex is culturally understood as being 'about genitals' and echoes social-culture's appreciation of intersex as a rare kind of freakish curiosity. Sarah-Jane has a press clipping from her local newspaper telling what the author calls the 'almost unbelievable story of a single human being with two separate identities, one male, one female' (Lomax 1996: 17). Billed as 'two people trapped in one body', a 'he/she', Sarah-Jane's life is described in hyperbole as 'incredible' (ibid.). Arguably, this kind of reportage of intersexed people – as with the use of the term 'hermaphrodite' – problematically reinforces the sense that intersexuals are freakish and 'other'.

Sarah-Jane revealed deep personal dissatisfaction with her condition: 'I wouldn't have minded being a boy or a girl, just not this' (interview 9 June 2004). In a second newspaper article she stated: 'I would not wish my genes on my worst enemy because the quality of life is non-existent ... most of the hermaphrodites I have met live very unhappy lifestyles' (Tanna 1999: 17).

This bleakness is what another 'hermaphrodite', Chris from Western Australia, describes as the experience of some intersexed individuals whose trauma is so extreme that they are completely alienated from the society they operate in and their self-worth is annihilated (correspondence 21 May 2004). Sarah-Jane's phenotypic presentation is tall, slim-hipped, with some slight breast tissue, and with closely shaved facial hair. Some of her mannerisms and gestures seem feminine, but there is also a mild sense of male effeminacy.

Sarah-Jane is forty-nine. When she was born there was some uncertainty over her sex, though the attending clinician told her parents that there was 'probably nothing too badly wrong' (Lomax 1996: 17). Sarah-Jane was registered female, but two male names – Antony and William – were included beside Sarah-Jane Victoria on her birth certificate, and the word 'hermaphrodite' was inscribed by hand in the corner. She describes herself as:

> neither male nor female. I'm a hermaphrodite, born with both sets of genitals: one ovary and one testicle, neither of which would ever work ... (interview 9 June 2004) essentially ... I am not a full male or a full female. (Lomax 1996: 17)

Kipnis and Diamond describe the continuum model of the external genitalia of intersexuals thus: 'external genitalia can be typically male, typically female, or virtually anywhere in between. A very large clitoris and a very small penis may be indistinguishable except for the term used to describe them' (1998: 404). While mixed sexual anatomy occurs, a fully-formed penis *and* a fully-formed vagina – that is, two sets of genitals – do not coexist in intersex (Chase 1998a). Sarah-Jane has genital ambiguity, but did *not* receive surgical treatment at birth 'for reasons she has never been quite able to fathom' (Glaser 2000: 25). She is angry and frustrated that nothing was done for her condition in infancy: 'The reason "my condition" was not dealt with at my birth was my Mum and Dad's fault ... if just one of them had had the guts to stand up to those wretched doctors ... I would not be in this mess now' (correspondence 17 January 2007). When pressed, however, Sarah-Jane could not say what exactly should have been done or how she should have been surgically 'sexed'. Her articulation of what it is to have been born intersexed with genital ambiguity is emotional: she 'could have lived with' surgery (interview 9 June 2004), but her inability to state how surgery might have helped testifies to her basic unhappiness with being intersexed: 'I cannot face what I really am ... that is breaking me mentally ... I don't know how much more I can take before I snap ... I cannot face in reality what I really am ...' (interview 9 June 2004).

Sarah-Jane's parents divorced when she was two. She has a letter from her mother confirming that Sarah-Jane is her *daughter* (Sarah-Jane's emphasis), but she bitterly describes her mother's disgust at her from infancy. In the custody of her father as a child, but parented by her older sister, she was never able to talk to her mother in any detail about her intersexuality as her mother 'finds it too painful' (interview 9 June 2004).

Holmes refers to a kind of 'terror' experienced by parents whose child is intersexed with genital ambiguity, and whose understanding of that word is 'female bodies ... with penises ... [and] ... male bodies ... with vaginas ...' (1994b: unpaginated). That is, they imagine their child as a freakish, uncanny, monstrous being.

The idea of intersex and their infant's ambiguous genitalia is undoubtedly disturbing to parents, and that is why parents struggling to understand the complex information they have been given should not make major, irreversible decisions about genital surgery for their child. The Intersex Society of North America advocates that such parents receive immediate counselling and be put into contact with other parents of intersexed children and appropriate support groups. Like Diamond and colleagues, ISNA argues that the child should be assigned a *sex of rearing*, named correspondingly and then be raised with age-appropriate explanations of their condition. ISNA maintains that there is likely to be an assertion of gender identity between ages six and ten, and if necessary name and sex assignment can then be changed. While this is a difficult path, it is more reversible than the surgical/hormonal alteration of infant genitals to match a decided upon sex identification in a newborn child. The child is at the centre of this issue, not the parents, however difficult they find the situation. And, as Chase notes: 'Gender is not so fragile that cosmetic surgery needs to be done early. Gender identity would not be undermined by asking the child about it' (Chase quoted in Yronwode 1999: unpaginated).

Sarah-Jane wanted to be 'normal', and the purpose of surgery on ambiguous infant genitalia is to achieve 'normality'. But, notes Chase, 'our experience as adult intersex people is that these kids are not going to be "normal"' (ibid.), and the implication is that to try to suggest that surgery can offer this is to add further distress to an already emotionally difficult life experience. The 'uncut' Sarah-Jane grew up feeling that she 'always was a girl' (interview 9 June 2004), and now refers to herself as 'an XXy Girl' or 'an Intersex-XXy-Woman' (correspondence 17 January 2007). She describes how her single testis remained undescended, her phallus 'was basically like a large clitoris' which 'didn't work', and she urinated sitting down (interview 9 June 2004). At puberty she was sexually attracted to boys. At sixteen, she was irregularly menstruating, a not unusual occurrence for intersexed people with ovarian tissue (Chase 1998a). Sarah-Jane's doctor informed her that although she was menstruating, and indeed capable of producing some seminal/vaginal fluid, she was sterile and her uterus was incomplete.

At seventeen, however, specific changes began which signalled to Sarah-Jane that there was 'something different and gruesome' about her (interview 9 June 2004). In response to testosterone secreted by her one testicle, Sarah-Jane's voice deepened, she grew in height to 185 cm and she developed body and facial hair, which she waxed. She began to feel sexually attracted to both men and women, and she experienced extreme hormonal mood swings (Lomax 1996). Chromosome testing at age twenty revealed that Sarah-Jane has an XXY genetic composition (interview 9 June 2004).

Typical male and female karyotypes are XY and XX respectively, while the karyotype for 'true hermaphroditism' is most usually XX, with XXY being a less usual variation. Sarah-Jane's response to her genetic diagnosis was one of alarm and shame: 'I was devastated, but it was not possible to talk to my parents about this, and when I confided in friends they were horrified and just didn't know how to react to it …' (interview 9 June 2004).

Sarah-Jane processed the information she was given by thinking of herself as 'a woman who basically had a bit of man in her' (interview 9 June 2004), and she acknowledges continuing conflict in gender terms: 'I'm at constant war with myself. The female side is much stronger, but sometimes it can be knocked sideways by my maleness' (Glaser 2000: 25). Confused about her gender from her early twenties onwards, she crossed between genders, sometimes successfully passing as Antony William. Sarah-Jane describes that she both despised and was curious about what she calls her 'male self' (interview 9 June 2004), and notes that her *self*-identification – even when passing as Antony William – was always as Sarah-Jane.

Sarah-Jane's Adult Choices

Sarah-Jane is now hoping to have the phallic tissue that she calls her 'male parts' – her small penis (or enlarged clitoris) – surgically removed. She is being psychologically assessed prior to genital surgery at the Elizabeth Garrett Anderson and Obstetric Hospital, London, and asserts that the sex specificity of this institution's provision confirms her *intersexed woman* status. Her consultant clinical psychologist there has also confirmed this status to her in writing. Sarah-Jane had breast implants in 2005, but also desires gender-affirming cosmetic hair implants and surgery on her nose to 'make [her] more feminine' (interview 9 June 2004) and a 'complete woman' (Tanna 1999: 17). She uses the words 'relief' and 'freedom' to define how she will feel. She currently takes Premarin – oestrogen therapy – to help with her feminization, but reports that she has suffered 'PMT everyday' since her teens, and is concerned that her body and face don't or can't match her ideal of herself (interview 9 June 2004).

It seems that Sarah-Jane may never be happy: not least because she has defined herself through her 'hermaphrodite' persona and yet she is unhappy with that persona. Sarah-Jane works variously in the sex industry as an escort, actress, model, pole-dancer/stripper, and is a 'submissive sex slave to four mistresses' (Mental Health Advocate on behalf of Sarah-Jane, correspondence 16 May 2005). Her intersexed body, in these worlds, is sometimes considered a 'unique selling point', and this perpetually reinforces her difference by focusing on the commercial desirability or not of her unusual physiology. To achieve the 'normality' she craves would be to erase that identification of herself, and risk loss of income and status within a particular social framework. Even in that sub-cultural world, however, Sarah-Jane exists 'between norms': 'I am rejected, but am I a reject? I have been used and abused ... I can not think of a single employer save for the sex industry who would employ me, and even they shy away ... I wonder if I will ever have any happiness?' (correspondence 17 January 2007). As an intersexual and self-identified woman sex worker, Sarah-Jane indicates that she should be able to access the health-care services she needs at Praed Street Clinic, London, but she has been refused support because that service declares itself *for women sex workers only*. The Praed Street Clinic referred her to the SW5 Health Services Project, which supports male and transgendered sex workers in her area, but she was refused access there *because she is not a man or a transwoman*. Sarah-Jane is therefore positioned between two sexual-health service providers, neither supporting her as an intersexed woman (Mental Health Advocate on behalf of Sarah-Jane, correspondence 16 May 2005).

Glaser, writing about Sarah-Jane's case, discusses how her parents might have 'saved her the trauma of an operation in adulthood' by requesting 'corrective' surgery for their child in infancy (2000: 25). Sarah-Jane was formally diagnosed as intersexed around age eleven when her aunt, who was a senior psychiatric social worker at the Middlesex Hospital, London, took her to the Gynaecology Department there for examination in 1968. Her genitalia, however, were ambiguous from birth, and Glaser suggests that early sex assignment surgery would have 'helped her lead a more conventional life' (ibid.). In doing so, though, Glaser reveals again the social-cultural stigma of intersex and the social-cultural requirement of the aesthetics of sex binarism. Glaser's concern for the surgery that might have been carried out on the infant Sarah-Jane is in respect of social-cultural convention rather than with regard to her health or sexual function. Had Sarah-Jane been subjected to infant clitoridectomy or clitoral recession, she would almost certainly not have had the erotically sensitive tissue she currently has. As an intersexed person, different upbringing, socialization, care and education could have assisted her to embrace her difference more readily. In adulthood *she* can be responsible for deciding her own surgical needs, and have autonomy over – and responsibility for – any decisions made about her body's form and function.

The 'Phallic Female'

Glaser (2000) indicates that surgery in infancy would also probably have removed Sarah-Jane's undescended testis. This secreted testosterone in her teenage years causing some virilization. But it is unlikely that this possibility would have been the primary surgical concern in infancy since reduction of the clitoris in female assignments is most frequently the focus of this intervention. Perceived 'oversize' in the clitoris arguably offends particular cultural mores by 'pathologically' mixing 'maleness' and 'femaleness' and upsetting the currency of feminine sexual propriety.

An average size of approximately 0.9–1.0 cm is proposed variously as the upper limit after which a phallic protrusion is not culturally 'acceptable' as a clitoris, even on a genetic female (McGillivray 1991 in Dreger 1998b; Diamond and Watson 2004b). Yet, interestingly, earlier reference was made to the *lower* limit for culturally 'adequate' *penis* size in infants as being 2.0–2.5 cm (Meyers-Seifer and Charest 1992, referenced in Dreger 1998b; Kessler 1990; American Academy of Pediatrics 2000). It seems that there is a 'grey zone' between the outer limits for an 'acceptable' clitoris and an 'acceptable' penis in an infant. A phallic appendage between the two outer limits is therefore judged as requiring surgical intervention. If one adheres to those outer limits then, for example, a phallus of 1.5 cm may be considered too small by some commentators to be a penis, and too large by others to be a clitoris. What might that organ then be? While sex remains undetermined, Lehrman (1999) claims it can be termed *either* a clitoris *or* a penis.

One can see how this approach to sex assignment for intersexed infants continues to speak to Money's claim for psychosexual neutrality in the first couple of years of life (Diamond and Sigmundson 1997b). For Money (Money and Ehrhardt 1972), ambiguous phallic tissue could be named as a clitoris *or* a penis as long as it is then named *decisively* before twenty-four months, as long as the infant is nurtured in accordance with the sex of naming, and as long as the genitalia are then surgically altered to concur with this determination. Such decisions are made by clinicians as speedily as possible (most frequently between six weeks and fifteen months), since lack of clarity between a penis and a clitoris potentially 'dilutes' culture's requirements of masculinity and 'coarsens' culture's understanding of femininity (Kessler 1990). In this protocol, one may detect the traces of particular readings of femininity as somehow 'delicate' and 'sexually retiring' (as evidenced in clitoral neatness), and masculinity as conversely 'strong' and 'sexually demanding' (as evidenced in penile magnitude). The 'phallic female' then in any shape or form is an affront to both these encultured 'norms'.

Ransley cautions that those most dissatisfied with their genital surgeries in infancy are those who are the most vocal, while satisfied or mainly satisfied subjects are most likely to be silent (interview 6 September 2005). Moreover, those old enough to provide adult testimonies refer to procedures carried out in their infancy, some time ago. Nevertheless, the experiences of 'phallic females' are cautionary, reminding us that consent continues to be given for surgical/hormonal 'solutions' to intersexed births today (Navarro 2004). Personal testimonies are an effective way of illustrating the confusion and emotional pain that can be part of being an intersexed 'other', and illuminate key features recurrent throughout this text: infant lack of choice; great pain and trauma; adult reclamation of some sense of self; then resolution, expediency, stoicism or silence.

Martha, a genetic female, was six years old when her clitoridectomy was carried out in 1958, removing a significant portion of her sexually sensitive tissue without her consent:

> When I learned of the impending surgery ... I knew this was about something between my legs. My chest felt tight and there was a rushing sound in my ears. I begged not to go. I didn't understand what was going to happen or why ... (correspondence 2 January 2007)

> It took the surgeon 30 minutes to make a U-shaped incision around my half-inch clitoris, remove it, put it in a specimen dish. He then closed the wound and stitched the skin up over the stump. (Coventry 1998: unpaginated)

Martha's clitoris was not diseased or misplaced. It was just larger than deemed appropriate for a girl of six. A 'stitched-up stump', however, must be inappropriate to any body. Ransley contends that there has been a shift in how such practices are currently handled. He believes that there is more caution on the parts of surgeons and more inclination – certainly in cases of smaller virilized clitorises – to leave them without surgery (interview 6 September 2005), and Creighton concurs (interview 9 February 2006). Ransley is aware, however, of the social-cultural implications of leaving a virilized clitoris alone, and tellingly indicates that it was probably easier for a girl to cope with a protuberant phallus 'in the age of the crinoline' than in the contemporary age of Lycra swimsuits or ballet class tutus (interview 6 September 2005). He reminds us of the practical problem for the 'phallic female' child of dealing with a visible atypicality in the charged region of her genitals. That child, Ransley suggests, will be less concerned about an unforeseen and unknowable future erotic life, and more concerned about the embarrassment of the now.

Avril was born with a protruding ambiguous phallus that was originally named a tiny penis, a closed over vagina and uterus, and both ovarian and testicular internal tissue (correspondence 30 November 2002). She was diagnosed as intersexed and announced as a boy. Avril's paediatrician, however, was apparently intrigued by the possibility that her ovarian tissue would allow her to be fertile – with assisted fertility technologies including *in vitro* fertilization – as a female in the future. Her phallus – virilized by the testosterone secreted *in utero* by her testicular tissue – was then removed and she was reassigned as a baby girl – albeit without a clitoris. Her ovotestes were removed at age eight in response to a perceived risk that they might become cancerous, so any possibility of future fertility was erased anyway. There are indeed some slight risks of malignancy in the ovotestes of certain intersexed people (Hughes *et al.* 2006), but these risks are considered to be small in pre-pubescence, and careful monitoring would be part of alternative treatment where they would be maintained intact while healthy, thereby allowing their endocrine effect up to and through puberty.

Avril had difficulties identifying with her female assignment. As a young woman she was attracted to women, but couldn't reconcile herself as a lesbian. In her late twenties, an older relative revealed her intersex status and her original assignment as a boy. She recalls this as simultaneously overwhelming, shocking and liberating. Her scarred genitalia, sexual dysfunction and deep-rooted emotional pain made sense. She suffered a breakdown, recovered and now lives as a celibate intersexed person, without further surgery, and with her original name of Avril.

Morgan Holmes described how at age four her 'body had been painted orange from navel to knees' without explanation (1998: 223). This was the iodine sterilization preparation for her clitoridectomy. She then remembers 'it hurt like hell to take a piss because it would run along the fresh wound that marked the spot where that piece had previously been' (ibid.). Her infant clitoris, her 'phallic femaleness' – enlarged by typical standards as the result of the virilizing effect of progestin given to her mother to avoid premature delivery – was recessed, removing the erectile parts of the clitoral shaft. Her words effectively communicate both her childish bewilderment and excruciating pain. In adulthood, she refers to herself as a 'mutilated intersexed woman' with 'stolen physical potential' within a 'silent and invisible population' (ibid.: 221).

Possible asymmetrical bias in decisions regarding infant sex assignment was alluded to earlier, with maintenance of a 'phallic culture' concerned not with the 'phallic female' but with preservation of the 'perfect penis'. Some odd decisions are certainly evidenced in the literature, and these generalized comments – reflective of a highly complex matrix of decision, opinion and practice – might be argued as having a social-cultural as well as medical agenda. For example, Kessler (1990) cites Money's assertion (1974) that in the case of *a genetic female infant with internal female reproductive apparatus* and an apparently fully formed penis that 'perfect organ' (in anatomical and cultural terms) *should not be neo-natally amputated.* In *that* 'phallic female', according to Money's thesis, the penis should be preserved but the femaleness erased. Kessler (1990) examines Money's now historical assertion that it is preferable to remove the ovaries and uterus of this subject (and with them any reproductive potential), to insert prosthetic testes and to administer male hormones for life, than remove an aesthetically 'perfect penis'. Embedded in this is a belief that preservation of that 'perfect penis', in terms of dimension and penetrative function, overrides genetic sex and potential fertility. If the penis is less than 'perfect', Money's contention was that conventionally it becomes understood to be an atypically large clitoris (a 'phallic female'), and should most usually be reduced through surgery with a vagina and labia constructed if possible.

Holmes (1994b) asserts that a *genetic male child* with a micropenis will also customarily be assigned female because of the culturally 'inadequate' size of the penis and the perception of its compromised penetrative capability. Diamond and Sigmundson contend that, in fact, a fertile male with a micropenis may not only father children, but can also have mutually satisfactory sexual relations (1997a). The micropenis and the atypically large clitoris then are dealt with in the same way: typically they are surgically reduced or removed, and the infant named as female (but not a 'phallic female'). The cultural icon of the penis is thus preserved exclusively as male, fully functional and respectably dimensioned, a potent symbol of masculinity. Clear and uncontaminated, culturally prescribed sexual divisions are maintained, as is the sex binary: 'what the physicians consider a greater good – keeping individual/concrete genders as clear and uncontaminated as the notions of female and male are in the abstract' (Kessler 1990: 23).

Fausto-Sterling poses a question in relation to all of this: 'Why should we care if a "woman", defined as one who has breasts, a vagina, uterus and ovaries and who menstruates, also has a clitoris large enough to penetrate the vagina of another woman?' (1993: 24). Why indeed. Well, for one thing, Fausto-Sterling's description above clearly images a 'phallic female' and this is a concept that is aberrant in wider culture. First, that image privileges a kind of 'lesbian symbolic' which still remains marginal and taboo in a cultural landscape where even male homosexual activity is becoming increasingly mainstream. Holmes (1995) is aware of a heterosexist agenda prevalent in intersex treatment, and cites emphasis on vaginal capability for receipt of a penis and female reproductive potential rather than erotic sensation for intersexed infants assigned female. Intersex is already culturally threatening – and Holmes detects a drive to negate the threat to the heterosexual binary framework that it implies. Female bodies that echo the taboo of the 'phallic female' – for which in this instance read the non-heterosexual female – are constructed as pathological, and are 'standardized' via partial or total clitoridectomy or clitoral recession: 'Behind these surgeries is a fear of homosexuality. There's this notion that girls with big clitorises will become lesbians and boys with small penises will be little, effeminate gay men' (Marcus Arana's allegations, referenced in Letellier 2004: 3).

Secondly, in relation to Freudian propositions regarding female maturation in the pre- and post-Oedipal stages, it is considered essential for the maturing female to go beyond her initial interest and indulgence in her pleasurable erotic organ and her desire to sport a penis in order to enter the mature phase of wanting a child instead (Freud 1925, 1931). Again, we see the privileging of the woman's safe arrival as a (symbolic) heterosexual, referenced here in maternalism. The 'phallic female' cannot be maternal for she lacks the symbolic equipment. She reflects a pre-mature stage of development, and in the adult woman is therefore taboo.

Thirdly, the 'phallic female' is a potent symbol of a castrator. She appears literally to have 'taken' the phallus, and the threat of *her phallus* is enormous to its 'rightful' owner, the male. Creed (1993) describes the castration anxiety of male spectators witnessing 'phallic femaleness' and deeming it monstrous. Creed cites, for example, the mythological *vagina dentata* and Medusa's 'frozen stiff' phallic hair as symbolic of the castrating threat of the 'monstrous-feminine' of the 'phallic female'. Given that Freud's representation of female genitalia conjures the 'shock of threatened castration' (Freud 1925: 257) anyway, the *phallic* genitalia of such females must be doubly powerful. And if, as Creed argues, societies use rituals to review and exclude the abject – that which transcends borders (Kristeva 1982) – then what better ritual for dealing with 'phallic females' than culturally condoned and medically sanctioned castration by surgery?

Finally, and Creed's text on the 'monstrous-feminine' is at the core of this, the 'phallic female' is a frightening monstrosity operating 'against nature' within culture. Creed makes reference specifically to the archetype of the witch, for example, with her long – symbolically phallic – nose. That witch, in another register, is a little girl with a larger than typical clitoris. And, like that witch, the little girl (again symbolically) cannot be permitted to survive (Creed 1993). Whereas witches are killed, little girls merely have their clitorises excised.

Kipnis (Kipnis and Diamond 1998) indicated that while there was no literature available detailing the hazards, psychosocial or otherwise, of having a large clitoris, research *is* available indicating that none of the clitoral reduction procedures in use reliably preserve full erotic sensitivity to adulthood (Schober 1998a; Creighton 2004b; Hughes *et al.* 2006). The Intersex Society of North America does not differentiate between clitoridectomy and the now preferred clitoral recession surgery. In the former, the clitoris is removed entirely. In the latter, the erectile parts of the clitoral shaft are shaved away. But, as Chase (referenced in Yronwode 1999) points out, Kinsey showed that women masturbate by stimulating that clitoral shaft rather than the clitoral glans. Clitoridectomy and clitoral recession remove that capability for erotic pleasure from the 'phallic female'.

Sex Liberated

The question of sexual self-identification is pertinent for intersexed individuals especially. Notably the Constitutional Court of Columbia ruled in 1999 that individuals have a constitutional right to define their own sexual identity, which significantly limited infant genital surgeries. Greenberg and Chase understand the ruling as 'forcing parents to put the child's best interests ahead of their own fears and concerns about sexual ambiguity' (1999: unpaginated), hence supporting the concept of freer development and definition of sexual identity by the subject alone.

The *customary* sexing of the body is simple: it works within a binary framework based on sex complementarity and mutual exclusion. Primary signification of sex is usually via consideration of either genitalia *or* gonads *or* karyotype, with arguably at least some concern for heterosexual reproduction. A sense of bodies as ontologically and historically stable and knowable, fixed and immutable is perpetuated, and the custom of sex identification is essentialist and absolutist. For the intersexed person, however, identification and determination of sex can be a much more complex journey. Gender theorists and psychoanalysts have written variously of the conflicted process of arrival at a sense of subjective sex for *all* human beings (Freud 1933; Butler 1993). Their broad implication is of an evolutionary arrival at a mature sexual identity or identities, a 'passage towards' rather than 'static event', even the self-constituting of what sex might be, and these are useful interruptions to the absolutism and essentialism outlined above, reiterating a challenge to a fixed and hegemonic system of classification of the sexed and sexual body.

If it was agreed that sex 'floats' between externally apparent characteristics of the body, those that are embedded deep within the body's organs and cells, and those that are intangible in the psyche, then a radical approach to sexing each body individually could be proposed. The 'assumption' by the subject of 'his' or 'her' own sex foregrounds the priority of that subject's 'believed sex' and, paradoxically, challenges the system that locates it. With the subject as the ultimate governor of 'his' or 'her' sex identification, and with the self-identificatory tool being the psyche rather than the physical manifestation of the body, there is real potential for liberation from the binary and a completely fresh approach to how sex is constituted or indeed – in more radical discourse – how many sexes there actually might be. Of course, most people – intersexed or otherwise – self-identify within the sex binary, and this text calls for a reshaped thinking that acknowledges intersex as an acceptable sex variation, but a further step would be to reshape social-culture to embrace intersex(es) as a norm.

Sarah-Jane's Wish

Sarah-Jane's life has tended towards the extreme: devastating periodic depressions, violent homophobic attacks, a number of suicide attempts, outstanding academic and professional success, a failed marriage, and cancer (Lomax

1996; correspondence 17 January 2007). Treatment for leukaemia left her vulnerable as the hair loss she experienced undermined her sense of femininity, leaving her looking more 'mannish' (interview 9 June 2004). This dislocation between Sarah-Jane's self-identification as a woman and the subtle masculinity of her appearance has been difficult for her, causing her to feel like a 'freak of nature' (interview 9 June 2004). This has been exacerbated by the 'mistaken assumptions, misunderstanding and prejudice' (Solomon undated: unpaginated) she has publicly suffered because she seems too masculine to fit social understandings of femininity, and she is by turn misread as a homosexual man, transsexual or transvestite. She states clearly: 'I have always behaved as a girl and, now, as a heterosexual woman ... Unlike ... [transsexuals and transvestites] ... I never had a choice which gender I wanted to be. On paper, I am a woman, yet in the flesh, people are less willing to believe me' (Tanna 1999: 17).

How might things have been better for Sarah-Jane? 'Hermaphrodites', she asserts, should be diagnosed correctly, make their own sex identification at an appropriate age, have access to medical and psychiatric help if they so choose, and not receive pressure from family, medical professionals or society as to how they should be (interview 9 June 2004). As to her family and her society, Sarah-Jane questions whether she can forgive or fit in: 'The tenderness of love is something I will never feel, I have become too hard and bitter ... I feel that this world has passed me by and I am either something that belongs in the past or to a future that has not arrived ... I feel my family sees me as society sees me, an object of ridicule ...' (correspondence 19 January 2007).

CHAPTER 7

Changes in Standards of Care?

Since 1997, many of the issues that are associated with medical concerns of the genitalia and the treatment of intersexuals have come under review and management techniques have been altered. It is likely that facets of intersex management will continue to occupy the attention of health care workers for years to come.

Milton Diamond, *Sex, Gender, and Identity Over the Years*

The North American Task Force on Intersex 2000

Between 1996 and 1998, a number of significant texts were published including Diamond and Sigmundson's critique of the David Reimer case (1997b); Diamond and Sigmundson's guidelines for dealing with genital ambiguity (1997a); and Reiner's critical reflection on sex re-assignment in a teenage girl (1996b). These challenged conventions of medical management for intersexuals and proposed alternative methods for their treatment and care. Chase's essay 'Affronting Reason' was published in 1998, as were Dreger's examination of the social-historical construction of biology *Hermaphrodites and the Medical Invention of Sex*; Kessler's interrogation of social-cultural systems of gender *Lessons from the Intersexed*; Holmes' text 'In(to)Visibility: Intersexuality in the Field of Queer'; and Schober's paper 'Early feminizing genitoplasty or watchful waiting'. These contributed to the growing movement for discussion, evaluation and change.

Also in 1998, the American Academy of Pediatrics' standards of care for intersex management were challenged, and three key recommendations were advanced in the US (Kipnis and Diamond 1998; Diamond 1999) seeking:

1. a moratorium on non-consensual cosmetic sex assignment surgery in the absence of evidence of its benefits;
2. continuation of that moratorium until comprehensive, qualitative retrospective research indicates the benefits of past treatment;
3. efforts to undo the effects of deception and secrecy characterizing past intersex management.

Diamond details the range of responses to these recommendations, as well as their developmental history, in his paper 'Sex, Gender and Identity Over the Years: A Changing Perspective' (2004c). He acknowledges that 'many physicians have changed their practices' (ibid.: 598), while 'many others are examining critically how the new and old research regarding intersex treatment should be evaluated' (ibid.: 603). Others still remain sceptical or wary of change.

The North American Task Force on Intersex formed in 2000 to follow up long-term outcomes of intersex treatment and management in North America, especially in relation to genital surgery for intersexed infants, and to consider the increasing numbers of adult intersexuals changing sex or gender roles (Preves 2000; Schober 2001). Its membership included surgical specialists, endocrinologists, psychologists, ethicists, psychiatrists, epidemiologists, geneticists, public health representatives and intersex advocates, including representatives from the Intersex Society of North America. The Task Force appears to have proved ineffectual, however, with apparent differences of emphasis between critics and advocates of traditional intersex management and lack of unbiased access to institutional records for retrospective studies cited as contributing to its demise (Chase, correspondence 27 July 2006).

The American Academy of Pediatrics 2000 and the British Association of Paediatric Surgeons Working Party 2001

In 2000, nevertheless, the American Academy of Pediatrics shifted their standards of care in recognition of new evidence in relation to the management and long-term follow-up of intersexed individuals (Diamond 2004a). This came only two years after the challenge to those standards of care that had produced the three recommendations above. One year later, in 2001, the British Association of Paediatric Surgeons issued their Statement on the Surgical Management of Children Born with Ambiguous Genitalia. While the US and UK bodies acknowledged the three recommendations of 1998, a moratorium on non-consensual cosmetic sex assignment surgery was not acceptable to either group. There were, however, some interesting differences in their positions (Diamond 2004c).

1. The US Academy continued to consider infant genital ambiguity a 'social emergency'. The UK Association, however, acknowledged parental desire for early 'corrective' surgery, but stressed that guidance towards fully informed consent required parents to also know the potential of non-surgical, psychologically supported treatment.

2. The US Academy maintained that virilized genetic females should be raised as girls because of their potential fertility. The UK Association indicated

that each sex assignment should be considered individually.

3. The US Academy asserted that clitoral reduction surgery was necessary for intersexuals raised as girls, but the UK Association acknowledged a 'strong case for no clitoral surgery in lesser degrees of clitoromegaly' (BAPS Statement 2001: unpaginated).

4. The US Academy accepted that genetic males with Partial Androgen Insensitivity Syndrome whose very small penises led to female assignments should have their testes removed, whereas the UK Association noted that such testes presented only a very small risk of malignancy.

These differences indicated a more flexible approach to intersex management in the UK than in the US, with full disclosure of non-surgical treatment options; individual assessment of cases; and a reduced emphasis on clitoral surgery and on removal of testes theoretically being more usual in the UK.

In 2001, the British Association of Paediatric Surgeons Working Party on the Surgical Management of Children Born with Ambiguous Genitalia acknowledged that 'the surgery of intersex conditions in childhood is complex and demanding', but aimed to present a 'fair and, above all, evidence based summation of current thinking and suggested practice' (BAPS Statement 2001: unpaginated). The precepts of the BAPS Statement represent the most current formal record of protocols for management of intersex signalled by ambiguous genitalia in the UK.

The BAPS Statement made clear that the range of intersex diagnoses requires a plurality of approach to policy on management of infant genital ambiguity. The current rapid changes in the field and the availability of more long-term data with improved record-keeping and research-sharing was acknowledged (Diamond, correspondence 2 December 2005; Ransley, interview 6 September 2005), as were evolving social-cultural contexts and medical attitudes, and the refinement of surgical techniques. The BAPS Statement described how current standard protocols were based on early diagnosis, sex assignment and surgery in infancy, but noted recent patient descriptions of such surgery as 'damaging', 'mutilating', 'essentially cosmetic' and performed without patient consent (2001: unpaginated). As in Diamond and Sigmundson's recommendations (1997a), the BAPS Statement emphasized the need for urgent multi-disciplinary treatment given the rarity and complexity of conditions contributing to ambiguous genitalia. It specifically recommended that the treatment team include appropriately trained paediatric surgeons and/or paediatric urologists, neonatologists, paediatric endocrinologists, geneticists, biochemists, psychologists and gynaecologists. As with Diamond, it also urged that easily accessible specialist psychological support for the child/adolescent and the family should be integrated with medical care.

While the BAPS Statement suggested that parents be advised of the possibilities of non-surgical treatments, it did not, however, extend as far as Diamond and Sigmundson's recommendation that cosmetic (as opposed to life-preserving) genital surgery and major prolonged steroid hormone treatment (except for preservation of life) be avoided until post-puberty to allow for changes at puberty to complete the child's sexual development, and also to permit the child to understand the consequences and responsibilities associated with a range of possible treatments (1997a).

Consensus Statement on Management of Intersex Disorders 2006

The British Association of Paediatric Surgeons Statement noted that further review within a few years would be appropriate. A consensus document reviewing intersex management and long-term outcomes, and proposing future studies, was published recently (Hughes *et al.* 2006). This paper draws on the knowledge and experience of fifty *international* experts, including two intersexed adults, and its evolutionary relationship to the recommendations of Kipnis (Kipnis and Diamond 1998) and Diamond (1999) and the BAPS Statement (2001) is clear. Hughes' key findings and recommendations are as follows:

1. 'Disorders of Sex Development' should replace the terms 'intersex' and 'hermaphrodite' for 'congenital conditions in which development of chromosomal, gonadal, or anatomical sex is atypical' (Hughes *et al.* 2006: 1). This would allow precise, clear and dispassionate classification of each individual's intersex condition.
2. A range of factors including *in utero* androgen exposure, which affects sex differentiation of the brain and subsequent behaviour, influences psychosexual development. This is still incompletely understood.
3. General concepts of care for infants with genital ambiguity should include: expert evaluation by a multi-disciplinary team; gender assignment for all subjects; open, participative and confidential communication with the subject and the family; involvement of support groups; preparation for possible gender re-assignment if assignment in infancy proves incorrect for the subject.
4. Where surgery is proposed, surgical sequence plus predicted consequences from infancy to adulthood should be clearly articulated, and emphasis should be on functional outcome (including erotic sensation and orgasmic capability) rather than on cosmetic appearance.
5. In infant vaginal surgeries, it must be acknowledged that revision surgery at puberty is highly likely, and vaginal dilation should not be undertaken prior

to puberty. Similarly, parents should not be given unrealistic expectations of penis reconstructive surgery and phalloplasty.

6. Testes should be removed where necessary in Androgen Insensitivity Syndrome female assignments, although the earliest reported malignancy in Complete AIS (discussed in Chapter 9) is at age fourteen. Streak gonads in cases of male-assigned Mixed and female-assigned Complete Gonadal Dysgenesis respectively (discussed in Chapter 11) warrant early removal. Sperm banking should be considered as a means for preserving fertility (Palmero et al. 1992), and it should be noted that the functional ovarian tissue in ovotestes is potentially fertile.

7. Management of hormone replacement in subjects assigned male or female should seek to replicate the typical changes of puberty, including development of secondary sexual characteristics, growth spurt, optimal bone mineral accumulation, and should support psychosexual maturation.

8. Quality of life, acknowledged in Chapter 4 as more difficult to gauge than penis length, number of sexual partners, or fertility (Ransley, interview 6 September 2005), should be defined as including 'falling in love, dating, attraction, ability to develop intimate relationships, sexual functioning, and the opportunity to marry and to raise children, regardless of biological indicators of sex' (Hughes et al. 2006: 5). Long-term outcomes of treatment should be measured in relation to external and internal genital manifestation, physical health including fertility, sexual function, social and psychosexual adjustment, mental health, quality of life, and social participation.

Hughes concludes that '[l]ong term data on sexual function and quality of life among those assigned female as well as male show great variability' (Hughes et al. 2006: 5). He calls for long-term, standardized and controlled clinical trials, and international collaboration to better evaluate surgical procedures over time, and to assess the comparative outcomes of early and later surgery.

Genital Ambiguity

The BAPS Statement delineated the range of common intersex conditions involving genital ambiguity thus:

1. Congenital Adrenal Hyperplasia (CAH)
2. Complete Androgen Insensitivity Syndrome (CAIS)
3. Severe undervirilization in genetic males, which can be caused by
   (a) Partial Androgen Insensitivity Syndrome (PAIS)
   (b) 5-alpha reductase deficiency
   (c) Testicular Regression Syndrome
   (d) severe hypospadias

4. True Hermaphroditism and Mixed Gonadal Dysgenesis.

Some of these – 'true hermaphroditism' and hypospadias – have been discussed earlier and the following chapters continue to examine intersex genital
ambiguity via selected personal testimonies collected in the UK and elsewhere.

CHAPTER 8

Lorna, Jessie, Sal and Congenital Adrenal Hyperplasia

When she was two, our doctor recommended that her genitalia should be repaired even though we didn't think it was very severe. My husband thought it was a bit ugly, but I was okay about it if I'm honest.

We saw a wonderful Pediatric Urologist and his surgery was very good. He did a careful reduction on her clitoris, and he told us it would have continued to grow as she got older, so we got it right at the best time!

She did really well, and she's home now looking just like a real little girl. My husband is mighty relieved and she'll be fine ...

Elizabeth, correspondence 11 February 2004

Congenital Adrenal Hyperplasia is by far the most common cause of ambiguous genitalia in infants.

Meyer-Bahlburg, correspondence 3 April 2002

Frequency and Symptoms

There are two forms of Congenital Adrenal Hyperplasia: Classical CAH and Late-Onset (Non-Classical) CAH. In its *Classical* form, CAH affects the foetal development of approximately 1 in 13,000–15,000 births, with some rare forms resultant from enzyme deficiencies rather than the more typical 21-hydroxylase deficiency (Blackless *et al.* 2000). In its *Late-Onset* form it affects as many as approximately 1 in 66–1,000 individuals (Blackless *et al.* 2000; CARES Foundation). Ethnicity is a factor in frequency statistics, with particularly high instances of Late-Onset CAH in, for example, populations of Ashkenazi, Hispanics and Croatians.

CAH is an inherited recessive genetic disorder affecting *both genetic males and genetic females.* During foetal development, when the external genitals in both male and female foetuses are incomplete, an enzyme absence or deficiency in the foetal adrenal glands results in the production of excessive androgens (male hormones including testosterone) as well as diminishing production of cortisol and of salt-retaining steroid (Conway 2000b). The resultant virilization is not an immediate issue for genetic male foetuses. In genetic female foetuses, however, it varies in severity but generally causes the clitoris to enlarge and the vagina to be narrow or closed (in Classical, but not Late-Onset CAH). Genetic female newborns with the virilized genitals of Classical CAH then are the archetypal 'phallic females' of anatomical science.

In 75 per cent of all babies (male and female) with Classical CAH, loss of salt from the body precipitates an immediate 'adrenal crisis' or 'salt-wasting crisis' following birth, and needs urgent attention as it is potentially life-threatening (Hendricks 2000). Its symptoms include vomiting, poor feeding, drowsiness, diarrhoea, dehydration and weight loss, and its appearance alerts physicians to the CAH status of these newborns (Conway 2000b). Without urgent treatment, these babies would go into shock and die. Treatment is identical for girls and boys, and consists of immediate and then long-term control of the levels of salt-regulating hormones. In both the salt-wasting and non-salt-wasting form there is also a need for life-long replacement of cortisol, the hormone that regulates the body's ability to cope with stress. Of those CAH babies who do *not* have a salt-wasting crisis, the genetic males will generally go undiagnosed since their genitalia are virilized anyway, while the genetic females will be diagnosed only if their genitalia are ambiguous. If the genitalia of these genetic females are completely virilized, it is also possible that they will be read as newborn boys.

Preparation for a salt-wasting crisis (and indeed avoidance or reduction of female genital virilization) is possible during pregnancy if the foetus' CAH status is known. There are those who argue for routine *in utero* CAH testing (possible only at around nine to ten weeks gestation), and currently this is usually reserved for families where one child already has CAH and there is likelihood of another child being affected. If CAH is a possibility in a pregnancy, virilization of the genitalia of genetic female foetuses can be prevented or diminished if the mother is treated with powerful steroids as soon as she knows she is pregnant, and ideally at four to six weeks gestation. In such cases, if sex testing – possible only at nine to ten weeks – indicates that the foetus is an unaffected genetic female, or a genetic male (affected or not), then drug treatment can cease. Statistically, however, this treatment exposes an average of eight foetuses to steroids in order to benefit one, and the long-term effects of pre-natal treatment on the child are unknown.

CAH affects genetic males and genetic females in the following ways:

CAH in Genetic Males

In genetic *male* infants who suffer a salt-wasting crisis at birth, diagnosis of CAH is made almost immediately and treatment can be undertaken. These subjects are usually prescribed cortisol medication to regulate their testosterone production to more typical levels (Conway 2000b).

In the genetic male infants who do *not* suffer this crisis, CAH may not be diagnosed at birth as there is no genital ambiguity, and the condition may go unrecognized entirely in infancy. In these instances, the subject will not receive the usual medication, and this can result in 'precocious puberty' with pubic hair growth, penis enlargement and rapid physical growth as early as age three or four. High levels of testosterone in men with CAH may also cause problems with aggression and 'excessive' sex drive, and there can also be enlargement of the testicles and diminished sperm count. These symptoms in adult males sometimes prompt the late diagnosis of CAH.

Genetic Females with Classical CAH

In genetic female foetuses with Classical CAH, the adrenal gland's over-production of testosterone produces varying degrees of virilization of the developing external genitalia. This can range from mild to severe enlargement of the clitoris (clitoromegaly) to fully male-appearing genitalia with partial or total fusing of the labia. The internal genitalia – uterus, ovaries and duct structures – develop along the typical female pattern since these form prior to the release of the excessive testosterone during gestation.

Genetic female infants experiencing a salt-wasting crisis after birth will be diagnosed as having CAH, and will be most usually assigned female, with surgery/hormone treatment to 'feminize' their ambiguous or fully virilized genitals (Pang undated). Those who do not experience such a crisis will not be diagnosed in that way, and, where virilization is severe, the genetic female infant – the baby girl – appears wholly male at birth. In such instances, since genetic testing at birth is not routine and sex determination is usually by visual inspection of the newborn's genitals, these infants are announced as baby boys. The clitoris is enlarged and appears like a penis, while the labia are swollen, fused in the middle and wrinkled like a scrotum. All girls born with CAH have a vagina, but the position, width or length can vary considerably. A small membrane may cover the vaginal opening making it invisible to cursory examination, or, if the labia are very swollen or completely fused, the vaginal opening can be hidden underneath. CAH in these instances may go undiag-nosed because the infant looks like a typical baby boy. The apparent boy, however, has internal female anatomy, and will go on to experience excessive hair growth, acne, irregular menstruation (from an opening not previously apparent) and rapid growth in height at puberty. In such severely virilized cases, *diagnosis of CAH and discovery that the apparent boy is a genetic female may not take place until puberty.* Interviewee Jean was raised as such a boy, who thought he was dying when he began to bleed from under what he considered his scrotum at thirteen (interview 13 March 2004). Following diagnosis, Jean elected to be re-assigned as female in her late teens because she felt that as a genetic female she should live as a woman. Feminizing surgery on her penile clitoris and on her vaginal introitus and cavity has created difficulties, with poor healing and slow progress in the use of plastic dilators to encourage expansion of her vagina. These issues have obliterated Jean's sexual desire, and consequently her loss of clitoral sensation is not especially a problem for her. She indicates distaste with 'everything down below there where the bleeding started', and alludes to being content as a boy before puberty (correspondence 18 January 2004).

In less severe cases of Classical CAH without a salt-wasting crisis, an infant's genital ambiguity will most likely prompt investigation and subsequent CAH diagnosis. Karyotype will be determined, and sex assignment – almost always as female, again with surgery/hormone treatment – will be undertaken.

Genetic Females with Late-Onset (Non-Classical) CAH

In genetic girls with Late-Onset CAH, genitals in infancy appear typically female, and those who do not experience a salt-wasting crisis will have no infant indicators of their CAH. The symptoms of virilization, including hair growth, acne and height gain, occur unexpectedly at any age, normally leading to investigation and diagnosis. Irregular menstruation can also happen at puberty, and an apparently typical girl with no genital virilization can be diagnosed with Late-Onset CAH when her periods fail to commence. Such symptoms are the first indicators of CAH in these girls, and therefore diagnosis happens when symptoms appear – before or at puberty – rather than at birth.

Girls with both Classical and Late-Onset CAH have unusually high testosterone levels. In the mildest cases conventional treatment with oestrogen can be sufficient to regulate their own production of testosterone from their ovaries (Conway 2000b). In less mild cases, endocrinologists typically prescribe and monitor treatment with steroid drugs such as hydrocortisone to regulate hormone levels and prevent the over-production of androgens. This treatment, of course, only happens where diagnosis has taken place. Careful monitoring of treatment is critical, especially during childhood, when the child's growth can be affected by over- or underprescription of steroid drugs.

The high levels of testosterone produced by the adrenal glands in genetic females with CAH can also interfere with ovulation. Endocrine treatment for CAH can help to improve this, but specific details on fertility in these cases are still not fully documented. Creighton (Creighton and Liao 2004a) suggests that the fertility potential of genetic females with CAH – even those with severe virilization – is a key consideration in the overwhelming tendency towards female assignment of these subjects. If pregnancy for CAH women does occur, the placenta lends protection to the foetus from the maternal hormonal imbalance, and generally babies born to mothers with CAH are born unaffected. Vaginal scarring resulting from earlier genital surgery or from genital virilization experienced during the mother's own foetal development, however, means that a significant number of these babies are not delivered vaginally.

CAH and Genital Ambiguity

As noted earlier, individuals with CAH can be genetic males or genetic females. It is those who are genetic females (with XX karyotype, ovaries, a uterus) who exhibit ambiguous or totally virilized external genitalia, and these individuals have traditionally frequently been referred to by the umbrella term 'female pseudohermaphrodites'. The current treatment protocol for genetic females with CAH seeks to maintain assigned sex (female) in tandem with the genetic sex (female) by keeping signs of virilization at bay (either by *in utero* steroid treatment or by surgery on the clitoris and/or vagina in infancy and childhood supported by feminizing hormone treatment).

As in Jean's case, it is possible to mistake the most virilized of genetic female infants for baby boys through non-recognition of the genitals at birth as those of a (typical) genetic female infant. There have also been rare instances where the virilization is so severe that parents and/or clinicians have consciously decided to raise the genetic female child as a boy – against genetic sex – and therefore without feminizing genital surgery. Diamond and Sigmundson (1997a) recommended a non-surgical course of action for severely virilized CAH genetic females (as detailed in Chapter 4). They proposed that surgery could then be undertaken *if desired by the subject* in adulthood to reinforce the masculine appearance of the genitals, or alternatively *the subject might choose* to reverse the sex of rearing and have feminizing genital surgery (clitoral reduction and surgery on labia and vagina).

Where genetic females with CAH have hypertrophied (enlarged) clitorises only, and their labia are separate rather than fused, Diamond and Sigmundson (1997a) still recommended avoidance of surgery, but suggested that such children should be raised – in accordance with their genetic sex – as girls, again until they can make informed choices about subsequent treatment (or not) of their larger than typical clitorises and possibly atypical vaginas post-puberty. Diamond and Sigmundson's recommendations are based on what they believe are the most likely gender identity outcomes in adulthood for the degrees of CAH virilization described. The implication in the literature, however, is that surgery of some kind is the usual course of treatment for infants and children recognized as having CAH, and that the timing and extent of this varies from case to case and from clinician to clinician.

Surgical Treatment Protocols

The BAPS Statement on the Surgical Management of Children Born with Ambiguous Genitalia (2001) described how *some* girls with CAH opt to change sex in later life in concurrence with their *in utero* virilization rather than their genetic sex. That is, they choose as adults to live as males and may seek surgery/hormonal treatment to reinforce this choice. Although we know the virilizing effect of androgens on the developing external genitalia of genetic female foetuses (their sex development) during gestation, there is as yet scant evidence about the virilizing effect of male hormones *in utero* on developing foetal brains (their gender development) (Hughes *et al.* 2006).

Kenneth Zucker of the Child and Adolescent Gender Identity Clinic, Child and Family Studies Centre at the Clarke Institute of Psychiatry, Toronto, examined the sexual function and psychosexual development of women with CAH (Zucker *et al.* 1996). One of his conclusions was that genetic females with CAH exhibited more 'cross-gender behaviour' during childhood than their non-CAH sisters and cousins, and that genetic female adults with CAH exhibited more cross-gender identification than the controls. Creighton too reports that girls with CAH have an increased likelihood of exhibiting a 'masculine' style of play, but are as likely as non-CAH girls to develop a 'female core-gender identity' (Creighton and Liao 2004a: 661). Hines also notes that 'females exposed to higher-than-normal levels of androgen prenatally [as in CAH] show elevated levels of male-typical playmate, activity, and toy choices in comparison to normal controls', and have 'higher-than-expected desires to change sex as adults' (Hines *et al.* 2003: 98). The BAPS Statement concludes, however, that the numbers of genetic female CAH subjects who choose to live as males as adults is low, and states that this should not *in itself* dissuade clinicians from undertaking feminizing genitoplasty in infancy. That being said, the BAPS Statement clearly notes that cases need individual consideration, and irreversible clitoral surgery must be approached cautiously if at all.

Feminizing Genitoplasty

The feminizing genitoplasty proposed for genetic females with ambiguous and virilized genitalia resulting from CAH consists of two procedures: clitoral surgery and vaginoplasty (these may additionally include some work on the labia). The debates surrounding feminizing genital surgery are undoubtedly 'emotive and distressing' (Creighton 2004b: 44) for many of those involved in the practice – patients, parents and clinicians. Its advocates variously cite improved gender identity stability; better psychosexual, psychosocial and psychological outcomes; diminished parental anxiety; and harmony between reproductive function and reproductive capability through the allowance of menstruation and intercourse as strong and persuasive reasons for permitting feminizing genitoplasty (Bailez *et al.* 1992; Gearhart *et al.* 1995; Rink and Adams 1998). Miller asserts that 'there should be little controversy regarding CAH patients' receiving what he terms the 'improvement of genital appearance' that such surgery brings (2003: 3,456), and he insists that it is 'cruel' to deny feminizing genitoplasty specifically to infants with CAH. Creighton (Creighton *et al.* 2001a; Creighton 2004b), however, notes that there is little published evidence of *long-term* and *objective* study of subjects of these surgeries, and therefore no concrete verification that they do indeed provide a better psychological outcome, a more stable gender identity, or for that matter that the child will necessarily accept the assignment of female sex. In her paper 'Long-term Outcome of Feminisation Surgery: The London Experience', Creighton suggests that while immediate cosmetic effects can be good following feminizing genitoplasty on an infant there is 'scanty evidence of a satisfactory *postpubertal* cosmetic or anatomical outcome [this author's emphasis]' (2004b: 45).

Girls with CAH are genetic females, with typical female internal structures. They exhibit a range of severity of virilization of their genitalia, and a small number are extremely affected. But what does this mean in reality? Creighton (Creighton and Minto 2001c) indicates that, while there are standard measurements for average clitoris size in female infants, clinical assessment of infant genitalia is often highly subjective and carried out by paediatric experts who may have little clinical experience of the great diversity of adult clitoral dimension and form. The genitals of newborn infants often look out of proportion anyway as they tend to be swollen and dark as a result of maternal hormones still present in the infant's body. Creighton (Creighton and Minto 2001c) points out that a clitoris that appears especially large on an infant body may well be much less relatively prominent in adulthood. Puberty also causes dramatic alteration of genital appearance (labial fat deposition, pubic hair growth) and this affects the proportional size of the clitoris to the rest of the external genitalia. Moreover, the continued production of higher than typical levels of testosterone by genetic females with CAH after birth and during childhood and adulthood can stimulate new or renewed clitoral growth, and poor endocrine treatment either by the clinician or through poor self-management by the patient can result in unanticipated changes to the dimension of the clitoris even after infant reduction surgery. Finally, as Cheryl Chase reiterates: 'a large clitoris ... represents no medical danger to its owner' (1994: 5).

Clitoridectomy is not new, historically having been used to quell 'unnatural' sexual appetites, to remove the cultural threat and affront of the 'phallic female' or to prevent masturbation in girls and women (Holt 1897; Sheehan 1997; Coventry 1998). There is arguably a social-cultural dimension to its continued, if refined, use. At birth, the infant is ignorant of its atypicality but its parents are frequently shocked and distressed, and there can be concerns articulated by parents of virilized girls that their child's larger than typical clitoris will result in lesbianism or nymphomania. In Channel 4's *Secret Intersex* documentary (2004), an infant with CAH, an enlarged clitoris and closed vagina was described. Her clinician articulated how the situation was 'extremely traumatic' for the infant's mother. Parental anxiety and mental anguish is frequently cited as a powerful driver in determining that feminizing genitoplasty should be done (Farhat 2005). Creighton points out, however, that there is no evidence that such procedures alleviate parental fears, and indeed there is anecdotal evidence to suggest that shame, fear, secrecy and anxiety typify parenting post-surgery (Creighton and Liao 2004a, referencing Liao 2003; Hughes *et al.* 2006). In any case, should any decision to enact a radical, surgical and permanent procedure on a baby be influenced by a desire to diminish the suffering of its parents? And, as Lih-Mei Liao, Consultant Clinical Psychologist at University College London, asks 'how can parents and surgeons be sure that these procedures are less traumatising for the child than the presumed catastrophe of non-intervention?' (Liao and Boyle 2004: 460).

For the baby in *Secret Intersex*, 'normalizing' surgery opened up her vaginal entrance, separating her urethral opening from it. Her clitoris was surgically relocated within her newly opened vagina, and she will need further surgery at puberty to release and reposition it. As with many CAH children, she will have hormone therapy throughout her life to attempt to keep her virilizing endocrine effects at bay. Paradoxically, there is both permanency, in the sense that surgery cannot be undone, and impermanency, in the sense that her feminization needs to be medically maintained. There is also certainty, in the sense of the determined nature of the treatment, and lack of certainty, in that her surgeon admitted that in this subject specialism surgeons are 'practicing blindly at the present time' (*Secret Intersex* 2004).

Gerard Conway, Consultant Endocrinologist at University College London Hospitals maintains that surgery for the vagina and urethra is more complicated and variable than clitoral surgery (2000b). Depending on the patient's anatomy, care needs to be taken with vaginal surgery that there is no damage to the bladder, and there are risks of urinary infection, stenosis and the formation of strictures or fistulae (Bailez *et al.* 1992; Rink and Adams 1998). Of course, where urinary stasis and/or infection are present already as a result, for example, of specific ambiguous genital configuration, surgery may be required to alleviate this. But it seems perverse to cut into a healthy infant and risk these complications in order to create a vagina that will realistically have no function until required much later for menstruation and/or sexual intercourse. Indeed, post-operative daily vaginal dilations to maintain the openness of the vagina in a pre-pubescent child are arguably unnecessary, and certainly harrowing (Hughes *et al.* 2006).

Few long-term follow-up studies are available for vaginoplasty in infancy, but there is likely to be a requirement for revision surgery for vaginal or introital stenosis (narrowing of the vagina or its opening) in adolescence when a vagina has been surgically created in infancy (Bailez *et al.* 1992; Alizai *et al.* 1999). Given the physical changes between infancy and puberty, such revision surgery needs also to ensure that the opening is large enough for sexual intercourse, use of tampons and unrestricted menstrual flow since these dimensions would be inappropriate to the infant. Creighton's study (2004b) shows that 98 per cent of her subjects would require revision of their infant vaginal construction before they could use tampons or have sexual intercourse, while 78.5 per cent of Bailez's subjects needed further surgery to allow intercourse (Bailez *et al.* 1992). Revision surgeries in adolescence or adulthood, on top of surgeries in infancy, heighten the probability of problematic scarring and sensory damage (Creighton and Minto 2001c). Certainly, performing fewer surgeries reduces the risk of scar-tissue build-up in and around the vagina, and this in turn lessens problems with non-pliability and non-lubrication. Since early vaginoplasty confers no obvious benefit for the young girl, it is arguably more directed towards alleviating parental distress. There seems to be a strong case for delaying it until just before the onset of menstruation, and Bailez, for example, conceded that 'reducing the number of reconstructive operations could be conducive to better long-term emotional health' (Bailez *et al.* 1992: 681).

Creighton (Creighton and Liao 2004a) notes that there is no data to suggest infant vaginoplasty is better in anatomical, cosmetic or functional terms than surgery carried out at adolescence or in adulthood. Referencing Alizai *et al.* (1999), she further reports that 28–46 per cent of a sample of subjects who had infant vaginal construction surgery reported unsatisfactory or poor cosmetic results, with vaginal stenosis in 36–100 per cent of cases (Creighton and Liao 2004a). Where the subject already has a shortened vagina, there are clinicians who are of the opinion that the potential for surgical scarring should be entirely avoided where possible, and dilation techniques used before and after puberty to slowly lengthen and widen the vaginal opening as an alternative to vaginal surgery. Hughes (Hughes *et al.* 2006), however, suggests that no one technique is best for all subjects.

The classic symbol of virilized female genitalia is the enlarged clitoris, as overt and apparent as the vagina is hidden. It is this that activates the cultural horror of the 'phallic female', and there is a range of procedures firmly in place for dealing with its 'affront'. *Total clitoridectomy or clitoral amputation* involves the removal of all visible parts of the clitoris (the sensitive glans and the protective hood) and some dissection and removal of the corpora, which is the embedded and sensitive body of the clitoris. Creighton (Creighton and Minto 2001c) believes that this procedure is now carried out only rarely in the UK although data is incomplete. *Clitoral recession* is an alternative procedure in which the clitoral structures are not removed, but are rather dissected out, then folded up and moved backwards under the symphysis pubis (the front join of the two large bones of the pelvis), while clitoral nerves remain connected to the clitoral glans (Creighton and Minto 2001c). This procedure, however, has been found to cause pain on clitoral engorgement and, while data is also incomplete, Creighton presumes this technique is also no longer used in the UK. *Clitoral reduction* is a third technique, although these techniques have variations and crossovers in the literature and in practice (Schober 1998a), which seeks to preserve the glans of the clitoris while the corpora is dissected and partially or totally removed. In this process, the clitoral nerves generally remain connected to the glans, and the glans may be reduced by 'wedge' excisions. Creighton concludes, however, 'there is no evidence that the retained glans functions well in sexual/orgasmic terms' (Creighton and Minto 2001c: unpaginated).

While falling short of the moratorium on non-consensual cosmetic sex assignment surgery recommended by Kipnis (Kipnis and Diamond 1998) and Diamond (1999, 2004c), the BAPS Statement indicated 'there is a strong case for no clitoral surgery at all in lesser degrees of clitoromegaly' (2001: unpaginated). In its Appendix, Creighton and Minto made their own recommendations regarding clitoral surgery (2001c: unpaginated), advocating that the following actions inform further development of treatment protocols:

1. that consultation is undertaken with intersex support groups, adult patients who have undergone clitoral surgery and parents of children who have experienced this surgery;
2. that all data on effects of sexual function should be discussed with parents, and the option to decline clitoral surgery must also be discussed;
3. that clitoral surgery should be avoided in mild and moderately virilized children;
4. that clitoral surgery on severely virilized children must be carefully discussed with all involved in the full understanding of effects in the future. The possibility of deferring surgery should be discussed with the parents, and the possible requirement for further revision surgery must be recognized.

In 2004, Creighton went further, stating:

Thus far the only known function of the clitoris is erotic pleasure.

Recent work on the neuroanatomy of the human foetal clitoris showed an extensive network of nerves surrounding the tunica with many perforating branches entering the dorsal aspect of the corporeal body and glans, making it clear that any incision to the clitoral glans, corpora or hood could risk damage to the dense enervation.

Past confidence amongst paediatric surgeons in unimpaired sexual function after clitoral surgery seems no longer tenable [this author's emphasis]. (Creighton and Liao 2004a: 660)

Why would we be surprised to find that there may be significant libidinal or body confidence issues for CAH women who have had genital surgery? Such women can exhibit anxiety about the prospect of sexual activity and have difficulty seeing or experiencing it as pleasurable (Conway 2000b). Anatomical function is only one contributor to good psychosexual adjustment, and others include the patient's own (and possibly partner's) assessment of the cosmetic appearance of the post-operative genitalia, the frequency of complications and need for revisions, the resultant quality of life for the adult, sexual satisfaction and general satisfaction with procedures undertaken. Because long-term study of outcomes has been so poor, and also because data from the past is incomplete due in part to significant numbers of cases of non-disclosure of true diagnosis, evidence for all assertions made in relation to new treatment paradigms tends to be based on smaller studies by individual medical practitioners.

Creighton and Minto (2001c) report two studies, one by May (May *et al.* 1996) and the other by Dittman (Dittman *et al.* 1992), which both concluded that women with CAH who were the subjects of feminizing genital surgery were less likely to masturbate, less likely to be sexually active and less likely to experience orgasm compared with a control group. May cautions, however, that while women with CAH 'do appear to have some sexual difficulties which are particular to their condition' (May *et al.* 1996: 491) these may not be solely medical/surgical, and may also be related to the psychological impact of CAH. Nevertheless, Creighton's own study at University College London Hospitals suggests that those of her study who *had* experienced clitoral surgery were significantly worse off than those who had not had surgery on their enlarged clitorises. Of this clitorectomized group, 26 per cent were unable to achieve orgasm by any means, and 28–46 per cent reported unsatisfactory cosmetic appearance (Creighton 2004b). Morgan's study (Morgan *et al.* 2005) at the Middlesex Hospital, London, examined eighteen genetic females with CAH, raised as female, some of whom had the feminizing genitoplasty described above. On a range of scales for social adjustment, all of the subjects fell within the 'normal' range as defined by the study. However, only four of the eighteen adult participants were sexually active, and of these only two rated any sexual enjoyment. As Melissa Cull, founder of the Adrenal Hyperplasia Network, notes:

> Depression and stress are often reported [by CAH women], particularly to do with relationships, with sexual difficulties after surgery ...
>
> Non-disclosure, shame, secrecy and stigmas attached to having ambiguous genitalia, and an intersex condition, and surgery to 'normalise' all place a heavy toll on a woman's psychological wellbeing. (Cull 2005: 341)

Crouch (2003) cites compromise of genital sensation and orgasmic function; Dittman *et al.* (1992) and May *et al.* (1996) point to sexual difficulties, pain on intercourse, and sexual anxiety; Cull (2005) describes loss of sexual privacy and self-esteem; Migeon (Migeon *et al.* 2002b) and Alizai (Alizai *et al.* 1999) even warn of the dangers of clitoral necrosis or tissue death which may be experienced by those whose surgeries were carried out non-consensually when they were infants. Cull also contends that repeat operations plus dilation are constant painful reminders for CAH women that they are genitally different. And Creighton (Creighton and Liao 2004a) is realistic about avoidance of genital surgery: she acknowledges that if feminizing genitoplasty is *not* carried out in cases of CAH genetic females with virilized genitalia, this does not erase these individuals' difference from typicality, with the resultant misunderstanding, social intolerance and sexual cruelty that can bring.

The 2001 BAPS Statement's conclusion that less severe virilization of genetic females with CAH need not be surgically treated has provided a benchmark for the beginnings of serious scrutiny of these practices. Creighton (Creighton and Minto 2001b) called for a long-term study of the outcomes of surgical management of conditions such as Congenital Adrenal Hyperplasia exactly because that management remains controversial. Such a study would help determine the effects of feminizing genitoplasty on the psychosexual and psychosocial development of its subjects. While there is slow movement forwards in terms of the collection and collation of long-term data, and its objective analysis, there are still many who advocate feminizing genitoplasty unreservedly for genetic female infants with CAH, and who state that there is still insufficient evidence for a systematic policy change in relation to infant genital surgery (Miller 2003; Farhat 2005).

Lorna's Story

Lorna wrote from California:

> I feel as though my little son died, and I've got a daughter I hadn't expected. It's confusing for me. I love her very much, this little girl. I just feel like I've lost my little boy … (correspondence 3 March 2005)

Lorna's child was born in 2003 looking exactly like a little boy. Lorna had been told she was expecting a boy following a routine ultrasound at twenty weeks into the pregnancy. She and her husband had decorated his room, bought lots of blue baby clothes and had chosen his name – Joseph. She had bonded with the son she believed was developing inside her, and had imagined what it would be like to be the mother of a boy, her first child.

Hours after Joseph's birth, however, their baby became seriously ill and was rushed to the neo-natal intensive care unit where he stabilized but remained very ill. During the next five days tests revealed that Joseph's testicles could not be seen or felt inside what appeared to be his scrotal sac, and the ultra-sound to see if they were still undescended from the abdomen showed that Joseph had a uterus. Lorna and her husband were in a state of complete shock. They had announced to friends and family that they had a son, and this news both devastated and bewildered them. Lorna will never forget that day or the pain and confusion she felt. She will also never forget the panic that her beloved little boy was a 'sexual freak' (interview 17 March 2005).

Lorna has since learned that her genetic female baby was born with Classical CAH. Her baby's larger than typical clitoris (1.3 cm in length) seemed to resemble a penis, and her baby's labia were fused together and wrinkled so that they looked like a scrotum. Internally, the baby had developed as a typical female. Five months later, renamed as Kellie, Lorna's child received surgery to separate her labia and reduce the size of her clitoris, but Lorna is still reeling from the shock of giving birth to Joseph, raising Kellie for five months with apparently male genitalia, and now having a surgically recon-structed little girl. Kellie had one additional genital surgery at the age of one, and her parents have been told that they should expect further work on Kellie's vagina just before puberty.

Lorna and her husband have come to rely intensely on each other as their respective families have had difficulty coping with Kellie's condition. Their 'perfect world', with its blue painted nursery, feels different for them now. Lorna's searches on the Internet have helped her to find more information on Kellie's condition, but she has also found criticism of parents who allow genital surgery on their infants. She finds the accusations of 'mutilation' diffi-cult to cope with, and asks: 'What would you do if it was your girl, and they told you this would let her go ahead and be a normal woman and maybe have her own children. What would you do if that was your little girl?' (Lorna, inter-view 17 March 2005).

Lorna and her husband remain desperately worried about the future. They are keen to try to have another baby, and hope that another child would be 'more normal, like, like a more normal baby' (interview 17 March 2005).

Jessie's Story

Jessie's father, Donal, described the 'joyful night that turned into a nightmare' when his wife gave birth to a child with very ambiguous genitalia and who also became rapidly very ill (interview 17 September 2004). Family and friends desperately wanted to come to the hospital to see the new baby, but Donal had to tell them not to come. Donal and his wife found the whole time 'so scary and embarrassing', and they struggled with not being able to call their baby 'him' or 'her' immediately. Jessie, who was named sometime after her birth, had no vaginal opening, an enlarged clitoris and almost-separate (partially fused) labia. An ultrasound indicated the presence of a uterus and ovaries, and a genetic test revealed that Jessie is a genetic female.

Surgery has reduced Jessie's clitoris, opened the vagina and wholly separated her labia, but healing has been difficult, and there have been problems with infections. Jessie remains a sickly little child whose situation is by no means yet resolved. Donal continues to experience difficulties coming to terms with his daughter's condition, but has no other solution. He was uncomfortable about the surgery, and it has caused difficulties between him and his wife. He concludes: 'there really wasn't anything else to do. I just hated the thought of my wee girl being cut in that way, but then I hated the thought of her staying like that. We just had to make the best of a bad job' (interview 17 September 2004).

Donal reports that his wife is dismissive of concerns about the surgery: the 'doctors knew best' and 'we'll cope with problems if they come', and Donal feels much less sure.

Sal's Story

Sal is about twenty years older than Kellie and Jessie, and describes the clitoral amputation she went through at three months of age as 'traumatic' (correspondence 2 April 2002). She still finds it difficult to come to terms with the judgement that her clitoris was oversized. She writes that she feels completely and totally female, and knows that even to have had a large clitoris would not have diminished that essential feeling: 'There was no medical problem with my clitoris, no disease, just an offence to somebody else. That was their problem, but I got to have my sexual part sliced up. It really stinks' (Sal, correspondence 2 April 2002).

When asked about parental fears that a daughter with a larger than typical clitoris would have lots of problems in school from other children, Sal is blunt. Schools should enact proper anti-bullying policies, talk to kids about difference and get on with things. Why should she be victimized because others cannot cope? Why should she have lost her ability to orgasm because some kids might have potentially bullied her, or because she might have embarrassed her parents? Sal understands that her clinician wanted to make her look more female, but she writes that she might look like a woman, but she can't have the joy of sexual sensation, and given that, what is the point of being one sex or the other anyway? Sal has come to terms with her parents' role in the decisions made, but still wishes they had managed to wait, think, learn, rather than being rushed forwards into consent by her doctors. Sal concludes: 'my folks were there to represent me because I was too little to speak for myself. They didn't deceive me about what was done, it wasn't a secret as I grew up, but to be honest – at the very beginning, when I was so small – I feel that they spoke badly for me' (Sal, correspondence 2 April 2002).

Another adult with CAH wrote about her experience. At birth in the mid-1970s, she was labelled as 'sex ambiguous' as her genitalia seemed to be incompletely virilized. Her parents were then assured that they really had a daughter, and five days later equally assured they had a son. They have subsequently managed to find humour in a scenario where their child travelled from 'a not-quite-sure to a girl with a boy's penis to an under-endowed little boy' in the space of a week (Anon, correspondence 17 May 2003). The diagnosis, however, meant that these parents had a chance to briefly consider the complexity and uncertainty of their situation, and they insisted that genital surgery was avoided as it seemed 'too fixed and too huge a responsibility for them to make' (Anon, correspondence 17 May 2003). This person was raised nominally as a boy, but without family emphasis on the male gender and with very careful parental consideration for privacy (for example, through home schooling and re-location of the family to a rural area). In this individual's later teens, having menstruated only occasionally, and with intact and healthy family relationships as a support, this person insisted on following *her* instincts with regard to *her* identity. She changed her name and began to live privately as a woman with the full back-up and encouragement of her family. She has made the decision not to seek surgery to alter her virilized genitalia, so she hopefully and positively anticipates an 'alternative' kind of relationship with a person who will understand her intersexuality.

Childhood Sexual Abuse?

In Chapter 3, Cheryl Chase was quoted as asserting that infant genital surgery creates 'emotionally abused and sexually dysfunctional intersexuals' (1998b: 214). The various exposures (for medical examination by clinicians and their students, as well as in medical photography) coupled with physical palpation and manipulation of genitalia (including digital penetration of vagina and rectum), are undoubtedly traumatic. Money and Lamacz, in a text defending clinical examination of genitalia and cautioning against contemporary 'victimology', nevertheless indicated that 'whether inchoately or explicitly, in the logic of childhood these experiences were equated with clinical sexual molestation or rape, hence the applicability of the term nosocomial [originating in a hospital] abuse' (Money and Lamacz 1987: 715).

In 1997, Tamara Alexander argued for a consideration of the medical management of intersexed children as an analogue for Childhood Sexual Abuse. Alexander noted that 'medical traumas share many of the critical elements of childhood abuse, such as fear, pain, punishment, and loss of control', while certain aspects of the medical management of intersex arguably incorporate the 'secrecy, misinformation, betrayal by a caregiver, and dissociative processes' reported by victims of Childhood Sexual Abuse (Alexander 1997:

unpaginated). She asserted that: 'Like victims of CSA [Childhood Sexual Abuse], children with intersex conditions are subjected to repeated genital traumas which are kept secret both within the family, and in the culture surrounding it' (1997: unpaginated).

Alexander contends that the sequence of treatments including infant and childhood genital surgery, examination and discussion have similarities with those of childhood sexual abuse. She lists depression, suicide and suicide attempts (Reiner *et al.* 1996a), failure to form intimate bonds (Hurtig *et al.* 1983), sexual dysfunction (Kessler 1990), body image disturbance (Sandberg *et al.* 1989) and dissociative patterns (Fraker 1996), noting that the recommendations for counselling made by the medical establishment are rarely followed through comprehensively, with many intersex cases being 'lost to follow-up'.

Alexander claims that because both clinicians and parents uphold the opinion that the treatment experienced by the intersexed infant, child or adolescent is necessary, the subject's feelings are frequently ignored or minimized. Of course, adults speak for children and make medical decisions for them throughout their childhood – that is their role. The difference in these instances is where treatment is cosmetic rather than life- or health-preserving. The child often feels supremely betrayed by the parent (Angier 1996), and, as with parental sexual abuse, this betrayal can damage that essential relationship irreparably. Shame, secrecy, sexual embarrassment and fear typify many testimonies from intersexed individuals recalling, for example, invasive medical photography, full body and genital examination in cases of precocious puberty and genital ambiguity, repeated scrutiny by a number of different clinicians, internal examination and catheterizations without permission or explanation. The anticipation of repeated treatments is equally damaging (Alexander 1997, referencing Freyd 1996), causing extreme anxiety, psychological torment, physical defensiveness and a loss of 'associatedness' with the physical body.

In Alexander's text there is no suggestion that clinicians or parents have any reasons other than the child's health behind the procedures they carry out or condone, and this is where any relation with Childhood Sexual Abuse, which is driven by needs for dominance and/or sexual gratification, breaks down. Nevertheless, the connections are startling: 'We are sexually traumatized in dramatically painful and terrifying ways and kept silent about it by the shame and fear of our families and society' (David 1995–6 quoted in Alexander 1997: unpaginated).

Part of that silence is about protecting the child, but it undoubtedly serves to perpetuate the taboo and the trauma (Anton 1995). This is the silence that allowed Linda Roberts' father to beat her (Hugill 1998: 7); that characterized David Reimer's 'blighted childhood' (Colapinto 2004: 282); that kept Jean 'in the dark' when she, thinking she was an adolescent boy, suddenly and shockingly menstruated from a vagina she did not know she had (interview 13 March 2004). This is the silence that prompted the confused announcements of Louise's infancy (interview 27 September 2005); that perpetuates Oluyemi's literal fear of death on being discovered intersexed (correspondence 7 May 2004); and that underpinned John Money's 'optimal gender policy'. It is the silence that interviewee Anja's T-shirt – *Schon mal mit nem Zwitter gesprochen? Hier ist die Gelegenheit (Ever talked to a hermaphrodite? Here is your chance)* – seeks to puncture. And it is the silence that permits medical photography without patient consent, and inappropriate storage, duplication, circulation and dissemination of such images (Creighton *et al.* 2002). Interviewee Edele, mother of a child with CAH, recalls attending a presentation by doctors who showed images of children's genitals to an audience of those with CAH and their parents:

> I felt very unsure, quite awkward when they showed us the photographs of kids and their private parts.
>
> They were really interested in showing how CAH kids develop, but they showed us the names of the children on the slides, and it really worried me. I kept thinking what if it was my child?
>
> I didn't feel like I needed to see pictures. It bothered me. What about the feelings of those kids up there on the slides? (Edele, correspondence 8 November 2005)

CHAPTER 9

Joanne, Ellen, Peggy and Androgen Insensitivity Syndrome

Androgen Insensitivity Syndrome (AIS) affects *only foetuses that are genetic males*. It used to be called Testicular Feminization or (as with similar intersex conditions) 'male pseudohermaphroditism'. In 70 per cent of cases, the condition is inherited from the infant's mother, and the remaining 30 per cent of cases have no apparent cause. There are two forms of Androgen Insensitivity Syndrome – Complete and Partial. Infants born with *Complete AIS* have female-appearing genitalia, while those born with *Partial AIS* have a range of genital ambiguities.

Frequency and Symptoms

The *usual* course of genetic male foetal development sees the Y chromosome trigger the formation of testes resulting in the production of testosterone. This male hormone typically initiates the growth of the internal male reproductive apparatus, as well as a penis and scrotum at around the seventh or eight week of gestation. In all cases of AIS, however, the genetic male foetus fails to respond to all (Complete AIS) or some (Partial AIS) of the male hormones (androgens) produced by its own testes. Consequently, in *Complete AIS* the external genitalia do not develop into a penis and a scrotum, but, by default, develop to appear as typically female. A short, often extremely short, vagina is formed and phenotype is female, but internal female apparatus does not develop. The testes, which began developing in response to the presence of a Y chromosome, are partly formed and remain undescended. They are located in the groin, the lower stomach or in an inguinal hernia in which the intestines bulge through a weak area in the muscles of the groin near the thigh. In *Partial AIS*, the foetus' failure to respond to its own androgens during development is only partial, and consequently external genital development is ambiguous, and the testes are as described above.

Blackless (Blackless *et al.* 2000) suggests that Complete AIS occurs in approximately 1 in 13,000 *apparently female* births, with Partial AIS being around one-tenth as common. While these figures are well-supported, there are significantly variable frequency rates proposed by other sources. Minto (Minto *et al.* 2003a) proposes that the estimated incidence of Complete AIS is between 1 in 13,158 and 1 in 40,800 live births, referencing both Blackless (Blackless *et al.* 2000) and Bangsboll (Bangsboll *et al.* 1992). And Ahmed (Ahmed *et al.* 2000) suggests that AIS is present in 1 in 20,000–64,000 male births. Some authors quote AIS incidence figures as a proportion of the *total* population, some as a proportion of the *XY (genetic male)* population, and some as a proportion of *apparently female* births. Consequently, statistics vary considerably.

Complete Androgen Insensitivity Syndrome

Infants with Complete AIS read as baby girls. Diagnosis of AIS in these infants can happen when an apparently female infant's hernia is found to contain a testis. But much more frequently infants with Complete AIS are 'read' as regular girls, are then raised as girls and are only diagnosed as having AIS, and as being genetic males, when menstruation fails to occur at puberty. Individuals with Complete AIS also have little or no pubic hair growth (since this is related to androgen secretion in both sexes), though some breast development does occur at puberty (Diamond and Watson 2004b). Although adolescents with Complete AIS are genetic males, development of male facial hair, male-pattern body hair, or the body muscularity that would be expected in typical male pubescence does not occur (Migeon *et al.* 2001). This is either because the testes were removed on early discovery or, if they are still intact at puberty, individuals with Complete AIS cannot respond to their own androgens at all.

Whether diagnosis of Complete AIS is in infancy, during childhood or at puberty, gonadectomy is emphatically the most usual course of treatment. That is, the internalized testes, or those discovered protruding within a hernia, are surgically removed. Hester (undated) notes, however, that there is a marked tendency for AIS gonadectomies to be explained as 'hernia repairs' or 'appendix operations', for non-disclosure of the male karyotype, and for the presence of testes in the apparently female child to be kept secret. And, from a particular perspective, one can see how this seems reasonable. These children appear to be girls: their genetic sex, which cannot be altered, is male, but the presence of testes, which can be removed, arguably both affronts the 'purity' of the seemingly typical girl and undermines the phallic obligation of the culturally iconic male. Hence, they are removed.

The British Association of Paediatric Surgeons Statement (2001) indicates how timing of gonadectomy remains controversial, and how inadequate data on this issue continues to be problematic. Those diagnosed with AIS in infancy are typically assigned as female. However, given that they cannot respond to the male hormones produced by their own testes anyway, there would not be any virilization to interfere with female assignment if testes remained intact. Moreover, their testes are internal (except when revealed in a hernia, which can be repaired) and are therefore invisible. Their continued presence would make a positive contribution to pubescent bone maturation, possibly to endocrinal balance, and to general body development. Diamond and Sigmundson argue that gonads should remain intact so that 'any genetic-endocrine predisposition imposed prenatally can come to be activated with puberty' (1997a: 1,049). So, why are they removed?

Clinical concerns centre around small risks of malignant change in the testes, yet Verp's comprehensive review of malignancy in the testes of Complete AIS subjects over age twenty-five suggested a 2–5 per cent risk, with risk being described as small prior to age twenty-five (Verp and Simpson 1987, referenced in the BAPS Statement 2001, and reiterated in Batch *et al.* 1992; Quigley *et al.* 1995). Alvarez-Nava (Alvarez-Nava *et al.* 1997, also referenced in the BAPS Statement 2001) reported no post-pubertal malignant changes in a study of seventeen Complete AIS subjects, and Diamond and Sigmundson (1997a) maintain that fear of malignant change in the gonadal tissue of AIS subjects should not precipitate gonadectomies in infants/children since these kinds of tumours have not been reported in pre-pubescence. Hughes points out that 'the earliest reported malignancy in CAIS is at 14 years of age' (Hughes *et al.* 2006: 4), and indicates that higher tumour risk occurs in cases of Gonadal Dysgenesis (discussed in Chapter 11) and in the intra-abdominal gonads of Partial AIS subjects, while risks are lower for those with Complete AIS or ovotestes.

Three treatment options are in fact possible:

- early gonadectomy: this is the usual course of action when diagnosis takes place in infancy or childhood, and diagnosis is most typically as a result of discovery of a gonad within a hernia;
- later gonadectomy: this takes place after puberty, most usually when diagnosis has been made then as a result of an apparent girl failing to menstruate;
- no gonadectomy.

Gonadectomy in infancy is often driven by parental concerns in relation to the malignancy statistics, but also arguably stems from parental inability to accept their child as a 'full girl', even with *internal* and *non-productive* testicular gonads. Better information for parents can assist them to consider not undertaking gonadectomy if the malignancy risks are perceived as small and the other health benefits of gonad maintenance are fully understood. In cases where gonads are maintained, long-term careful monitoring of them for cellular changes must be part of the treatment and must be emphasized to parents. Subjects must be fully and appropriately informed as they grow up of their condition, of the rationales behind treatment decisions made, and of possible implications (Diamond and Sigmundson 1997a). Maintenance of the gonads also permits the subject to understand and come to terms with diagnosis, and take informed and consensual responsibility if gonadectomy is decided upon later.

Improved procedures for 'harvesting' sperm from testes now make it technically possible for a person with Complete AIS (a genetic male) to be fertile as a male provided testes are preserved. A small quantity of sperm is aspirated from an intact mature testis and used to fertilize an ovum *in vitro*, and this is then implanted in a woman's uterus (Creighton and Liao 2004a). Some discussion has also taken place about cryopreservation of testicular tissue from the testes of AIS subjects who are undertaking gonadectomy, in order to ensure their future fertility should they wish to pursue this. Ethical issues relating to cryopreservation are unclear even in the general population and the BAPS Statement (2001) does not recommend this possibility in the absence of further information. Nevertheless, the possibility of sperm aspiration overturns previous understandings of Complete AIS patients as infertile. Most are assigned as female, or are inadvertently raised as female if undiagnosed, and *as females* they lack reproductive apparatus and are therefore infertile. This process permits possible *male* fertility, and arguably prompts reconsideration of Complete AIS subjects as only really socially functional as girls and women. This strengthens the argument for delaying gonadectomy until puberty in order to at least allow subjects to consider their fertility themselves.

Hines' study of twenty-two subjects with Complete AIS concluded that 'psychological development in CAIS is typically feminine' (Hines *et al.* 2003: 97). Nevertheless, there *are* some individuals with Complete (and Partial) AIS who wish to live as males after diagnosis, following karyotype rather than anatomical appearance. There is still little experimental data on the administration of male hormones in these instances (Diamond and Watson 2004b), and it seems that the effectiveness of such treatment depends on the specific details of individual cases. Grino (Grino *et al.* 1989) notes that in *some* cases, and with large hormone doses, significant phallic growth has been achieved, and this is acknowledged as of great importance to those opting to live as males. Retention of the testes allows time for digestion of the diagnosis by a maturing subject without the loss of a significant symbol of maleness, should such a symbol be desired.

Arguably, gonadectomy on diagnosis – driven by a perceived cancer risk – is also propelled by the same kind of perplexing and unsettling social-cultural anxieties that perpetuate clitorectomies for 'phallic females'. Given the 'ease' with which Complete AIS subjects can be raised invisibly as girls, and the widespread and uncritical use of feminizing genitoplasty to allow those with the genital ambiguity of Partial AIS also to be raised as females, gonadectomy arguably operates as another kind of erasure of 'phallic (gonadal) femaleness'. If testes are taken away in infancy, there will be no need for 'embarrassing' revelation that an apparently 'normal' girl is a genetic male (and indeed one with testes if not a phallus). The BAPS Statement acknowledges parental 'difficulty in accepting a female phenotype whilst testicular tissue is present' (2001: unpaginated), and this must be considered as a significant element in the decision-making process for parents and clinicians. It is also undoubtedly a difficult journey of acceptance for the AIS subject: Diamond reminds us that the female-assigned individual needs to 'reconcile that they are living with an anomalous karyotype, are born with testes, will not menstruate, and will be infertile; they will miss many of the social milestones of the typical female' (Diamond and Watson 2004b: 636).

The great majority of those with Complete AIS are comfortable with being identified as female (Hines *et al.* 2003; Diamond and Watson 2004b). However, some do express reservations. In Diamond's study of thirty-nine subjects with Complete AIS, 18 per cent did not believe that they felt the same as they would if they had been born as genetic females, and 56 per cent felt that at times they had to 'work at being a woman' (Diamond and Watson 2004b). Most disturbing is Diamond's finding that 62 per cent of his Complete AIS subjects had contemplated suicide, and 23 per cent had attempted it. Of his subjects who had Partial AIS, 61 per cent had considered suicide and 3 per cent had attempted it. Reasons given for consideration of or attempt at suicide include later discovery of diagnosis having been reared as female and/or problems within a relationship (Diamond and Watson 2004b); the emotional strain of repeated medical examinations perceived as invasive by the subject (Bragge 2005); and unexpected phallic enlargement in mid-childhood for an apparent girl with undiagnosed Partial AIS whose intact internal testes (which she was unaware of) produced some testosterone, causing a partial reactive virilization and resulting in gonadectomy which the patient went on to regret (Beth, correspondence 7 August 2004).

Joanne's 'Monstrous-Feminine'

Joanne is twenty-six and has Complete AIS:

> When all my girl friends at school were beginning to get their periods, I was told a big lie. My doctor told me that my ovaries had been screwed or twisted up ... or curled up in some way ... before I was born.
>
> He told me I'd been lucky this was noticed, and there would have been major cancer in my ovaries in a few years. He said they had been got out just in time and I wouldn't

get periods the same as other girls. But I should be happy I wasn't dead. I didn't think
to ask how they'd know this when I was born.

My mother and my Dad stood by and listened to this lie.

My doctor gave me hormones to help me be more 'womanish', but he said not to
expect any babies.

That was it, nothing was spoken about again. In my family, we just shut it all down
and acted like nothing was different ... I just feel like it doesn't matter and it really
matters a lot to me ... (interview 3 October 2003)

Joanne's experience is shared by many individuals with Complete AIS who
are subjected to gonadectomy as much as those with Congenital Adrenal
Hyperplasia have clitoral and vaginal surgery without consent and without
being told of their diagnosis as they grow older. Diamond also refers to the
'secrecy, shame and stigma' (Diamond and Watson 2004b: 626) characterizing the experiences of those with AIS. He writes of the 'gut feelings' (ibid.)
of several of his research group who self-diagnosed through Internet and
library research having sensed that there was something about themselves that
they had not been told. Diamond further notes that, of his research subjects,
only 51 per cent were told following diagnosis by their physicians that they had
AIS, with only 16 per cent being offered counselling (Diamond and Watson
2004b). Diamond reports subjection to repeated examinations, display of the
subject's genitalia to medical students, photography without permission, reference to the outdated term 'testicular female', and stunning general insensitivity as the most usual experiences relayed to him by his AIS study group.
Margaret Simmonds of the Androgen Insensitivity Syndrome Support Group
(UK) indicates that the 'main issues of concern to our members (in terms of
the majority situation) are:

a) secrecy and paternalism (non-disclosure of diagnostic information), leading
   to isolation from peer support, stigmatisation, etc.
b) lack of psychological support within the healthcare system
c) offensive medical terminology and being displayed as freaks to trainee
   doctors
d) anatomical/medical issues such as vaginal hypoplasia (under-development),
   non-consensual (childhood) or pressurized (adult) gonadectomy, conse-
   quent loss of their natural testosterone, problems with oestrogen-based
   HRT, high osteoporosis risk in CAIS, obtaining carrier testing for relatives,
   etc.' (correspondence 28 April 2004). And as Kitzinger concludes:

The hushed conversations, the embarrassment of doctors, the explanations which don't
add up, lead women and girls with AIS to the belief that they have a defect so monstrous that nobody is willing to discuss it. (2000: 388)

That 'monstrous-feminine' again (Creed 1993) ...

Joanne's story continues: curiosity about the removal of her (supposed) *ovaries* in infancy, and some feeling that something did not quite tally, drove her to carry out some personal research. Her medical records did not provide details of a surgery in infancy, and yet Joanne had been told that her ovaries had been removed when she was an infant. This fuelled her suspicion and Joanne began to search the Internet for details of such surgeries in babies. Some weeks later, having realized that the story given her by her doctor at adolescence was not correct, and by scrutinizing older medical documents online, and through a chance online discovery of an AIS-related blog, Joanne emerged with the belief that she was a 'male pseudohermaphrodite' whose testes had been removed. Her father verified her self-diagnosis in a subsequent conversation, but then refused to discuss the topic further. Joanne was devastated and terrified by this, and humiliated by memories of having been examined by medical students and a range of doctors, all peddling the lie that she was an unfortunate girl whose potentially cancerous ovaries had been luckily removed in infancy by a particularly alert paediatrician. The organs removed were not ovaries, they were testes, and they had been removed because they might present a slight risk to health, because they affront social-cultural norms in relation to the sex binary, and because they are arguably uncanny. That is, the 'monstrosity' of a 'girl with testes' is as disquieting and unsettling as the archetypal 'phallic female', causing as much upset and even fear. While the sex binary is pretty robust, stable and entrenched, and social-cultural confidence in it is reasonably intact, this type of uncanny or monstrous body surely troubles it.

Joanne recalls feeling numb from the waist downwards. She has not yet come to terms with the fact that her body is not the body she thought it was (interview 3 October 2003). Her trauma is one of estrangement and dissociation: she feels that she wants to purge herself of her male genes, but of course that is impossible. She wants her gonads back inside her body, but at the same time she wants them to be the ovaries she thought she had. She mourns the loss of her sense of womanhood, which paradoxically was confirmed in her mind by the menstruation that never happened and the babies she cannot have. She feels that her self-identity has been annihilated and that she is a 'foreign body'. Most of all, she described her mother and father as 'traitors', and cannot forgive their 'wilful deceit of me when I was old enough really to be able to hear this all back then' (interview 3 October 2003). As Liao concludes:

> Evasive answers appear to have failed to 'protect' people from knowing their difference, rather delivering a message of unspeakable shame ...
>
> Medical secrecy also means non-consensual treatment, and consequently an absence of thorough evaluation of cosmetic, psychological, social and sexual outcomes from both clinician and patient perspectives. (Liao and Boyle 2004: 460)

Joanne was too traumatized to return to her doctor and withdrew from her family. She stopped taking her oestrogen treatment, administered from puberty to induce and maintain female physical development, not having been made aware that this would adversely affect her bone density. After three years, Joanne has resumed oestrogen therapy, and, having decided against further surgery, is using a dilator to try to lengthen and widen her short blind-ended vagina, one of the characteristics of AIS. The BAPS Statement (2001, referencing Costa *et al.* 1997) notes that a range of dilation techniques is available, and reported success rates can be in the region of 85–90 per cent. Liao, however, is less enthusiastic, noting that a dilation regime may be 'distasteful or painful' (Liao and Boyle 2004: 460) and, where vaginoplasty has been undertaken, may need to be prolonged indefinitely to 'maintain the constructed vagina in readiness for intercourse' (ibid.). Joanne has not yet had a sexual partner, and she admits that her current low self-esteem probably precludes a satisfactory sexual relationship for some time. Vaginal dilation is not a pleasant or pleasurable experience for a young and traumatized woman, but Joanne is dogged in persevering with the process.

Minto's (Minto *et al.* 2003a) survey of sixty-six adult women with Complete AIS indicated that 90 per cent have sexual difficulties, most commonly infrequency and avoidance of sexual intercourse and difficulty with vaginal penetration. It may well be that those individuals coming forwards for such a survey are those who are experiencing difficulties separate from their diagnosis, and that there are greater numbers of individuals with Complete AIS who are living sexually contented lives than Minto's statistics show. Nevertheless, this is a significant study and it illuminates certain key aspects of anatomical particularity in this group of people. Seventy-seven per cent of Minto's group perceived their vaginas as small, but in fact on genital examination only 35 per cent had vaginal underdevelopment or incomplete development (Minto *et al.* 2003a). This study described a mean vaginal length of 8.4 cm in subjects all of whom had either undergone surgical vaginal lengthening or who were sexually active adults. Minto concludes that both partial anatomical completion of the vagina in Complete AIS subjects and negative psychological feelings related to the discord between their female 'social sex', their female external appearance and their male genetic sex created sexual difficulties of some magnitude. On top of this, Minto indicates that low levels of testosterone cause sexual demotivation, and indeed 66 per cent of these subjects experienced sexual infrequency resulting from their difficulties (Minto *et al.* 2003a).

Joanne continues to receive poor psychological support, and is isolated and suspicious about the medical profession. She is now beginning to be aware of what living with AIS means for her, and is in contact with a support group in Australia. She describes her initial contact with the support group as both transformative and deeply upsetting. She cried for hours when she first made contact, and now realizes that it is impossible for her to cope without the friendship of others who share her experience.

It is vital that intersexed individuals in general are not perceived as 'pitiable victims of nature', or indeed 'of culture'. Diamond's study (Diamond and Watson 2004b), for example, indicated that 85 per cent of a group of thirty-three AIS subjects, who had received gonadectomies in infancy, were content with their surgeries. There are worst- and best-case scenarios for all of these conditions, and many women with AIS lead happy and contented lives.

Partial Androgen Insensitivity Syndrome

As with Complete Androgen Insensitivity Syndrome, Partial Androgen Insensitivity Syndrome affects genetic males only. In subjects with Partial AIS the external genitals are not completely female in appearance, but are ambiguous. This is because the genetic male foetus has only *partially* responded to its own androgens, and therefore has not received the full androgen effect that a typical male foetus would. Their ambiguous genitalia

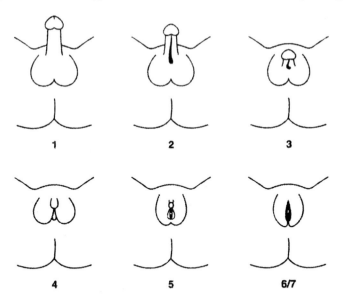

Figure 1 Schematic representation of a grading scheme for clinical classification of AIS. 1. Grade 1: typical virilization *in utero*. 2. Grade 2: male phenotype with mild defect in virilization, e.g. isolated hypospadias. 3. Grade 3: male phenotype with severe defect in virilization – small penis, perineoscrotal hypospadias, bifid scrotum or cryptorchidism (undescended testes). 4. Grade 4: severe genital ambiguity – clitoral-like phallus, labioscrotal folds, single perineal orifice. 5. Grade 5: female phenotype with posterior labial fusion and clitoromegaly (enlarged clitoris). 6/7. Grade 6/7: female phenotype (grade 6 if pubic hair is present in adulthood; grade 7 if no pubic hair is present in adulthood)

can range from appearing almost indistinguishable from female genitalia, but with undescended testes and short vagina, to hypospadic but apparently male genitalia with a scrotum and descended testes. For example: 'the genital tubercle is larger than a clitoris but smaller than a penis, a partially fused labia/scrotum may be present, the testes may be undescended and perineal hypospadius [sic] is often present' (Migeon *et al.* 2001: IV).

Those in between the absolutes of male and female genital appearance are those who are immediately diagnosed as intersexed, and the same issues of sex assignment as have been described in sections above are mobilized. At puberty, individuals with Partial AIS are likely to experience female breast development, generally with a small amount of pubic and axillary hair. Diamond (Diamond and Watson 2004b) provides a schematic representation of a grading scheme for clinical classification of the genitalia of AIS subjects. Their image is adapted from that of Quigley, C. *et al.* (1995) Androgen Receptor Defects: Historical, Clinical and Molecular Perspectives. *Endocrine Reviews* 16: 3: 271–321 (*Copyright 1995, The Endocrine Society*). It is reproduced with full permission.

Ellen's 'Phallic Female'

Ellen was born with Partial AIS, and ambiguous genitalia which looked more male than female. Karyotype testing immediately confirmed that the infant Ellen was a genetic male, and her mother was told to treat her as a little boy, to call her by a little boy's name, to keep her (his) genitals covered up at all times and to await surgery at an optimum time. Ellen was raised as a boy until age eighteen. At eighteen months, surgery was carried out to *masculinize* her genitals in keeping with her assigned gender and her genetic sex. Ellen's penis was hypospadic, with a misdirected urethra, and she had a number of surgical procedures to try to rectify the position of the urethral opening. Her undescended testes were left intact inside, and her apparent labial folds (scrotal sacs) were opened up to incorporate prosthetic testes at puberty.

Breast development occurred at age thirteen, and a double mastectomy was carried out with little meaningful discussion with Ellen. Ellen had been told that her small penis would grow at puberty, but this proved not to be the case. She describes her phallus as 'like a bit of dead flabby meat that pee came out of but in an off-centred way' (interview 3 March 2004), and it really was unviable in any way as a functional penis. Blockages and infections in the urethra and the bladder continued throughout childhood and adolescence, with Ellen habitually needing to have a catheter fitted and also needing frequent hospitalization. She experienced constant pain, embarrassment, awkwardness and a feeling of being unclean. Her condition was described in the extended family as 'some strange hernia in the groin' (interview 3 March 2004), which reinforced her sense of shame.

Ellen – as a boy – sat to urinate, had no apparent testicles and she knew in childhood that she was not 'normal'. At thirteen, with a new 'normal' baby sister, Ellen was beaten by her stepfather and told by him that she was a 'freak of nature' and a 'dirty dyke' (interview 3 March 2004). Ellen describes feeling like a 'walking dead man', a kind of ghost that was neither male nor female, and certainly was 'not of this world'. She had no friends, could not bring herself to attend a doctor, had no support system and considers that she was deeply betrayed and damaged by the actions of her adult 'carers'.

Ellen fortunately drifted into a group of people who happened to include a person with another intersex condition, and she received enough respite support to take stock of her situation. At age eighteen Ellen began to live as a woman, and adopted the name of Ellen, which she continues to use. That identification felt much more 'normal and comfortable' (interview 3 March 2004), and although Ellen continued to live a marginal life with few close associates, she was less vulnerable than before. She had another surgery at age twenty to shorten her urethra to reduce opportunities for further infection, but there continues to be considerable scarring and anatomical malconfiguration of her genitalia: 'The scar tissue gave me agonizing problems. I've never had a full sex life because I can't, and so I've never had a relationship. I can't have children anyway ...' (interview 3 March 2004).

Four years ago, Ellen took the decision to go ahead with some feminizing treatment, to have the scarified and dysfunctional 'penis' removed and to try to find a more comfortable way to urinate. Although she has not had vaginal construction work, her surgery to remove her 'penis' has made a great difference to her urinary function and well-being. Oestrogen therapy has allowed her to grow some breast tissue, and she feels more 'womanly'. She still indicates, however, that she is resigned to being celibate because she 'wouldn't show anybody that mess below' (interview 3 March 2004). Ellen is remarkably positive about her solitude. She says that in spite of everything she feels better about herself than she ever did as a boy. Whereas in her childhood she felt disembodied, she has now managed to associate emotionally with her body and to begin to enjoy being 'bodily'.

In other circumstances, physicians have warned parents that their children might kill themselves on discovery of clitoral enlargement at puberty caused by the presence of undescended testes. Martha Coventry (1998) evokes how frightening and devastating this was for her interviewee's parents to hear of this possibility. As a result they offered no explanation for their child's genital surgery:

It was never addressed to me that they were going to amputate my clitoris. I woke up in a haze of Demerol and felt the gauze, the dried blood. I just couldn't believe they would do this to me without telling me.

I put my hand down there and felt something like the crusty top of some horrible

casserole, like dried caked blood where my clitoris was. I wondered why no one told me
and I figured it was the kind of thing decent people don't talk about. (Coventry 1998:
unpaginated)

Peggy's story

Peggy's case history to age seventeen was cited in publication by Crawford
(1970: 168-170), and subsequently by Money (1991) and Preves (2000). She
cites Dr John Money's writings as 'particularly helpful' to her in understanding
her situation and in making her eventual decision to live as a woman. Peggy
thinks highly of Money's work, especially referring in her correspondence (5
and 12 January 2007) to how Money communicated frankly with children
(like her own cousin with PAIS) about sexual matters when providing information about treatment options.

Born in the USA in 1953, Peggy was named, announced, taken home, and
baptized as a girl, but her parents were advised to bring her back to hospital
for specialist investigation of an apparent anatomical variation consisting of
slight clitoral enlargement and partial labial fusion. After subsequent evaluation, Peggy was diagnosed as having 'male pseudohermaphroditism'. Her
physicians, a gynaecologist and a paediatric endocrinologist, noted that 'Of
course, this is a boy' [quoted from medical records]' and decided that she
should henceforth be treated as a boy and have masculinizing genital reconstruction. Peggy takes up her own story:

> A happenstance that may have been crucial was that the pediatric urologist who was to
> evaluate (and presumably operate on) me was out of town, so I was sent home with the
> idea that this evaluation was not urgent and could take place later on. When the urol-
> ogist did examine me, over a year later, he wrote that "The prospect of creating an
> acceptable penis in this patient seems to me very remote. There is nothing there except
> a slightly enlarged clitoris ..." [quoted from medical records] and noted that it would
> be better if I were "oriented as a female". The endocrinologist had also administered a
> course of hormones that were expected to cause phallic enlargement. The hormones
> had little effect other than breast budding, which is virtually the definition of AIS, but
> at that point my doctors didn't know there was such a condition.
>
> My parents had a meeting with the doctors. The issue of my gender assignment was
> reopened but my parents had gone through a difficult time socially telling people that I
> was not a girl but a boy and the doctors did not want to actually say that their initial
> recommendation that I be a boy was a mistake – so a boy I remained.
>
> Did I "know" instinctively that I should have been a girl? How would I? Children's
> curiosity about sexual matters being what it, I learned at an early age that I was different
> from other boys, that, in fact, I looked more like a girl "down there" but the adults in
> my life did not encourage questions about sex. All I found out from them was that some
> boys are different from others and that I would eventually have some kind of normal-
> izing surgery.

If I had grown up as a girl, I might have been a tomboyish one (the railroad tracks and the woods were among my favorite childhood playgrounds), but I made a somewhat girlish boy. I would have loved to learn to sew and knit and to play with dolls, but that was strongly discouraged, while I was encouraged to be interested in sports and to defend myself in fistfights, both of which I just avoided. That was even less acceptable to the other children than to adults, so I didn't fit in socially. Besides which, I was supposed to keep my genital difference a secret, which was difficult to do during the class's twice-daily trip to the boy's room. To avoid revealing that I could not stand up to urinate, I just stopped using the bathrooms at school, a practice I continued until age 18.

Towards the end of my grammar school years, I became fearful that I might be required at school to undress in front of classmates for gym class or for a physical examination. This wasn't something I felt I could bring up with teachers or with the school authorities – I didn't think they knew and was not sure what would happen if they did find out. I just lived from day to day, dreading the day (which never actually came) when my terrible secret would be unmasked. Around my 13th birthday, this became even more worrisome as I began growing breasts. Gym class twice each week was an ordeal as I had to remove my outer shirt and reveal the contour of my breasts getting larger month by month. (correspondence 12 January 2007)

Peggy, raised as a boy and believing the adults who told her that she was 'supposed to be' a boy, was asked, with no preparation, counselling or explanation of her condition, if she wanted to stay a boy or be 'made into' a girl. Paediatric endocrinologist Crawford later described Peggy as an 'unhappy adolescent' boy, with breasts removed but with a 'totally inadequate' response to 'high circulating levels of testosterone' (1970: 168, 170). For Crawford, a 'far more satisfactory outcome' was experienced by another patient, also with PAIS, but assigned as a girl at birth, surgically feminized and reported as planning to marry at age nineteen. At the same time, however, Crawford commented on this other patient's 'tomboyish antics' (ibid.: 177), seemingly suggesting that male assignment may have been the better choice in these 'genetically male' patients with PAIS – if only surgical and hormonal masculinization would work. Peggy continues:

My breast development led to a visit with the pediatric endocrinologist. Unknown to me, my father must have mentioned to him that he would be supportive if I wanted to change to being a girl. In my own perception, though, there was no such possibility. I was supposed to be a boy, albeit with some unheard-of medical condition. That's what I had been told, and why would adults tell me anything but the truth? At this visit, the endocrinologist, believing [according to his own notes] that my father was "pressuring" me to change to living as a girl, asked me point-blank – do you want to stay a boy, or do you want us to make you into a girl? Completely shocked by this unexpected question, I gave the answer I knew he expected, that I wanted to be a boy. That was the first and last time I talked about my gender identity with anyone until I was past age 21, over eight years later. I had mastectomy the following summer.

Through my teenage years, I gradually became aware that I had the same sexual feelings as most people my age, but I never revealed them to anyone. I just felt that area of life was closed to me. Also, my attractions were always for boys and took the form of obsessive infatuation for particular friends. These were typical teenage crushes, except that there was no place to go with these feelings. My future was an enormous question mark. How was I going to get along? How would I endure my unfulfilled sexual and romantic longings? How could I keep the secret of my physical difference, especially now that it seemed I would be smooth-cheeked, unmuscular, high-voiced, narrow shouldered and wide-hipped for the rest of my life? As a substitute for the social life I was missing, I retreated into fantasy and daydreaming.

When I entered college at age 18, I discovered that the library had textbooks that actually covered AIS, and there I found an enormous revelation. Other people with the same condition as I were girls and women, and they were sexually active and even married! Things began to make more sense, especially the way the vague idea of eventual masculinization was being continually projected into the future. It was a mistake and I was supposed to be a girl! That thought was immediately followed by the realization that I had already had a choice in the matter, had had mastectomy, and that there could now be no turning back. It was three more years before my feelings of denied sexuality and social isolation built themselves into a crisis, and before I discovered that breast reconstruction was a possibility. Only then did I mention how I felt to another person, and at age 23 I moved to another state to begin my new life – nearly all my adult life – as a woman. (correspondence 12 January 2007)

Peggy had her labial fusion divided in adulthood, but has had no clitoral reduction surgery, so her genital appearance is still close to what it was at her birth (correspondence 5 January 2007). She has also had breast reconstruction. As a woman, not menstruating has not been a problem for Peggy (although she acknowledges that she did not go through puberty with female peers), and she has 'not been extremely troubled about infertility' although she likes children and indicates that she would 'love to have my own child to care for' (correspondence 5 January 2007). Peggy has, happily, 'found a man to be my partner in life, an unremarkably heterosexual guy who accepts my condition and my history matter-of-factly' (correspondence 12 January 2007).

Peggy refutes the idea some have suggested to her that 'it must have been hard being treated like a boy but knowing inside you were really a girl'. In relation to 'ideas about "identity" and gender politics as formulated, for example, by Preves (2000)' Peggy asserts that 'Intersex isn't necessarily all about "identity"' (correspondence 2 March 2007), and insists that her later desire to live as a woman 'was motivated mainly by desire to have more of a social life and a sex life' (correspondence 7 January 2007).

Sex of Rearing

As Figure 1 indicates, there is great variation in the genitalia of genetic males with Androgen Insensitivity Syndrome. From the female appearance of Complete AIS this ranges through mild to severe virilization including hypospadias, apparent clitoral enlargement or small penis, split scrotum or labial fusion, and undescended testes. Diamond and Sigmundson (1997a), advocating no surgical interventions, made specific suggestions as to the *sex of rearing* for infants with AIS related to the genital appearance and likelihood of satisfactory outcome post-puberty (see Chapter 4).

In a later text, Diamond (Diamond and Watson 2004b) describes how he found significant gender ambivalence among a small study group of eighteen individuals with Partial AIS, those who tend to exhibit genital ambiguity. Thirty-three per cent raised reservations about the gender to which they had been assigned, with four (50 per cent) of those raised as males (in accordance with their genetic sex) deciding in adulthood to live as women. Of the ten sub-jects who were raised as females, two (20 percent) switched in adulthood to live as men. In total, a significant 33 per cent of Diamond's study group changed gender role in adulthood, and the ages at which these changes were made ranged from eighteen to forty-six, averaging at just over thirty-three. Where sex of rearing has been affirmed by surgical/hormonal intervention, these shifts are especially problematic. Diamond reports that the two individ-uals raised as girls and now living as men are 'angry that they were brought up as girls and are particularly bothered that, without their knowledge or informed consent, they were castrated and subjected to vaginal reconstructive surgery and from puberty on were given estrogens to feminize them somatic-ally' (Diamond and Watson 2004b: 629).

What these testimonies illustrate first is the danger of permanently altering a child's body non-consensually and in such a fundamental way. Secondly, they illustrate the predominant social-cultural adherence to a sex binary, even when the evidence of some bodies troubles that. Individuals with AIS – genet-ically male, and with female-appearing or ambiguous genitalia – are *intersexed*. That is, they have an alternative sex descriptor separate from the 'absolutes' of male or female precisely because they mix the characteristics of male (kary-otype, presence of testes, possible partial virilization) and female (possible female-appearing genitalia). But by being less needy of naming people one or the other sex, and allowing intersex to be acknowledged as a sex variety among a number of sex possibilities, might that not shift our emphasis more happily towards how an individual then operates (how they live, look, love) within social-culture? Gender identity is permanent for each person – this is what gives rise to the discomfort of intersexuals who have been sex assigned 'incor-rectly' in discordance with their gender identity. But gender role is not fixed, and an intersexed person can surely choose a gender role best suited to their gender identity without needing to be subjected to the depressing determinacy of the kinds of surgeries in infancy and childhood described above?

An anonymous interviewee with Partial AIS describes how she (her choice of pronoun) has come to identify more readily with intersex as a sex descriptor, and reports personal weariness over 'years of simply trying to be this thing called a woman – I just failed all the time doing that' (Anon, correspondence 2 September 2006). Appreciating parental fear and concern, and understanding her parents' desire to make their intersexed child 'normal', this interviewee contends that the early surgery and secrecy that generally prevails and that she experienced 'took away my chance – or even my right – to understand, or accept, or change what is after all *my* difference' (correspondence 2 September 2006). Parental need to feel that a wrong has been 'fixed', that an aberration has been 'normalized' and that sex stability has been regained is – according to Virginia Slocum, a social worker and Certified Marriage, Family and Child Counsellor in the US – so much less important than the needs of the intersexed child (Slocum 1995: 7). Slocum contends that 'healing and a kind of wholeness and equanimity are possible' (ibid.) if intersexual difference is at least openly acknowledged. To do anything other, she maintains, is to risk that children who are born with any of the range of intersex conditions will 'never be comfortable in their own bodies and never at ease with the world around them' (ibid.).

CHAPTER 10

Severe Undervirilization in Genetic Males

In Western societies, a large penis in men obeys contemporary fashion rules …
Sarah Creighton, *Changing Attitudes to Sex Assignment in Intersex*

Phallic Culture, Gonads and Testicular Regression Syndrome

The Statement of the British Association of Paediatric Surgeons Working Party on the Surgical Management of Children Born with Ambiguous Genitalia (2001) indicated that among the range of common intersex conditions producing genital ambiguity were those causing 'severe undervirilisation in genetic males'. The most straightforward manifestation of undervirilization is the micropenis, that is, a penis that is typically developed, but smaller than usual. The newly formed testes of the genetic male foetus release their first *in utero* androgens to initiate the differentiation of the previously indifferent genital tubercule towards male development. In micropenis development, this stage proceeds without issue and the penis begins to form. However, the second androgen effect on the male foetus occurs later in gestation, and where this is insufficient to promote typical penis enlargement, a micropenis forms. In these instances, testes – the other signifier of the male – are already present.

While development of a micropenis diminishes the scale of social-culture's signifier of virility, other specific conditions – Partial AIS (discussed in Chapter 9), 5-alpha reductase deficiency, Testicular Regression Syndrome and severe hypospadias (discussed in Chapter 5) – variously interfere with the typical development of male external genitalia. That the BAPS Statement distinctly mentions this collective interference highlights the importance of its challenge to the cultural prominence of the penis as a symbol of male prowess.

Testicular Regression Syndrome, for example, is a very rare condition sometimes referred to as XY Gonadal Agenesis Syndrome. It includes a range of genital anomalies in genetic males resulting from regression of the development of the testes between eight and fourteen weeks of gestation. The phenotype of these individuals depends on the timing of the onset of the foetal testicular regression. If this happens between eight and ten weeks of gestation the resultant external genitalia may be female in appearance, or exhibit ambiguity, and there will be absence of gonads, an underdeveloped uterus and rudimentary genital ducts. If the testicular regression happens between twelve and fourteen weeks of gestation the foetus will grow towards the male phenotype, with penile development, but with absence of testes or presence of rudimentary gonadal streaks lying undeveloped in the abdomen. Intermediary phenotypes can also appear, with various ambiguities of the internal structures and the external genitalia (Sarto and Opitz 1973; Edman *et al.* 1977; Josso and Briard 1980; Rosenberg *et al.* 1984).

In this condition, not only is the penis sometimes unformed or poorly developed, so too are the testes. Their role as actual and symbolic virilizing agents must not be overshadowed by focus on the phallus. Typically, infants with Testicular Regression Syndrome would be assigned as female, with supporting feminizing genitoplasty to cosmetically align the external genital appearance of these genetic male infants more closely to those of a female. The subject is infertile, and, while virilization does not happen at puberty, oestrogen therapy may be administered to produce breast development in alignment with sex assignment.

Phallic Culture, and 5-alpha Reductase Deficiency

In Chapters 3 and 4, specific reference is made to the conventional tendency to surgically assign genetic males demonstrating 'phallic inadequacy' as female. This practice arguably ensures the primacy of the penis in terms of its 'appropriate, adequate and acceptable' dimension; shape/colour; urinary, erectile and 'at rest' capability; and conduction of urine/semen. With phalloplasty still no guarantee of phallic 'adequacy', and suicidal despair billed as the experience of 'failed males' with small or absent penises, there is little question that culture demands that penises are 'good enough' (Kessler 1990: 13) to warrant their name. Away from the symbolic, however, Reilly and Woodhouse's study of adult males with smaller than typical penises indicated potentially good outcomes in terms of erectile and orgasmic function (1989). Indeed Creighton questions whether 'the re-assignment of boys with micro or absent penis to girls constitutes *cultural practice* or evidence-based medicine [this author's emphasis]' (Creighton and Liao 2004a: 660), while Kessler argues that the exacting cultural and medical standards for an 'acceptable' penis ensure perfection via regulation: 'as long as "male" is defined as the possession of a "good-sized" penis, more infants will be assigned as female than as male' (1990: 13).

As with Androgen Insensitivity Syndrome discussed in the previous chapter, 5-alpha reductase deficiency affects genetic male foetuses only. There are no reliable frequency statistics for this condition (Blackless *et al.* 2000), but it is extremely rare (Herdt 1996). During genetic male foetal development, gonads typically differentiate into normal testes, and secrete appropriate amounts of testosterone (initiating separation of male and female external genitalia), but foetuses with this condition cannot convert their testosterone correctly into the more potent dihydrotestosterone (DHT) due to deficiency of the 5-alpha reductase enzyme. Consequently, these foetuses, with testes already formed, then continue their development along the default female path. They develop ambiguous external genitalia: their penis resembles a clitoris; their scrotum looks like labia majora; and they may develop a short blind-ended vagina. Their internal structures are typically male, and the testes are functional and potentially fertile, but do not descend. Some infants with this condition appear closest to male at birth, but in significantly undervirilized subjects, the child will appear wholly female at birth. The great majority of children with 5-alpha reductase deficiency are raised as female, but they will not menstruate at puberty and vaginal penetration will be impossible.

At puberty, subjects with 5-alpha reductase deficiency *usually* produce some testosterone from their intact testes, and this causes *some* virilization. Effects include increased muscle mass, voice lowering, reasonable axillary hair growth (with little or no facial hair growth), some phallic development, descent of testes, and sperm production if the testes remain intact (Migeon *et al.* 2002b). This begs the question as to why the permanency of surgical feminization in infancy would be considered appropriate to such cases?

5-alpha reductase deficiency (also referred to as Pseudovaginal Perinoscrotal Hypospadias or 'male pseudohermaphroditism due to 5-alpha reductase') has been studied in populations in, for example, the Dominican Republic and Papua New Guinea where there is a tendency towards greater frequency (Herdt 1996; Diamond 2004a). There, subjects are raised as girls (which they most resemble) *without* surgical intervention, and then follow their tendency to virilize at puberty. The condition is known in the Dominican Republic as 'penis at twelve', and in New Guinea as 'changing into a male thing' (Herdt 1996: 426, 432). Imperato-McGinley *et al.* (1991) reported an almost 100 per cent assumption of the male gender identity/role following puberty in these cultures, and not having assigned female sex surgically allows this to happen without somatic trauma (Herdt problematizes this with a thesis of 'third sex' within a two-gender system). In the 'medical West', however, most physicians recommend gonadectomy before puberty for children diagnosed with 5-alpha reductase deficiency to avoid pubescent virilization. Such children are raised as girls, and surgery/hormonal treatment is used to make permanent that assignment. Feminizing genitoplasty, with all the attendant arguments given previously, and oestrogen therapy after gonadectomy are used to support the continuance of female assignment post-puberty. Rarely, where a child seems to naturally migrate towards a male role during childhood, gonads are allowed to remain intact and the child is re-assigned as a male. In such cases, however, it is acknowledged that the penis will be less than 'adequate', and phalloplasty will be recommended to attempt to 'normalize' that important signifier. Arguably, this lack of 'adequacy' in male assignment for individuals with 5-alpha reductase deficiency asymmetrically informs the assignment decision, and operates the cultural erasure of undervirilization in 'men'.

Historically, individuals with 5-alpha reductase deficiency were considered infertile. Raised as female, they have no female reproductive apparatus, while as genetic males they tend to have low sperm volume with high viscosity or a total lack of sperm in their ejaculate. As noted in the previous chapter, advanced fertility techniques now allow the possibility of removal of sperm from undescended testes and optimization of low sperm volume to maximize effect on implantation in an ovum (Creighton and Liao 2004a). Consequently, theoretically 5-alpha reductase deficiency need not necessarily preclude fertility as a male (Katz et al. 1997).

Jennifer's Story

Correspondent Jennifer is the adoptive parent of a 6-year-old with 5-alpha reductase deficiency. She describes how her child, adopted 'in Asia', was pronounced male at birth (correspondence 2 October 2004). The adoption agency was aware of genital ambiguity in this child, and organized a second examination in the United States. As a result of this, the infant was re-assigned as female. Was genital maleness insufficient for the phallic culture of US America, but adequate for generalized 'Asia'?

Jennifer took over parenting when the child was age twenty months and being raised as a girl, without surgical intervention, in the US. Jennifer had a range of consultations with several paediatricians, and the little girl was formally diagnosed as having 5-alpha reductase deficiency and as being a genetic male. Genetic sex is often a 'fall-back', a kind of sex origin, in cases of ambiguity, and Jennifer agreed that this was a determining factor for her in the decision to then re-assign her child as male at age thirty-two months. The authoritative voice of her next statement echoes with the same tone as Money's 'optimal gender policy':

> we decided our child was actually a little boy so we began raising him as a boy ... a three surgery process has been planned for him ... (correspondence 2 October 2004)

With certainty, Jennifer concurred with those claiming psychosexual neutrality and sex malleability for the young child (Money asserted this was the case *until around twenty-four months*, somewhat younger than when Jennifer enacted *her* 'decision' for her child). As with Money's 'theory of neutrality', this decision then required genitalia to match and reinforce it. Jennifer's assertion that her child 'has begun to have some discomfort with the current configuration of his genital area' (correspondence 2 October 2004) rationalized her choices, and eased the next stage of the process – initiation of masculinizing surgery on a child of six. One must question, however, whether this child's 'discomfort' is personal or socially engineered, a medical difficulty or a cultural one.

Following the first surgery Jennifer declined to continue corresponding. Her child was announced male at birth, female in early infancy, male again at age three, with confirmation of that decision by surgery commencing at age six, and with anticipation of some virilization at puberty. One must hope that all surgical outcomes are good for this undervirilized genetic male child in a culture of the 'perfect penis'.

Undervirilized Males, Genital Ambiguity and Sex Assignment

Migeon (Migeon *et al.* 2002b) contends that undervirilized genetic males with genital ambiguity including a small phallus and perineoscrotal hypospadias are the most difficult subjects to treat in relation to determination of sex of rearing. There is current lack of agreement as to which sex of rearing is the better for harmony between ultimate gender identity and the sex assigned, and further lack of agreement over the optimum treatment approaches (surgical or non-surgical) to maintain or achieve best genital function and/or appearance. Migeon (Migeon *et al.* 2002b) reports that female sex assignment for those genetic male infants presenting with undervirilized ambiguous genitalia or micropenis – supported by feminizing surgery/hormone treatment – is generally usual, but acknowledges that there are significant testimonies from genetic males raised as or assigned as females who are, after puberty or later, deeply dissatisfied by their treatment.

Kessler (Kessler 1990) believes that phallocentric heterosexism is at the heart of sex assignment practices, and argues that the emphasis on the penis' capability for vaginal penetration indicates the privilege afforded conventional heterosexual relations. Strict conceptions of 'normal' male and female sexual anatomy, as well as 'normal' sex behaviour, arguably for her underpin prevailing treatment protocols, and are sexist in their asymmetrical definitions of male and female anatomical 'adequacy'. The privileging of size and penetrative capability over the penis' erotic sensation, coupled with the widely held view that genital surgery towards female appearance and function is more effective – or indeed easier – than that towards male appearance and function (Schober 1998b), results in genetically male intersexed patients with micropenis and/or testes most often being assigned as female (Phornphutkul *et al.* 2000).

The alternative – masculinizing surgery on genetic males to repair hypospadias in particular – is described by Migeon (Migeon *et al.* 2002b) as having a
64 per cent post-operative complication rate in his study, with repeated surgical procedures resulting in complicated scarring and loss of tissue, and with
adverse effect on sexual function. Creighton proposes that decisions as to sex
of rearing are 'largely influenced by the supposition that the construction of a
"functional" vagina (i.e. capable of receiving a penis) is technically more fea-
sible than that of a "functional" penis (i.e. capable of erection and penetration)' (Creighton and Liao 2004a: 659). Consequently, she maintains that
there is a tendency among surgeons to favour female sex assignment
(Creighton and Liao 2004a, referencing Wilson *et al.* 1998).

We have already seen examples of female assignment for genetic males that go
wrong, most notably in David Reimer's case history reported in Chapter 4.
Phornphutkul *et al.* (2000) reference Bradley's (Bradley *et al.* 1998) study of
another genetic male surgically assigned female at age seven months after acci-
dental loss of penis at age two months. In that case, however, the individual was
raised as and has remained as a female (as of age twenty-six). In other references,
however, long-term outcomes in cases where genetic male intersexed children
were raised as female show subsequent post-adolescent self-assignment as male
(Gooren and Cohen-Kettenis 1991; Reiner 1996b). In Migeon's (Migeon *et al.*
2002b) long-term study of genetic male adults over twenty-one, who presented
as infants or children with ambiguous genitalia (including microphallus and
perineoscrotal hypospadias), and who were raised as either males or females, the
conclusion was that either 'male or female sex of rearing can lead to successful
long-term outcome for the majority of cases of severe genital ambiguity in 46,XY
individuals' (ibid.: 1). Nevertheless, in Migeon's study 23 per cent of subjects –
almost equally divided between those raised as male and those raised as female
– were dissatisfied with their sex of rearing.

Phornphutkul *et al.* (2000) presents a detailed case study of a genetically
male infant, born with ambiguous genitalia manifesting as a microphallus with
the urethral opening at its base, resulting from the mother's ingestion
throughout pregnancy of a prescribed anti-convulsant drug. Gonads were
found in what seemed to be the labia majora, but no uterus was detected following rectal examination. The infant was assigned as female four days after
birth, and the parents – at first informed of their child's genital ambiguity –
were then told to raise the child as a girl. They were assured that the child
would identify as a girl. The parents were also told that the child had testes
that needed to be removed as there was a risk of cancer forming in them, and
at three weeks of age this was done although no malignancy was subsequently
detected in the removed testes. Phornphutkul (ibid.) reports the mother's full
acceptance of the child as a girl, although the mother apparently had no rec-
ollection of having been told the child's karyotype.

The child began oestrogen replacement therapy at age ten, and at sixteen began preparations for surgical construction of a vagina. By age sixteen, Phornphutkul (ibid.) reports that the child's phallus (clitoris) had enlarged to approximately 6 cm in length. The child began to question her condition, deciding ultimately to discontinue her oestrogen therapy, to seek mammo-plasty to remove the breasts she had developed as a result of that therapy and finally changing her name and announcing herself as male. The subject began testosterone replacement therapy and developed an additional 1.5 cm of phallic length. Phornphutkul reports that the subject's mother disclosed that he had always 'acted like a boy' (ibid.: 136), while the subject described having felt like a 'boy trapped in a girl's body' (ibid.) throughout childhood. While caution is advisable with patient or parent hindsight, this testimony neverthe-less suggests that this subject's core gender identity ultimately could not be overridden by alteration of genitalia and prescription of hormones.

The David Reimer story, and studies presented by Reiner (1996b), Gooren and Cohen-Kettenis (1991), Migeon (Migeon *et al*. 2002b) and Phornphutkul *et al*. (2000), support the theory that gender identity cannot simply be imposed on a presumed 'sex-neutral' child. That is, early sex assignment as female of individuals who are genetic males, and who have ambiguous or female-appearing genitalia, does not guarantee that the subject will self-identify as female as s/he matures. It seems reasonable to conclude that human infants are not psychosexually neutral, and that there is some hormonal effect on the brain of the developing foetus that imprints a gender predisposition of some kind. Moreover, while the David Reimer story, and the studies provided by Reiner, Gooren, Migeon and Phornphutkul suggest female assignment may not be appropriate to those genetic males discussed, we cannot with authority determine either that male assignment would suit other subjects with the same genetic maleness and the same genital ambiguities. Nevertheless, a number of significant studies indicate that undervirilization or a micropenis in genetic males need not preclude a high frequency of 'normal, heterosexual function' (Reilly and Woodhouse 1989; Bin-Abbas *et al*. 1999).

Phornphutkul *et al*. (2000) conclude that the sex of assignment should be based on the underlying diagnosis of the intersex condition in the individuals presenting, and concede that this may result in sex of rearing being selected which does not fall in harmony with the apparent size and functionality of the phallus. Phornphutkul asserts the patient's gender identity should be part of the decision-making process as to the eventual sex designation, and conse-quently urges avoidance of genital surgery until the patient can incorporate his or her gender identity into any decision regarding surgery. Phornphutkul's paper acknowledges that 'gender identification is a complex biological and psychological process that most certainly has prenatal and postnatal compo-nents' (ibid.: 136), although their interrelationship is still not clear.

CHAPTER 11

'Hermaphroditism' and Gonadal Dysgenesis

The British Association of Paediatric Surgeons Statement (2001) indicated that among the range of intersex conditions that particularly present with genital ambiguity are 'true hermaphroditism' and Gonadal Dysgenesis. 'True' and 'pseudohermaphroditism' are discussed in Chapter 2, although the terms are used loosely in relation to a number of intersex conditions and this is noted throughout the text.

Complete Gonadal Dysgenesis

The Complete form of Gonadal Dysgenesis is proposed as occurring once in every 150,000 births (Blackless *et al.* 2000). It affects genetic males (46,XY karyotype) and genetic females (46,XX karyotype), as well as individuals with the 45,XO karyotype (which is described in relation to Turner Syndrome in Chapter 13). In Complete Gonadal Dysgenesis, the typical differentiation of the gonads as either testes or ovaries does not occur. They form atypically as underdeveloped and undescended streak gonads, and there is complete absence of ovaries, testes or ovotestes. Streak gonads differ from ovotestes (which contain both ovarian and testicular tissue) being undeveloped whorled gonadal structures without germinal or secretory cells. They fail to produce the androgens necessary for masculine differentiation of the genitalia, and consequently female-appearing external genitalia form. Streak gonads are also incapable of ovulation or oestrogen secretion. Clitoral hypertrophy (enlargement), and sexual infantilism (delayed or absent puberty) may also be experienced (Jha undated).

Mixed Gonadal Dysgenesis

Fausto-Sterling describes Mixed Gonadal Dysgenesis as a 'catch-all category' (2000: 52) covering individuals whose gonads fail to develop properly. Where Complete Gonadal Dysgenesis is typified by the development of *exclusively* streak gonads, individuals with Mixed Gonadal Dysgenesis will 'usually have a differentiated gonad on one side and a streak gonad or streak testis on the other side' (Kim *et al.* 2002: 1,013). That is, they will have a formed gonad (a testis or an ovary) on one side, and an underdeveloped gonadal structure on the other. Mixed Gonadal Dysgenesis affects individuals who have a 46,XY/45,XO mosaic as well as those who are genetically male (46,XY). The condition manifests variously, with individuals appearing phenotypically like those with Turner Syndrome (see Chapter 13) to phenotypical males, and with a range of genital presentations between.

Blackless (Blackless *et al.* 2000) reports that there are no reliable estimates of frequency for Mixed Gonadal Dysgenesis. The BAPS Statement (2001) acknowledges that individuals with these conditions are few, and they share common concerns and issues with subjects with Congenital Adrenal Hyperplasia, Complete Androgen Insensitivity Syndrome and others with non-specific severe undervirilization. The BAPS Statement (2001), however, clearly warns that 'there is unequivocal evidence of a greater risk of malignant change in dysgenetic and streak gonads' in these individuals, and this is supported by Hughes (Hughes *et al.* 2006). Its recommendation is that streak gonads and gonads 'inappropriate to the sex of rearing' should be removed in infancy. Where testes are retained, the advice is that they should be relocated if necessary into a palpable position to aid subsequent careful surveillance.

Swyer Syndrome: Anja's Story

Swyer (or Swyer's) Syndrome – first described in the 1950s by Dr G. Swyer – is also known as XY Gonadal Dysgenesis. It is a chance occurrence affecting genetic males, and does not run in families. In 30 per cent of Swyer Syndrome cases, the cause is a specific change in part of the Y chromosome, but in the remaining cases the reason is unclear. Usually, a Y chromosome encourages male development in the foetus and prevents the development of a uterus, and the gonads (testes in a male foetus) are instrumental in this. In Swyer Syndrome, the gonads and the Y chromosome do not function in the usual way. A vagina, clitoris and labia develop and the external genital appearance is that of a typical female. However, internally, the development is more unusual. A uterus forms, but the gonads are present only as small streaks located near to it. Those with Swyer Syndrome are genetic males who appear phenotypically female. Their streak gonads cannot produce either oestrogen or androgens, and although they appear female they will not develop breasts or a female body form without hormone replacement treatment. Migeon (Migeon *et al.* 2002a) reports that all of a group of women (his term) with Swyer Syndrome who were being studied by him and who received oestrogen treatment subsequently commenced menstruation (this hormone replacement also assists with bone health and helps allay osteoporosis later in life). Individuals with Swyer Syndrome are presumed infertile as there are no eggs and no functional or fully formed ovaries. Migeon (Migeon *et al.* 2002a), however, reports an instance of such a person with this syndrome successfully carrying pregnancies with *in vitro* fertilised donated eggs – as there is a uterus – and with hormone treatment required to support the pregnancy.

Assisted fertility affords increasingly interesting opportunities to those traditionally considered infertile. Ransley also commented on the advances in assisted fertility, assisted conception and their implications for intersex reproduction (interview 6 September 2005). He provided a different example from his experience of a 'true hermaphrodite' with two ovotestes, no uterus, a reasonable vaginal length, a moderate-sized phallus and an XX karyotype. Ransley makes the point that in the past there would have been a choice as to whether to raise an infertile male (since, Ransley notes, the testicular element of two ovotestes would be highly unlikely to be fertile) or infertile female capable of sexual function. Historically then, Ransley asserts, the assigned sex would be determined by consideration of hormone exposure *in utero* and size of phallus. Now, however, Ransley contends that there is the possibility of harvesting an egg from the ovarian part of her ovotestes, of having that egg fertilized *in vitro* and carried by a surrogate. A new perspective on intersex fertility ...

Anja is a person with Swyer Syndrome, living in Germany and in her mid-thirties. She began her correspondence with 'I was born ... the most important thing for me is that I was born at last' (15 September 2005). Anja embraces her life, with intersex, and both she and her mother are refreshingly open about where intersex should be in society: 'Intersex must go into public so that many people know about it' (correspondence 22 January 2004).

Anja was originally diagnosed with 'Pure Gonadal Dysgenesis', which she then learned was Swyer Syndrome. Her karyotype is a 46,XY/45,XO mosaic, with tests indicating that 97 per cent of her karyotype is typically male, and 3 per cent is without the Y chromosome. Incidentally, her birth certificate and her passport state that she is female, and she began her second marriage in December 2005.

Both Anja and her mother were interviewed in Hamburg on 10 September 2005 (unless otherwise indicated all quotations in this chapter are from that interview).

CH: ... it is wonderful to have a mother and a daughter who will talk to me for this book ...

Anja: ... if it's a daughter!!! (*laughs*). I don't know a word for me in English and neither in German as well. Because there is only daughter and son, and boy and girl ... so we are missing a whole vocabulary, and that is terrible ...

I was born ... when I was born everyone thought I was a girl because I looked like it, and I think I look like a girl now!? Or not!

> Some of us, when they are born they recognize it at once, but not for me. So as
> I growed up, I thought I was a girl. And everyone thought I was a boy because
> I had such short hair, and I wore trousers, and very seldom skirts and dresses.
> And when someone called me 'boy' I always claimed 'no! I am a girl!' And it was
> so important for me to state that I am a girl because I thought I was and when
> I look back now I would love to be five again and then someone would call me
> 'boy' and I would tell them 'no! I am not a boy, and I'm not a girl either!'
> (laughs) ... Because now I can tell them I am neither a man nor a woman.

Anja raises a key issue in her opening words – that of gender identification.
Gender role – that acting out of the social role of the woman or the man –
strictly speaking lies beyond the remit of this text. But, there is no question
that it lies only just beyond its remit, and there are many instances where intersexed individuals first note their difference – long before they are aware of their
intersexed status – because they *feel like* a boy or *feel like* a girl (gender identity). Or, indeed, parents report that their child *plays like*, or *acts like* or *wants
to dress like* a boy or a girl. There is no question that part of gender role is social
construction, but there are also strong arguments – not least those that indicate how little is known about the hard-wiring of the brain by hormonal
washes *in utero* – that articulate the proximity of sex and gender identity. Anja
is circumspect about this aspect of her wish to dress and act in a masculine
fashion as a small child, but to assert herself as a girl:

> *Anja*:   And today I think I just wanted to be like the other boys. From in me? I don't
> know. You can say that is from the intersex, and you can say that is because
> there are many boys out there ... I don't know.
> *(Anja's mother intervenes in German here and converses with Anja)*
> ... other people told us how I behaved like a boy, and that they really could
> think how I should be a boy because I was climbing at the highest trees – my
> behaviour was more 'ruddy' than girlish. And I always hated that – when
> people told me that. At about ten, I had long hair because I wanted to know
> what it is. Then I went to the male haircutter and cut it off. When they said to
> my parents 'your son' or 'he' *(Anja indicates distaste and annoyance)* – everytime,
> 'no! I'm a girl!'

So Anja grew up as what might be called a 'tomboy' (see Diamond and
Sigmundson 1997a: 1,048, referenced in Chapter 4, in which they note that
'the child is special and in some cases might, before or after puberty, accept
life as a "tomboy" or a "sissy" or even switch gender altogether'). Anja
describes how all the girls in her class at school eventually began menstruation,
and how she was relieved not to experience this. She indicated here that she
was not clear then about how to use a sanitary towel and she had not wanted
to talk to other girls about this. There is a sense of distance and reserve in
Anja's relation to this 'female rite of passage'. Anja decided not to tell anybody

that she had not menstruated, and thought that maybe she could just carry on as normal without referring to it. Anja reports how she avoided the vaccination for rubella measles at school when she was fourteen, and how there was discussion of the implications of rubella measles for pregnant woman. In hindsight, Anja remembered feeling that she would not need to be immunized for a condition that would threaten a pregnancy:

> *Anja*: And then I was sixteen, I was out of school, and one day I thought about that I had not had my menstruation until now, and then I thought I am infertile. I don't know where the thought came from, but I thought that. And after that it seemed normal to me that I don't get my menstruation.

At age seventeen, Anja's mother asked her about it, and when Anja told her that she had not had a period, her mother made a doctor's appointment. Hormone testing led to a referral to a specialist doctor, and that was when Anja was discovered to have a 97 per cent genetic male (XY) and 3 per cent XO karyotype. In spite of the mosaicism diagnosed, Anja is clear about her self-identification: 'I think myself as 46,XY [genetic male]'.

Revelation is a key moment for intersexed individuals, and the articulations of correspondents and interviewees of that moment when they discover that they are more complex than those who are typically male or typically female are deeply affecting. There are many testimonies indicating that diagnosis – however traumatic – verified something that intersexed individuals knew or felt anyway:

> *CH*: What did it mean to you when you got your diagnosis?
>
> *Anja*: The very first thought that came in my consciousness was that I was right. Once I consciously thought that I should be infertile – I thought that really – and then I heard it [the genetic diagnosis] from the doctor, my first thought was 'I was right' … I just was right …
>
> *CH*: And had you ever heard of such a thing – a 46,XY woman, or even an intersexed person – before?
>
> *Anja*: I never heard about such a thing, that I should be, I never heard about that. But I did know – do you know the word 'zwitter'? It's like 'hermaphrodite'.

Anja tells a story of a 'zwitter' in her extended family: the son of an aunt of her grandmother's new partner was a 'zwitter'. And Anja's narrative replicates some of the mythology surrounding intersex in social-culture:

> *Anja*: I hardly knew what was a 'zwitter', and then she [Anja's mother] told me maybe he has both genitalia … So, I knew one, but at this time I didn't know that I was a 'zwitter'. I'm not a 'zwitter' actually, but I behave like one. Because there are so less 'zwitters' in the world, real 'hermaphrodites', I'm medically called a 'pseudo-hermaphrodite', but who is looking forward to being called a pseudo-anything?

And so for me now a 'zwitter', or a 'hermaphrodite', is now someone who's neither man nor woman, and therefore just living a little bit different from men or women.

CH: This 'zwitter' that you had heard about, and that had been described to you as both a man and a woman, with possibly ambiguous genitalia rather than necessarily any 'double' genitalia – that must have seemed a very different thing to you then receiving this diagnosis and thinking 'but my body is not giving me those kinds of external signals ...'.

Anja: Yes, well, I thought I was a girl, but the doctor told me okay I will be a 'real woman'. So, I have these male chromosomes, but that doesn't matter, the nature wanted to have me as a woman. So, I thought everything is okay, I am a woman, and I have these chromosomes, but I don't have to care. I have to get surgery, and that was it. I would have to get surgery for the ovaries, because they could build cancer, and we didn't want that. So I didn't know I was so similar to the 'zwitter' I knew ...

There are parallel narratives always from parents of those children who either manifest with genital ambiguity at birth, or who are diagnosed as intersexed later. Via Anja's translation, Anja's mother initially experienced 'no shock at all' at the diagnosis because she was so relieved that Anja was not suffering from cancer. Secondly, Anja's mother felt enormous relief that Anja was not devastated by the fact that she was infertile. And finally, her mother indicates that she loved her child regardless of anything: 'My history is a little different from other ones because in my family my intersex was "no big deal" without being closed away and silenced' (Anja, correspondence 22 January 2004).

But some parents whose newborn baby presents with ambiguous genitalia have a different – instant – experience of having to think about how they are going to cope and deal with that circumstance. When pressed on the fact that, until she was seventeen, nothing was really discussed because nothing was diagnosed, Anja was clear about her parents' love preceding her diagnosis and therefore surviving intact through that diagnosis:

Anja: My parents had seventeen years to know they have a child, and when there are parents who have a child with ambiguous genitalia [from birth] then they don't know the child. They have to learn to know that – their child – and then to know it's different. But all parents I know, after they are told the truth, it was better. It is so.

Some parents are told 'well, the child is maybe a little bit different, but it's nothing, you have a good girl', and so on. And that's not really ... you have to know the truth, and then you can cope best. Otherwise it's not good.

Anja markedly notes that her doctor was also relieved about this aspect of her diagnosis 'because he was afraid to tell me that'. Anja was just seventeen, and she describes how the doctor advised her to have surgery to remove her gonads on the basis that her chromosome mosaic held a 25 per cent chance of gonadal cancer. Anja was offered an exploratory biopsy, but she did not want exploratory surgery followed by the major gonadectomy, so she 'just told him "get it out". Whatever it is, I don't need it'. She describes how frightening the statistical possibility of cancer presented to her by her doctor was, and also notes 'for some of us who were told 30 per cent, we now know today it is less than 5 per cent [coughs ironically]!'

Anja's gonads were removed at age eighteen, and 'we just got into our normal life one day later'. The doctor told Anja that the gonads removed were ovaries, but she does not believe that. She is convinced that they were 'testes, but not grown as they should', and that she was told 'they were ovarian because I looked female'. Anja is still 'very angry' about this because she now knows that, given her condition, the gonads removed were neither testes nor ovaries, but were 'streaks, actually with the same mosaic as my blood – 97 per cent 46,XY and 3 per cent XO'. She has this in writing from copies taken of her medical files. Anja is circumspect, however, about the value of her gonads to her since, as streak gonads, they would not have had any endocrine effect. She has met other intersexed individuals whose *functional* gonads were removed and she counts herself lucky in not having experienced that degree of loss. Anja acknowledges that had she been told when she was eighteen that her surgeons had removed functioning testes, she would have experienced 'half a horror that I could be a man'. Today, however, she is better informed, and her grief at their removal is concerned with her fifteen subsequent years spent 'trying to be a woman', when she is intersexed:

> *Anja*: … and I never got it, never not one day. And now I know I didn't even have to try because there's no way [I am a woman] … the doctor told me I am a 'real woman', and that was the worst mistake he could ever do …

Anja acknowledges how common the stories of half-truths and semi-lies from clinicians are in relation to intersexed people. Migeon also confirms that from his study of 46,XY adults 'Almost half of the patients, reared male or female, were neither well informed about their medical and surgical history nor satisfied with their knowledge' (Migeon *et al.* 2002a: 1). Anja's doctor also told her that she would probably not meet any other intersexed people in her whole life, implying that intersex is extremely rare. Anja struggled with language to address this issue, and then became most fluent:

> *Anja*: They try to protect from this truth, but they don't do, they just make a delay. When someone has bone cancer in the arm and they have to cut this arm off, then they have to tell them the truth…With us, they can't do. They just tell us

we are a woman. And we try to be women, and we try to ... and we wonder our whole lives why do we feel that way. And when they tell us we have testes, then maybe it could be quite a horror, a shock, but we have to deal with it. And it's better then ... (*impassioned*)

CH: A clinician told me that he is concerned to tell patients. Not everybody hears the 'shock' and then learns to cope. He is worried about people who will commit suicide, have a nervous breakdown ...

Anja: But then you can tell him, more people he will not tell will commit suicide. Then he will tell them the truth. Because the truth is a good power. He could try to tell the parents that they have a dog instead of a child, they won't believe him, because the truth is they have a child. Think of a child that has diabetes, then the parents have to do certain things that the child won't die, so they have to tell the truth. And that is not less shocking for parents than intersex. Parents [of intersexed children] don't have to do something daily – you know, when you have a child with diabetes, then you have to do certain things every day, and that could be harder than to have an intersexed baby ...

But was there not something different about intersex? Was there not some kind of cultural fear – something that is going to challenge binary sex – some great taboo in our society? Isn't that different for a parent than having a child with diabetes, or something that they can tell their neighbour more easily?

Anja: I think it's just a fear for the unknown, and diabetes – we know what it is! And any disease we know – or even a disease we didn't know so far – then it's a disease. But intersex is a state of human.

(Anja consults her mother)

She told me when she talked with neighbours, and the topic came around, and she tells the neighbours or whoever about it, if it is intersex or diabetes, she doesn't care. But some would care – she told me some care about that – because they don't know what it is. And when she tells them what it is, then it's ok.

But there are still some who are afraid of intersex people because they think the order of society is breaking up!! And that's very dangerous! I think they think intersex is as dangerous as unlocking every door in the country!!

Anja then tells a story from her mother's childhood (around 1954) of another 'zwitter' who lived in their neighbourhood. This individual lived as a woman, 'but nobody would talk to her, and she was totally isolated'. Anja's mother was told by *her* mother that if this person came along, she must go to the other side of the street. And this was the common practice of the neighbourhood towards this person. Anja expresses outrage and annoyance – 'I want a time machine – I think I would go to her, and walk with her, with this T-shirt!!' Anja's T-shirt is inscribed *Schon mal mit nem Zwitter gesprochen? Hier ist die Gelegenheit.* Anja enjoys using the word 'zwitter' as a form of reclamation of 'a bad word that everyone knows' and she believes in heightening the visibility of intersex in society. Reactions to the T-shirt are frequently fear and embarrassment – 'they look, and they look away'.

CH: I think you and your mother are much further along the road of acceptance than many people. The reason why I am writing this book is because I didn't know such a word existed when I grew up …

Anja: Oh!?

CH: No, I come from a rural background, but there was a person in my local town when I was a child and when I look back now I am convinced this person was intersexed and was treated very badly …

Anja: Oh …

CH: And it stuck with me as a child, and I don't like bigotry, or people being isolated because they are different …

Anja: Yes …

CH: And that's why I'm writing the book …

Anja: Oh!

CH: I didn't know anybody before I began to research this …

Anja: Well, I know about fifty …

CH: And I'm writing the book because I don't like the kind of isolation you've described …

Anja: But, you know, when there is a rare postage stamp, it's worth much more. And yet people who are very seldom in the world, they are left outside? It's not logical!

At the time of Anja's diagnosis at age seventeen and her gonadectomy at eighteen, she recalls, a '"zwitter" was always someone who has both genitalia, something outside', and she did not have that (nobody has dual genitalia) nor did she have a noticeably large clitoris. Consequently, Anja and her family did not make any connection between being a 'zwitter', being intersexed and being Anja. As far as they knew, from what the doctors told them, 'ovaries' had been removed because of a cancer risk. Anja was aware of her mosaical karyotype but she did not translate this into being intersexed – 'there was no change because no-one thought I am a "zwitter"'. Anja's passport and birth certificate asserted her femaleness, and so she 'just lived and tried to be a woman'. In her twenties, she married and was divorced (for reasons unrelated to this issue), and she describes the 'normal' course of social development for a woman as 'you grow up, you marry and you have children. And when you don't do this, then you are a bad woman'. Anja knew she was infertile, but was circumspect. She was, however, aware that something was different.

Anja's road to full discovery of her intersex status began when she had a job that allowed access to the Internet. She recalled that Klinefelter's Syndrome (described in Chapter 12) had been mentioned in relation to her, and she searched on the Internet for this. Most Klinefelter's Syndrome individuals identify themselves as male, and, as Anja discovered, their karyotype is

47,XXY. Anja persisted:

> *Anja*: And then I searched, and I found medical pages for intersex information and
> forms of intersex, and three days later, I found XY-Women, a web-based self-
> supporting group. At first I couldn't believe it, and then I thought – oh that's
> me. I sent an email, I joined the group and next day I had six emails!

This happened in September 2002, and in March 2003 Anja attended her first
meeting with twenty-five other intersexed people:

> *Anja*: It was very good. And the first time in my life, I felt that I belonged to that
> people. Like I imagine when girls find out some day that there are girls, and –
> oh, I belong to this; and boys – oh, I belong to them. And I sat there, and – oh,
> I belong to them. I am not girl or boy. There are groups of people – people, ok?
> – neither that nor that …
> From then on I know some, and we have all similar opinions about being alone,
> and telling the truth and so on. And we can recognize each other from that – just
> like twins growing up separated and then coming together thirty years later, and
> they are both the same.

Finding others who are intersexed – in spite of the assertion of her doctor
that she never would – and embracing the language of being a 'zwitter' has
been enormously liberating for Anja. She identifies herself as intersexed, and
reflects 'we are born with intersex … we are intersexed, we stay intersexed'.
She describes how some of her intersexed friends and acquaintances feel more
comfortable if they adopt a male or female gender role, appearance, behaviour,
and maintain either male or female in their official documents. Anja, however,
wants intersex to be a recognized category in society, and she believes that
many of those intersexed whom she knows would want this to be formalized
and fully accepted also. She asserts that she is 'not a woman and not a man',
but notes that this is a recent shift for her – 'it is really a short time that I know
where I am and what I am'. Anja's parents have completely accepted her full
diagnosis as intersexed, and she acknowledges that this is unusual and that she
is lucky:

> *Anja*: There was absolutely no change in their behaviour in front of me. If I had got a
> tattoo it would have been more of a shock to them! And when I told other 'her-
> maphrodites' in the group, they couldn't believe that …

Anja looks like a woman, is genetically male (excepting her 3 per cent of
mosaic), and feels like neither. She was very lonely before she was in contact
with other intersexed people, and she acknowledges that however many
friends and family she had around her, she was 'really alone before, completely
alone, terribly alone'. She describes the feeling of not belonging to anybody.

She also narrates how, as she became aware of intersex through her Internet searches, at first she was concerned about the implications of acknowledging that she was neither male nor female:

> *Anja*: I didn't want to hear anything about that because I was so sure I was a woman. And I didn't want to break up the society.
> And one year later, it just came. I knew, I felt it was the right thing. And I do so until today.

Anja is now an advocate and activist for intersex rights. She works to stop surgeries for intersexed children, which are permitted by parental consent, and believes that intersexed children must make decisions for surgery themselves. She wants it also to be possible for intersexed children to remain as intersexed people. Anja is exasperated by the current state of play, where surgery is the norm, and where there is denial of subsequent problems:

> *Anja*: We can cut it away, so let's do that. And then no problem will come up? What to me is so important to be in your book is that I want to tell the people – I hope many people are reading this book then – that there is a possibility that parents are not crying, running away, shouting "what – we have a monster child?!"
> Intersex is in this world! There are parents who started to cry when they saw their child, and I think most people think that intersex must be something very hard when you have it … For parents and for children as well it doesn't have to be so hard …

Carina's Story

Carina is the mother of a child with Mixed Gonadal Dysgenesis. At birth a slight enlargement of the apparent clitoris was noticed, but since the child was three weeks premature it was concluded that this was insignificant. Nevertheless, the paediatrician organized genetic testing and, when her daughter was ten days old, Carina was told that her little girl was a genetic male. Carina insists that her child's genitals 'still looked like a little girl's, although a little bit large' (correspondence 3 August 2004), and so she heard all the information with a mixture of 'shock and just awe – could this be right?' Her child was not only genetically male, but the daughter she continued to insist that she was also – it transpired following further investigation – had no womb, only a very short vagina leading to a dead end, and also an undescended gonad. Treatment suggested was a gonadectomy before the end of the first year, with simultaneous clitoral reduction surgery. Vaginal surgery coupled with hormone treatment was recommended for somewhat later in the child's development.

Carina and her husband sought advice from medical sources and a support group where they live, and made their own decision as to the treatment their daughter should have. Carina tells me that, in spite of her genetic composition, she immediately understood her daughter as a little girl and her instinct has informed her decisions. Her child will not be fertile, or experience any of the usual female rites of passage – menstruation, natural breast development, giving birth – but she is, Carina insists, still a girl and not a boy. Consequently, they decided to allow the gonad to be removed in case it would have a virilizing effect at any point, and they have already agreed together that they will permit oestrogen treatment as their daughter comes near to puberty. They have, however, not agreed to clitoral or vaginal surgery. Carina indicates that their journey towards these decisions has been difficult. They have not been able to seek support from friends or family for fear of rejection or opposition, and they want to protect their child from others who might see the situation differently or try to influence them or the child. Their stress is evident, but they are committed to their decisions for now.

Carina does acknowledge that she and her husband have had to 'play God' (correspondence 3 August 2004), and she hopes that their daughter will have a female gender identity that will match the instinctual decisions they have made about raising her as a girl. They acknowledge that whatever happens in their daughter's uncertain future, they intend to keep loving her. And they understand that this might include her choice to change gender role or sex in adulthood.

A New Paradigm or Pie in the Sky?

Belinda is forty-eight and now knows that she has Mixed Gonadal Dysgenesis. For much of her life, however, she did not have a name for her condition and simply knew she was very different from the 'norm'. Her self-understanding has evolved over a lifetime starting with the explanation, from a specialist endocrinologist in her thirties, that she had 'not virilized particularly effectively' (correspondence 6 October 2004) from before birth, and had undergone a series of contradictory surgeries on her ambiguous genitalia, taking her first towards a female assignment, then towards a male assignment. Belinda's androgynous adult body form and facial characteristics are notable, and her genitals are dysfunctional in terms of erection, ejaculation or sexual sensation. She is critical of medical treatment protocols that still promote a concept of 'fixing' intersex through surgery, but she is also conscious that many medical practitioners genuinely struggle with very difficult ethical and practical decisions (correspondence 6 October 2004). She detects that protocols are gradually being revised for the better, and contends that it is essential that a resolution be found for the great lack of trust intersexed people feel for the medical profession. Those who feel they have been harmed by their experience of medical management cannot be dismissed, she asserts, and the medical establishment must address that. She also advocates that the evidence pointing to intersex as a type of sex is acknowledged, and urges that it be embraced in a new sexual paradigm. When asked about letting those who are intersexed be intersexed as opposed to wanting to define them as males or females, however, Philip Ransley is direct:

> I think it's pie in the sky. Now, if you were to wipe the slate clean with intersex, and say 'in order to start we need to know what the natural history of intersex is, so don't do anything to any of them, leave them be, see how they get on' ... then you need 50 years to work out what the suicide rate is, and ... how many disasters, and there would be a number ...
>
> At least we would know, but ... Obviously we can't go through that process so we have to continue to try and just refine our process by experience. (interview 6 September 2005)

Ransley cannot see society changing sufficiently rapidly to accept different sex diagnoses in time for it to be of use to any patients that he currently sees. He acknowledges that there have been massive adjustments in society in relation, for example, to access for those with disabilities, but he believes the subject of sex differentiation is much more complex and controversial:

> when you get onto what toilet do you go into, do you provide three, or four, or five, or do we go down to one? And society's not in a mature enough state to do that ... (interview 6 September 2005)

CHAPTER 12

Sex Chromosome Variations: Klinefelter's Syndrome

During the past century, as sexologists and later anthropologists and social historians encountered numerous instances of fuzzy sex and gender categories of individuals who seems to be neither clearly male nor female, feminine nor masculine, the strong central tendency has been to reduce the variations to the male or female sex.

Gilbert Herdt, *Mistaken Sex: Culture, Biology and Third Sex in New Guinea*

Male or Female?

Klinefelter's and Turner Syndromes, and the chromosomal variations that underpin them, are often referred to in the literature on intersex (Fausto-Sterling 2000). Many of those who exhibit their symptoms, however, as well as their collective support groups, and the clinicians who work with them, refuse to acknowledge the term intersex in relation to these syndromes, insisting that Klinefelter's and Turner are syndromes specific to males and females – not intersexuals – respectively. In order to do justice to the range of opinions on intersex, it seems appropriate that Klinefelter's and Turner Syndromes are included in this text in order to illuminate these divisions.

The processes of foetal sex differentiation are described in previous chapters as a developmental sequence from fertilization through a series of stages during gestation. Each stage builds upon the preceding development, and any atypicality during these stages results in non-standard sex development. Genetic sex differences – typical and atypical – are present from conception and cannot be altered. Chromosomes, spaghetti-like strands of genetic material donated to the foetus from each parent, are found in the nucleus of all the cells of our bodies (Bock 1993). That material is usually organized as a series of forty-six chromosomes in each cell, and two of these – the sex chromosomes – indicate genetic sex (46,XX – or XX – for genetic females, and 46,XY – or XY – for genetic males).

The 'genetic paradigm' dictates that the Y chromosome in a karyotype indicates a male. Yet Hambley is less certain of the 'purely ... genetic view of reality', and he provides a number of examples where individuals with a Y chromosome grow up to 'differ radically from the paradigm' (1999:

unpaginated). For example, he indicates that some persons with an XXY karyotype fail to virilize in typically male fashion, and argues that they – with their high voices, lack of male hair pattern and small underdeveloped penises – prove that the Y chromosome does not always effectively create 'absolute maleness'. Similarly, Hambley indicates that there are XXY individuals who identify as female, or 'something in between the typical dichotomy of culturally constructed genders' (ibid.). This chapter considers whether some individuals with karyotype atypicality of this kind can be considered as intersexuals.

This question is timely. The UK's Gender Recognition Act of 2004 overturned Omrod's landmark judgement in the Corbett versus Corbett case (1970). In that famous divorce case involving the transsexed woman April Ashley, Omrod effectively attempted to define sex in relation to chromosomal, gonadal and genital configuration (presupposing these to be always in harmony and unambiguous). Broadly speaking, the Gender Recognition Act signifies an important shift in UK law, to permit a form of self-definition of sex in relation to gender identity rather than in relation to somatic (bodily) presentation. This is not unproblematic, but in essence for the purpose of this text, it significantly begins to divorce sex from anatomy, constructing what is arguably a new, healthy and helpful paradigm.

To go back to genetic sex, amniocentesis testing and chorionic villus sampling (respectively of the fluid and membrane surrounding the foetus in the uterus) provide information on a range of genetic conditions (such as Down Syndrome) and structural defects (such as spina bifida). There is possibly an increased risk of general foetal chromosomal abnormality with older mothers (Samango-Sprouse 1999), and consequently older pregnant women in the UK are often offered these tests. With Klinefelter's Syndrome, some sources indicate that increased maternal age is considered a risk factor (Bojeson 2003), while others disagree (Nielsen undated). Just as sex differentiation *in utero* is not always typical, neither is genetic sex. As will be seen, some insist that unusual or ambiguous karyotypes are merely variations of the male and of the female, while others argue them as evidence of intersex. These deliberations are as pertinent to the discourses of sex as are considerations of genital ambiguity as either variation within the sex binary or evidence of entirely other sex configurations.

Genetic Sex and the Extra X

Unless specific *in utero* genetic testing has been carried out, the sex of the foetus and the newborn is usually determined by ultrasound or visual examination respectively. Determination by eye supposes sex to be always tangible, visible and literal, and in a great majority of cases it is. Putting aside discovery of genital ambiguity, however, the method ignores the possibility of sex anomalies in the *endocrinal* and *genetic* constitution of the baby, as well as overlooking the chances that *internal* anatomy and even possibly the hypothalamic construction of the brain (Zhou *et al.* 1995) may be in disagreement with the *apparent* sex suggested by even unambiguous genitalia. The term 'sex chromosome anomaly' is used specifically in medical parlance when karyotyping indicates atypicality in the sex chromosomes, and locates difference very much within the sex binary – these are disorders of the XX/XY pattern rather than another category of (inter)sex (Fausto-Sterling 2000). Such anomalies, however, are considered *by some* to be symptomatic of genetic intersex.

In approximately 80 per cent of those diagnosed with sex chromosome anomaly one extra X chromosome is present in each cell and this karyotype is referred to as 47,XXY (Nielsen undated). For those who argue that sex chromosomes determine sex, it is this 'extra X' that gives rise to consideration of this karyotype, and others equally atypical, as evidencing intersex. In the early 1970s, international researchers screened large numbers of newborn *male* (by visual inspection) babies in order to identify those with this additional X chromosome (Bock 1993). Their studies revealed that the XXY karyotype appears to be one of the most common genetic variations known, with suggested frequencies of 1 in 500–1,000 (*apparent*) *male* births (Hambley 1999). Persons with the XXY karyotype are most usually defined in medical literature and by Klinefelter's Syndrome support organizations as *male*. There are those who share that karyotype, however, like interviewees Sarah-Jane or Chris, who have ambiguous anatomical characteristics. And there are some with this karyotype who do not identify as male.

Dr Harry Klinefelter

The XXY karyotype was discovered in the late 1950s, and the historical route to that discovery is important. Researchers did not seek the chromosomal anomaly in the general population, but rather *in men with the already determined Klinefelter's Syndrome*, who were all then found to have an extra X chromosome (Bock 1993). These individuals exhibited the symptoms of a syndrome named earlier by Dr Harry Klinefelter and diagnosed in a group of only nine men who had *enlarged breasts, sparse facial and body hair, small testes and an inability to produce sperm*. Klinefelter's sample of nine adult men – or, for the sake of historical accuracy, nine individuals who by visual inspection were understood to be male – was unscientifically small. It was also selected on the terms of symptoms manifest, rather than on examination of a selection of the whole population to determine a sample of those with the chromosomal anomaly. Klinefelter's sample, however, has powerfully shaped how screening for XXY infants developed. That is, because Klinefelter's subjects were *understood to be male*, it was only *male* (by visual inspection) newborns who were subsequently screened for the chromosomal anomaly. Those then found to have XXY karyotypes were consequently understood to be male in spite of some evidence that this may not be entirely the case.

Klinefelter's original observations emphasized the *apparently male physical presentation* of his notably adult subjects, *discounting* their developed breasts, scanty body and facial hair, *forefronting* their small testes and male-patterned genitalia, and remaining ignorant of their internal anatomy. The question is, might subsequent investigations of XXY karyotypes have examined the possibility that XXY individuals might be females (XX) with an additional Y chromosome as much as males (XY) with an extra X? Certainly, for those who choose to note the development of 'feminine characteristics, little body hair, breasts, pear shape' (Mark, interview 11 May 2005) Klinefelter's Syndrome might arguably suggest some kind of female-oriented intersex.

Although karyotype is fixed from conception, Klinefelter's Syndrome is an *adult* condition, since the specific syndrome can only occur with pubescent changes. And *adult individuals* with XXY karyotypes may exhibit all, some or even none of the symptoms of Klinefelter's Syndrome. Diamond, for example, points out that 'the clinical features of KS are extremely variable' (Diamond and Watson 2004b: 632), and diagnosis of Klinefelter's Syndrome therefore tends to occur more frequently in those displaying prominent rather than mild symptoms. Interviewee Sarah-Jane (Chapter 6) exhibits no evidence of being a Klinefelter's male, and yet she has an XXY karyotype. The variability of the XXY karyotype, of the symptoms of Klinefelter's Syndrome, and of the individual is frequently reiterated and seems to be key to understanding this issue: 'Since your extra X is just one out of 47, you have a lot of other genetic material that affects you in a variety of ways, and the extra X can differ in genetic coding from individual to individual' (Hambley 1999: unpaginated).

Frequency and Diagnosis

The Klinefelter Organisation (UK) suggest 1 in 1,000 *male infants* have an XXY karyotype, while the Klinefelter's Syndrome Association UK and the US-based Klinefelter Syndrome and Associates both offer a 1 in 500–1,000 frequency rate. Fausto-Sterling's (2000) rate for Klinefelter's Syndrome is 0.0922 per 100 (1 in 1,084) live births, while Ratcliffe and Paul (1986) present a median figure of 1 in 750.

Variants of 47,XXY occur less frequently. For example, more than one additional X chromosome may be present (48,XXXY or 49,XXXXY) (Preves 2003), or more complex variations appear such as 46,XX (male); 47,XYY; 48,XXYY; 48,XXXY. Research into these karyotype variations is sparse, but their management is likely to be not dissimilar to that of their

47,XXY counterparts (Hambley 1999). The more complex of these karyo-types are, however, statistically more likely to demonstrate physical problems and mental issues including learning difficulties (Diamond and Watson 2004b).

In approximately 6 per cent of cases, a chromosomal mosaic manifests, wherein the additional X chromosome(s) are only present in *some* cells (Nielsen undated). In these, the proportion of XY cells to anomalous XXY or variant cells determines the severity of the mosaic, and unless all of the body's cells are tested, which is impossible, then it is also impossible to know the actual extent of the variation or mosaic other than by its outcomes (Rolla 2004). The most common mosaic is XY/XXY. Other forms – complicated atypical chromosomal configurations – range in frequency from 0.2 per cent to 0.08 per cent of the population.

Realistically, many of those with few or no symptoms of their variant karyotype remain undiagnosed (Samango-Sprouse 1999). Tony McCabe, of the Klinefelter Organisation (UK) notes the 1 in 1,000 frequency rate for XXY karyotype is based on genetic testing at birth of *male newborns* over a period of time. He questions where these 1 in 1,000 are in the adult popula-tion given the small numbers of those with Klinefelter's Syndrome that he is aware of who are receiving medical treatment or indeed who are members of his support group. The implication of Tony's enquiry is that there are many undiagnosed symptom-free adults who have not been karyotype tested in infancy and who therefore are unaware of their genetic anomaly. McCabe (2003) suggests the frequency statistics for Klinefelter's Syndrome in the adult population are inflated. Arguably, however, they are more accurately *evidence* of a karyotype presence in the newborn population that is then not surfacing in the numbers presenting with Klinefelter's Syndrome post-puberty. The low rate of diagnosis of individuals with Klinefelter's Syndrome may also be attrib-uted to the majority of XXY and variant males not experiencing problems of sufficient severity to warrant them seeking help or advice. Diagnosed or not, emergent as Klinefelter's Syndrome or not, the XXY and variant karyotypes evidence a sex chromosomal make-up that is certainly atypical for male or female. While the great majority of foetuses, infants and children with these anomalous karyotypes are named as male, and the vast number of adults with them self-identify as male, are there any other characteristics that might further disturb the customary binary sex distinction?

Intersex or Not?

McCabe questioned why XXY and variant karyotypes, and Klinefelter's Syndrome, were being discussed in this book, asserting 'KS is not strictly an intersex condition' (interview 29 April 2004). Klinefelter's Syndrome, Turner

Syndrome (discussed in Chapter 13) and their related karyotype anomalies are frequently cited in the literature of intersex. Fausto-Sterling, for example, classes Klinefelter's Syndrome among the 'common types of intersexuality' (2000: 51). Yet the almost entirely 'normal male' birth presentations of XXY and variant babies (Nielsen undated) is alluded to several times by interviewees. The Klinefelter's Syndrome Association (UK) notes that 'babies with KS are unrecognisable from XY babies at birth' (correspondence 8 May 2004), and Bock reports a NICHD-funded study which concluded that 'XXY babies differ little from other children their age' (1993: 3,202). The Klinefelter's Syndrome Association (UK) strongly asserts that 'We are born male' (correspondence 8 May 2004).

Marie is the mother of a 20-year-old with 48,XXXY karyotype. Her child was not diagnosed until he was ten, and she recalls thinking of her newborn as her 'perfect baby' (interview 11 May 2004) since there were no external signs of any atypicality. In subsequent correspondence (18 May 2004), when asked about her child's genitalia in infancy, however, Marie clarified that he had small but descended testes and a small penis. She indicated that 'there was talk of penile enlargement at some stage but nobody has mentioned it for a while' (correspondence 18 May 2004), and made clear that this would be something that she would want her son to decide on for himself. All parent interviewees for this chapter describe being initially unaware of any physical difference from a male 'norm' in their newborns. That being said, it is unlikely that most parents would want to acknowledge a difference at birth unless it was so overt that it required comment, and a mildly undervirilized infant penis and testes would not necessarily at that point be either noteworthy or memorable (Hambley 1999).

Stefan is stepfather of a child with XXY karyotype who was diagnosed *in utero*. While his partner was aware of the chromosomal atypicality of her child, Stefan indicated that it would not have been possible to discern anything unusual from visual examination at birth. Stefan himself has an XXY/XY mosaic karyotype, and his parents reported 'no visually recognisable anomalies' (interview 10 May 2004) at his birth, although he has smaller than average testes in adulthood.

K's 3-year-old child has the XXYY karyotype, and she indicates that 'at present he looks like all other little boys' (correspondence 21 May 2004). Pressed for details of the route for his diagnosis given her assertion of absence of infant symptoms pointing to genetic anomaly, K did not respond to further correspondence. Nic, the mother of a now 13-year-old with the same karyotype as K's child, said her child is 'definitely a boy' (interview 23 May 2004), although she notes a feminizing of his figure as he develops. She describes this as having a waist, 'soft tummy, shaped hips, and extremely soft almost girlish skin', noting that he also has very little body hair (correspondence 9 February

2007). In these respects he differs markedly from her other two male children. Undescended testes were straightforwardly rectified at birth, and investigations towards a diagnosis of autism led to chromosome testing at age five. Debra and Keith's son was diagnosed at the age of one week with 49,XXXXY karyotype: they insist 'there are no characteristics that would lead someone to believe that he is part female. He has no female organs' (correspondence 25 May 2004).

These examples typify a dominant model for infants diagnosed as having XXY and variant karyotypes. That is, 'we are born as baby boys and there is no ambiguity over our sex, therefore we are not intersex' (Tony, interview 1 May 2004). There are, however, some clinically reported differences in newborns with XXY and variant karyotypes. Ratcliffe (Ratcliffe and Paul 1986) notes that these babies can tend to be rather smaller and lighter at birth than average, and with a slightly smaller head circumference. She indicates that their genitals are no different to those of an ordinary male baby and the penis is usually of normal size, but does point out, however, that occasionally testes are still internal at birth, and a minor operation is required to guide them into the scrotum. Since the testes are the glands responsible *in utero* for the secretion of the male sex hormones, stimulating the development of the male reproductive system and secondary sex characteristics, this may or may not be a significant tendency. Stefan and his stepson did not experience non-descent of testes, but, in his advocacy and educational work, Stefan has encountered 'some boys and men who had undescended testicles that required surgery to be dropped into place' (correspondence 17 May 2004). And, a parent's letter in *The Link*, newsletter of the Klinefelter Organisation (UK), non-specifically suggests some form of obvious difference: 'When my son was born I was devastated that things were obviously not as I had imagined ... I was coming to terms with his development delay and what the future may hold for him ...' (Anon 2002: unpaginated).

There is no suggestion in the various reports detailing the occasional occurrence of undescended testes in XXY and variant infants of there being Testicular Dysgenesis, or of the testes being anything other than what they appear as. And indeed non-descent of testicles is neither exclusive to these children nor necessarily indicative of any issue of atypical sex differentiation. That being said, and with no conclusion in relation to these cases of undescended testes, some individuals with XXY karyotypes also have ovarian tissue.

XXY Troubled ...

There is general consensus among support groups for Klinefelter's Syndrome, with many parents and in general medical texts also that birth presentation for infants with XXY and variant karyotypes is essentially, straightforwardly and apparently male. But the question remains: what does that extra X do?

While the external anatomy associated with XXY and variant karyotypes seems relatively uncomplicated, internal anatomy and indeed the 'look' (phenotype) of XXY and variant individuals may not always be as uniformly male as commonly suggested. Thangaraj *et al.* (1998), Schmid *et al.* (1992) and Saavedra-Castillo *et al.* (2005) all report on 47,XXY *females*. Schmid's 'unusual' case study describes a child aged six, found to have a 47,XXY karyotype, with female-appearing external genitalia with enlarged clitoris, a uterus and incomplete female duct structures, and with gonads located inside the labia majora (these were removed and found to be testes). Diamond (Diamond and Watson 2004b, referencing Cossey 1991) recalls that Carolyn Cossey, a 'James Bond girl', was raised as a boy and changed sex to live as a woman in her late teens. Her karyotype is 48,XXXY. And Röttger (Röttger *et al.* 2000) reports the case of a 47,XXY female who has one son and two daughters. One of her daughters has the same 47,XXY karyotype. To their knowledge this subject is the first known *fertile* XXY human female.

These instances of 47,XXY females – each reported in respected medical journals – represent a challenge to assertions of the male exclusivity of the XXY karyotype, and further upset what physical manifestations can be understood with certainty to be associated with that karyotype. Here we have research citations of *females* with the karyotype that is necessary for the development of Klinefelter's Syndrome, a collection of symptoms conventionally associated entirely with *males*. Might XXY then potentially be considered as near to *XX (typical female karyotype) with additional Y* as *XY (typical male karyotype) with additional X*? The answer patently requires a non-generic understanding of how genetic material affects different individuals (Bock 1993). How would Klinefelter's Syndrome support groups square these *females (including a mother)* with their assertion that their subjects are always and entirely *male*? Furthermore, earlier assertions stated that there must statistically be many people with XXY and variant karyotypes out in the population who are undiagnosed as such, and who are therefore not included in what is still patchy research knowledge of these genetic differences. Might some of them be living as *females*?

And finally, are there individuals with XXY and variant karyotypes who have had breasts removed and who have had testosterone therapy when adolescent, but for whom such treatment was inappropriate to their sense of intersex-identified (or even female-identified) selves.

Chris Somers XXY: An 'Epicene' Person

Chris' karyotype of 47,XXY was diagnosed when s/he was twenty-seven (Chris prefers to use personal sex-neutral language). Like many with this karyotype, Chris was a 'normal'-looking male-appearing infant. S/he had a regular childhood, although s/he remembers never intrinsically feeling like a little boy. At puberty, however, s/he developed breasts. In spite of horrendous bullying during his/her school years, Chris was drawn to the idea of living as 'both male and female – or a person in between, a different gender' (interview 22 May 2004). While Chris' parents were supportive, they were concerned about the 'terrible pressure' s/he experienced living as an *apparent* adolescent male with breasts. At age sixteen, s/he and his/her parents agreed that a double mastectomy was advisable: 'I felt that to live in a world I was in, I couldn't survive as a normal human being. I would have needed an enormous support network. And I was only just a young person' (Chris quoted in Kerr 2005: 10). Chris has subsequently noted that this was a 'reluctant bi-lateral mastectomy … an operation I never ever wanted' (correspondence 6 February 2007). Ultrasound investigation later revealed the presence of internal gonadal tissue and a collapsed vagina (Somers 1999). The configuration of the upper vagina has also suggested the possibility of some uterine structure, but a laparoscopy would be necessary if this was to be confirmed. Thangaraj *et al.* (1998) acknowledge that this internal configuration, and indeed a female phenotypic appearance, is possible, though less general, in individuals with a 47,XXY karyotype.

Chris identifies particularly as *intersex*, stating that s/he may look like a stereotypical man but [s/he] do[es] not always live as one', and insisting that s/he does not identify as male (correspondence 6 February 2007). Chris believes that the numbers of those with XXY and variant karyotypes, internal anatomy that may be female and external genitalia that are male-appearing, might be greater than is generally believed. S/he advocates that much wider research is carried out to determine whether this is the case, arguing in a range of texts and correspondences for these female internal organs to be sought out via ultrasound in known cases of XXY karyotype as well as in the general 'male' population. These internal organs would then become a kind of phys-ical and (by ultrasound) visual evidence that karyotype atypicality can be equated with intersex.

Chris uses the physical evidence of his/her internal female anatomy revealed by ultrasound to affirm personal feelings of androgyny, concluding that the anatomy and the feelings were present always in tandem, and were contrary to the societal 'norm' that insisted that s/he was male. In the absence of belief in the validity of *feelings* of intersex as a kind of self-identification of sex, and with the problematically intangible 'proof' of intersex that an XXY karyotype can bring, there is evidently some relief for Chris in discovering his/her intersexed internal anatomy. Indeed, it is these internal and hidden physical structures that allow Chris to 'prove' intersex in contradiction of assertions that XXY universally signifies the male. It seems that female breast development in XXY karyotype individuals like Chris can be rather persuasively argued as not necessarily indicating any kind of bodily *femaleness* per se, particularly since some genetically typical XY men also experience breast development.

Chris uses the presence of the 'female bit' (the extra X) in his/her karyotype to evidence the mixing of usually complementary and exclusive physical characteristics in intersex: 'Male and female is an over simplistic categorization of the actualities of the world of human and other biology' (Somers undated: unpaginated). This is complex territory, and Chris further illuminated his/her ambivalence towards binary sex and its signifiers in interview (22 May 2004). Chris pointed out that, in his/her opinion, society was much too convinced that there are only two exclusive sexes. S/he could see how 'terrified' parents are to acknowledge that their child may not be male or female, and acknowledged how enormous peer pressure makes it extremely difficult for those diagnosed with XXY or variant karyotypes in adulthood to open up about the possibility of not being sexually 'normal'.

Chris' own sex history is complex. As well as the bilateral mastectomy, his/her generally perceived non-virilization was also treated with male hormones post-puberty (interview 22 May 2004). *Now*, in problematic hindsight, Chris states that s/he would have resisted this treatment and insisted on his/her sex ambiguity. S/he self-classifies as 'an epicene person' (correspondence 15 May 2004), with a tremendous personal desire to 'offer ... another way of seeing us and others':

> epicene is a kind and beautiful word where hermaphrodite had been used mostly in derision at those who are in the lived experience ... I use the word hermaphrodite and am not ashamed of it [but] I am aware of the terrible hurt directed at those of us who are/were ... by a population ignorant of the reality. (Chris, correspondence 19 May 2004)

Chris is reclaiming an *intersex identity* from societal insistence on binarism as a way of acknowledging and strengthening his/her self-identity. Via breast removal and testosterone treatment in adolescence, Chris was effectively assigned sex in a not dissimilar way to that by which infants with ambiguous genitalia are assigned sex (through surgical/hormonal intervention). That is, a normalizing decision was made and carried through by others: 'I personally had felt very differently for years, feeling more feminine than I did male, yet neither one nor the other – ever since I was a very young child ... A real mixture of both in almost every respect, but who would believe or understand me ...' (Somers undated: unpaginated).

Vague feelings of partial femininity were reiterated by a number of interviewees with 47,XXY karyotypes, most of whom resolutely identified as male. Stefan, for example, was aware of 'something not quite right' from around age five (interview 10 May 2004), while Tony registered 'a shift of 30 per cent toward a feminine side' (interview 1 May 2004). Marie noted her son's tendency to be 'more gentle than the others' (his brothers), and to engage specifically with what she calls 'girls' toys', but indicated – correctly – that 'it is hard to know if this is due to his chromosome make up' (correspondence 9 May 2004). It is difficult to differentiate between what interviewees meant by gender as opposed to sex, and Marie's assertion that 'he has never indicated an inclination towards a female side' is interesting.

Chris considers adolescent testosterone treatment and breast surgery as a kind of 'pseudo-sex assigner', used to normalize maleness in an uncertain body, to erase breasts and virilize body/testes that fail to do so 'naturally', and thereby ignoring internal configuration, chromosomal alignment, lack of physical virilization. But s/he also concedes that testosterone is administered not only to promote the development of male characteristics but also for some health-enhancing reasons in *males* who do not produce their own hormones satisfactorily. Chris was told, for example, that testosterone treatment would help strengthen his/her bones, which were susceptible to osteoporosis, and indeed this is the case in many instances. Chris, however, currently has medium to severe bone degeneration despite almost thirty-two years of testosterone treatment and did not experience the bulking of muscle mass and the considerable hair growth most often associated with testosterone treatment (correspondence 6 February 2007). For 47,XXY people who *feel male*, the testosterone shots can be invaluable, helping them develop physically as typical men, especially through puberty. For Chris, however, who felt s/he leaned more to the female (if anything), the lowering of voice, the alteration of smooth skin texture, and the slight shifts in musculature and hair patterning experienced after testosterone treatment began were difficult for him/her. Recently, Chris has asked if s/he could receive oestrogen or mixed hormone treatment instead of simply testosterone, but this has so far been refused for medical reasons (correspondence 6 February 2007). A great deal more research is needed, but an idea lingers. Might there be *boys who look male externally*, but have female organs inside; who have sexually ambiguous chromosomes; who develop breasts at puberty; and who are then placed on testosterone therapy and have their breast tissue removed in order to essentialize their maleness, but who actually should be left to develop in an ambiguous way until they can decide for themselves how they wish to be and who they want to be?

There is no doubt that peer pressure has a major influence on decisions by parents and clinicians to treat breast development by surgery and undervirilization by hormone replacement. While Chris is happy now to embrace his/her 'epicene' identity, in more formative years s/he 'was not psychologically strong enough … to deal with the situation I found myself within. I was … in a boys' boarding school and you might imagine what that was like

... in the shower rooms which were very public' (correspondence 19 May 2004).

Chris is now happily married to a woman. His/her only regret is that s/he had to state that s/he was male in order to marry. As Chris rightly said, there are many marriages in many countries where XXY individuals or XY women with AIS are married *against karyotype and in keeping with their gender identification – individuals whose genetic sex and anatomical sex are unaligned*. As a genetic intersexual, with anatomical evidence of intersex, Chris recognizes 'many intersexed people would prefer to remain in the safety zone of being classified as one of the 'norms' within the binary concept of sex and gender' (correspondence 19 February 2007), but Chris would like *intersex* to be understood as his/her sex, and states that s/he 'is not alone in this way of thinking, many more the world over are becoming less afraid to acknowledge their differences with courage' (correspondence 19 February 2007).

Malcolm's Story: A Boy with Breasts

Chris' feelings about his/her mastectomy are that it represented a huge personal sacrifice to fit the 'social norm', describing it as 'a violation of his/her own personhood, however well intentioned people may have perceived otherwise' (correspondence 19 February 2007. But his experience at the hands of his school peers echoes another very different testimony from Malcolm, whose adolescent breasts were also seen by his classmates in the school changing rooms:

> I knew I'd been seen ... all these lads like a pack turned on me. They were one big gang, spitting, hitting, and laughing at the 'titty freak' ...
>
>   I had some kind of faint or blackout, and then we never went back to that school. My mother insisted we moved away and we didn't talk about that particular episode after that ... but I never got over it. I feel it broke me up in some way. (correspondence 3 March 2005)

Malcolm's devastation has persisted over three decades after this episode in spite of his breast removal surgery when he was nineteen. Mastectomy erases tissue but not feelings. This ghastly episode reveals how deeply unacceptable to social 'norms' of maleness any difference is, especially difference that appears to feminize the male or threaten the primacy of the 'perfect penis' as the cultural icon of maleness and masculinity. In the 'male with breasts' configuration of some Klinefelter's Syndrome subjects, we see the symbolic converse of the 'phallic female' – a 'mammaried male'. The threat to the symbolic binary of sex is witnessed here as immense, even primal, and the behaviour of the locker-room bullies testifies to their fear and horror at the supposed abjection of a male body whose boundaries are traversed so visibly by the breast-signifier of femaleness.

Perhaps the most culturally disturbing symptom of the XXY karyotype, and of Klinefelter's Syndrome, is the gynaecomastia or breast development described above. For possibly 50 per cent of youths aged thirteen to fourteen with Klinefelter's Syndrome, as well as for a third of youths with straightforward XY karyotype, breast development takes place (Ratcliffe and Paul 1986). Where it is temporary for other youths, for those with Klinefelter's Syndrome it may persist and indeed increase, necessitating either testosterone treatment and/or surgical removal of the breast tissue if an appearance of typical maleness is to be maintained (Nielsen undated). The incidence of breast cancer in Klinefelter's Syndrome subjects is also significantly greater than for typical males (Diamond and Watson 2004b), although notably lower than for genetic women. Breast removal is not necessarily a solution to this, and it has been suggested that such cancer may be linked to the hormonal imbalances in Klinefelter's Syndrome rather than the presence of the breasts per se. McCabe suggests that around 80 per cent of adult men with Klinefelter's Syndrome have breast development of differing degrees of severity, with 10 per cent of those warranting a double mastectomy (correspondence 2 May 2004).

Dr Arturo Rolla explains that greater than average production of oestrogen by XXY and variant individuals 'increase[s] the tendencies to develop toward a feminine physique (breasts, hips, decreased muscle mass etc)' (1999: unpaginated). He indicates that levels of testosterone in XXY and variant persons differ between subjects, but its low or absent levels cause the testes to work hard to try to secrete testosterone and this in turn causes an increased oestrogen output. That oestrogen surge is typically that which would be 'normalized' by testosterone therapy (Rolla 1999). Rolla adds that increased amounts of fatty tissue in many XXY persons also contribute to oestrogen production as a result of androgen conversion in that tissue, although this is highly variable from individual to individual. It is clear how the development of breasts interferes with a reading of a particular body as male, and fuels the inexcusable bullying detailed above. As Nic says about the possibility of her XXYY child developing breasts: 'that might twinge me a bit ... that's physical evidence of something less than masculine ... nobody sees a small penis or testicles ...' (interview 23 May 2004). And Nic's inclination would be to want any developing breasts on her son to be removed, 'so that he doesn't get stigmatized by other people, ignorant people' (interview 23 May 2004).

In the vast majority of cases of Klinefelter's Syndrome, breast growth is disturbing but not necessarily challenging to an individual's *fundamental* sense of being male – if that is intact. Marie's son, Peter, for example, developed breasts at puberty, and was distressed by other people's reactions, as well as their incongruity with his sense of maleness (Marie, interview 11 May 2004).

Marie also found their growth difficult, and she was supportive of his acceptance of surgery at around age thirteen. Peter's considerable learning difficulties – only sometimes attributable to karyotype anomalies – meant that he was
intellectually unprepared for the consequences of his surgery. He believed that
he would wake up from his operation with no trace of the breasts ever having
been there – a complete erasure – and he was unable to rationalize that there
would be healing time, it would be painful, that there would be scarring and
indeed that there was also some fatty tissue left behind by the surgeon. While
Peter eventually came to terms with the experience and residual traces of
gynaecomastia (breast development), Marie is adamant that counselling for
him and her, which was not given, should have been available. As she said,
parents who are going through this experience with their sons are doing it for
the first time, whereas medical professionals know the pitfalls, and being properly prepared would have alleviated much of her son's pain and distress. As
stated above, mastectomy erases tissue but not feelings...

'Sex Essentialism'

Correspondent and interviewee Stefan, who is a 47,XXY man, acknowledged
that at one time he was 'upset and angered' by being associated with intersex
(correspondence 5 May 2004). For him, this is no longer the case. Without
wishing to undermine those who provide great support and guidance for those
with XXY and variant karyotypes, there is a tendency among the range of
support groups to insist on the XXY karyotype, its variants and Klinefelter's
Syndrome as conditions of an iconic *male*, and to discount the possibility of
individual self-identification as either intersex or female. The Klinefelter's
Syndrome Association in the UK indicates that its members were most likely
to talk 'from the point of view of refuting any argument that they are intersexed individuals' (8 May 2004), making categorically clear that:

> The Klinefelter's Syndrome Association ... does not accept that Klinefelter's Syndrome
> is an 'intersex condition' ...
>
> Those with Klinefelter's Syndrome are born male. Many need hormone supplemen-
> tation through puberty and throughout adult life. Some may need other treatment, but
> this in no way diminishes their essential maleness. It should certainly not lead to them
> being considered 'intersex' individuals. (correspondence 27 April 2004)

And Tony McCabe of the Klinefelter Organisation (UK) wrote: 'I still
believe that the only true people who are intersex are those born with indeterminate gender and not those born with Klinefelter Syndrome' (McCabe 2003:
2). McCabe acknowledges that he could see how the chromosomal addition of
an 'extra X', the tendency of many to develop breasts, the propensity of some

to carry 'female-distributed' weight, the lack of facial hair or typical male muscularity in the absence of testosterone treatment could result in an intersex labelling. But he refutes this: 'yes we have an extra female sex chromosome and this does cause us problems physically and mentally and we might feel more in tune with our female half and have female tendencies but we are still ultimately male' (ibid.).

The insistence on non-intersexed maleness is what most people searching the Internet for support and guidance for XXY and variant karyotypes and/or Klinefelter's Syndrome encounter. Such sex stereotyping must surely be problematic in the face of evidence of some such individuals who do not identify as male. Not represented in the characterization of their membership by most support organizations, *these* individuals are then labelled *by default* as transsexual, gender dysphoric, etc. The Klinefelter's Syndrome Association (UK) advises that those with XXY and variant karyotypes – whether or not they actually call their condition Klinefelter's Syndrome – who do not identify as male are 'the exception rather than the norm' in their experience (correspondence 27 April 2004). Logically – statistically – even in a group of typical XY men, there will be those who are transsexual, gender dysphoric and indeed exceptional. Therefore from the position that asserts XXY and variant karyotype as essentially male, there is a good statistical likelihood that there will be individuals – exceptions albeit – who are the XXY equivalent of those within the XY population. If one does not accord with the assertion of XXY and variant karyotypes as essentially male, there appears to be little room for dissent within mainstream informal support networks.

Perhaps the whole debate as to whether XXY and variant karyotypes evidence intersex is immaterial if the child is healthy and happy. The compromise of 'maleness' for many young people with XXY and variant karyotypes is hard. Breast development, curvy or pear-shaped body, scant or no facial hair, no deepening of the voice, etc. appear as an erosion of masculinity, and those involved are frequently mocked, and especially mocked as effeminate or gay, both still being in some way deemed undesirable.

Parents too are often driven by a great range of emotions at their child's diagnosis, and operate a variety of strategies to 'normalize' them:

We have never considered [our child] intersexed ... I have never heard the term used especially in regards to Klinefelter Syndrome or its variants ...

it bothers me to have someone think that my son is of both sexes ...

he knows the difference between boys and girls and will tell you that he is a boy ...

he has never had a tendency to play with dolls, etc. but would rather play with cars or swordfight his brother ... (Debra, correspondence 25 May 2004)

For other parents, like Marie, there is a reliance on the child to identify any difference – 'Peter has never implied or said that he feels anything other than male' (correspondence 9 May 2004). In her mind, his mother Marie can understand her son as 'male and female in the one body' (interview 11 May 2004), and she can understand how Klinefelter's Syndrome gets linked to intersex. That being said, she is most interested only in these ideas if that kind of understanding can help her child. In society, for her and those who know him, however, she asserts that her son is male. There continues to be a potent sense of social stigma surrounding the sex-related aspects of Klinefelter's Syndrome. Marie spoke of other mothers with whom she is in contact who have told nobody, and who work alone to cope with information about their children which they feel to be shameful and taboo (interview 11 May 2004). And a particular sadness is there for Nic:

> what I find heartbreaking ... is the almost certainty that he may never have kids ... it wasn't that I'm not going to be a grandparent, how will he cope ... that pierced me ... the poignant thing? Would I change everything? If I could change him to 'normal' I would ... if I could wave a magic wand ... intersex just doesn't ring true for S ... (interview 23 May 2004)

There is parental disbelief, too, which is powerfully intuitive: 'I cannot see how anyone could consider any variant of Klinefelter's as intersex' (Keith, correspondence 19 May 2004), and a kind of collective refusal of the terminology of intersex: 'Like the majority of parents I do not see my son as being intersex ...' (K, correspondence 21 May 2004). Secrecy is frequent for fear of peer reprisal. Tony indicates how his mother, who has never accepted her son's condition, has told him never to tell anybody that he cannot have children biologically, and she has perpetuated a myth that Tony has never wanted to be a father and has in fact had a vasectomy. While this fear is more on the part of Tony's mother, concerned for what *her* peers would say or think, there is genuine fear on the part of parents of younger children that 'a malicious or thoughtless child may tell all the neighborhood children that his former companion is a "freak" because he has an extra chromosome' (Hambley 1999: unpaginated).

David: A 'Beautiful Variation'

David also has an XXY karyotype, a 'small male phallus' (correspondence 11 February 2007), and developed breasts in adolescence. He has been told he is a 'mutation', but he prefers to self-identify as a 'beautiful variation', and chooses 'to say that I'm not a man or a woman; I'm a blend, an androgyne' (David quoted in Letellier 2004: 3). David is also gay.

The desire to 'normalize' XXY and variant karyotypes, to assert individuals with these karyotypes as essentially male in an uncomplicated fashion, to insist that these genetic atypicalities are endocrinal (hormonal) imbalances curable by hormone replacement therapy, appears to be strong. David believes that there is a homophobic and transphobic agenda also in operation that colours how parents of intersex children, including those with his karyotype, respond to their children: 'I'm not seen as a real man because I'm queer, and many of these parents only want their kids to be male heterosexuals. They don't even want to hear the word "intersex"' (David quoted in Letellier 2004: 3).

While homophobia is the experience of many typical XY homosexual men, the issue becomes sharply focused where there is a chromosomal challenge to 'heterosexual normality'. In fact, homosexuality is no more common in male-defined individuals with XXY and variant karyotypes and/or Klinefelter's Syndrome than in the average male population. Yet it is interesting that it came up overtly in several interviews with heterosexual XXY adults who identified themselves as male. And by implication in interview with Tony: 'I wasn't turning into the man my father wanted me to be' (interview 1 May 2004). It is as though the 'threat' of any degree of feminization resulting from karyotype variation also 'threatened' the possibility of homosexuality with its still culturally embedded nuances of femininity and lack of masculinity.

David has been having testosterone treatment for twenty-seven years, and 'passes' well as a tall and imposing man. Yet his self-expression is more fluid: he describes a kind of 'sexless genderless energy' (interview 19 June 2004) and a feeling of being 'other' to the binaries of male or female. He embraces the terms *androgyne* and *intersex* specifically: the former because it best contains his sense of gender identification, and the latter because it speaks accurately to his anatomy and his chromosomes. He is aware that part of the difficulty of the intersex discourse is that the terms sex, gender and sexuality get muddled, and he believes that the muddle helps nobody.

David's birth, just after the Second World War, was, as far as he is aware, unremarkable. At puberty, however, 'typical' development failed to occur as his testes 'failed to normalise and remained small and undescended' (correspondence 11 February 2007). He remembers his main concern at that time was whether he would be able to have children when he grew older, and he was reassured by his doctor that everything would be fine. He grew tall, attaining a height of 6 feet, 9 inches at age fifteen, and had a smooth androgynous body form. In subsequent discussions, however, his doctor referred to him as a 'deficient male' (interview 19 June 2004), and he remembers reading in a biological textbook at high school that 'giants' are usually sterile (another of the mythologies, although David *is* in fact sterile).

In 1971, David broke an engagement to be married: his low sex drive and general lack of energy were problematic, but he rationalized it by admitting to bisexual relations. In his heart he knew at this stage that he was gay. In his twenties, David grew prominent breasts, and he was happy with them: 'I had beautiful breasts and a beautiful smooth body' (interview 19 June 2004). Investigation for low libido led to a karyotype test, and on diagnosis of his 47,XXY chromosomal configuration, David was placed on testosterone treatment without consultation or description of its effects. David knew he was taking male hormones, and indeed hoped for increased sex drive, but the other effects were almost immediate and not understood by him. He developed a beard, male-pattern baldness, and his physiology became hirsute. His prostrate began to grow and he had difficulty urinating (causing a problem which he has had now for twenty-two years). Once on testosterone, David's breasts reduced significantly, and he began to struggle with his feelings. He was unable to stop taking testosterone because its effect was so significant on his libido, and to stop would have been – he states – to have experienced permanent testicular 'atrophy' (interview 19 June 2004). After a long journey, and now in a 26-year gay relationship, David has come to be at peace with himself as an 'androgiant'. He is convinced that 47,XXY is an intersex condition because without hormone intervention 'our bodies look androgynous' (interview 19 June 2004).

Liam's Story

Liam was born in 1964 in the UK and now knows that he has a 47,XXY karyotype. His intersex condition is, however, different from those discussed in this chapter, but his story is located here as a foil to the certainties at work within the XXY and Klinefelter's community.

To doctors and parents alike, Liam appeared to be a healthy newborn baby boy and he was raised accordingly. What was not apparent was that Liam had a semi-formed uterus, plus one undescended testis and an ovary inside. His external genitalia appeared male, as his fused labia seemed to contain testes, and also covered the opening of his vagina. As Liam grew up, he describes his outward appearance as 'relatively normal' (interview 2 May 2004).

When male puberty failed to occur, Liam's parents took him to the family doctor, who initiated a series of tests to try to determine the cause. Liam remembers being suddenly quite acutely aware that 'something was wrong' (interview 2 May 2004) although he had felt content and comfortable during childhood. A Partial Androgen Insensitivity Syndrome diagnosis was made: it was an incomplete diagnosis, however, as Liam exhibited male-appearing external genitalia, but had partial internal organs of a female. Liam's doctor told him and his parents that in these cases the subject should always be assigned as female, and described to them how – if this had been discovered at birth – there would have been 'corrective' feminizing surgery. Liam was fourteen, and was being asked by his doctor to 'become a girl!!' (interview 2

May 2004). He describes how he was informed that if he decided not to go ahead with feminizing surgery, inevitably his life would be shorter, and he describes as 'spooky' the thought that 'if you don't do as they say, you die earlier' (interview 2 May 2004). Nevertheless, Liam could not countenance what was effectively a proposal for a sex change at fourteen. His relief at having a diagnosis for his absent puberty was overwhelmed by anxiety about what he should do next.

Liam was offered female hormones, and he agreed to take them from age fourteen onwards because the doctors said it would be easier medically for him, and that his body would prefer to be female than male. Liam recalls being deeply worried about what would happen when the female hormones began to take effect. Pressure for surgery continued from his doctors, and Liam's parents continued to deliberate in a kind of panic as to what to do for the best. There was a growing sense of urgency, and Liam was told that the decision about his future was to be made in the school holidays. Liam's mother sought advice at the Charing Cross Gender Identity Clinic, London, but there was little data available to reassure her or assist her with the decision to be made. Liam remembers that there was nothing on television, nothing in magazines, no Internet and just a taboo subject about which they kept quiet.

Liam's mother was supportive of him throughout this dilemma, although she blamed herself for Liam's condition. His father was shocked by the situation, but continued to offer Liam his support in whatever decision was to be made. Finally, Liam's parents asked that he make the 'daunting' (interview 2 May 2004) choice of whether to change sex or not. In hindsight, Liam believes he was lucky to have this control over his life, but at the time he found it a difficult and frightening decision to make. In order to cope, he rationalized his condition as somehow 'cool because it wasn't quite normal' (interview 2 May 2004). He spoke to no peers about the issue.

Liam decided that it would be easier to change over to being a woman, and wavered several times during the six months before surgery was booked to take place. During this period, he did not attend his original school, and a new school and female name were chosen. One month before surgery he cancelled. He then remembers a huge row ensuing during which he was asked why by his doctors and was told that they knew best what was good for him. Ultimately, however, the doctors admitted that they were unsure of the outcome of the proposed surgery, but that they were convinced that without it he 'wouldn't make thirty' (interview 2 May 2004). In this situation of uncertainty Liam refused to go ahead with surgery and refused to take any more female hormones. He felt that it would be unbearable to him to have his penis surgically removed, and that was his deciding factor. He notes that he certainly 'grew up a lot quicker having to think about this' (interview 2 May 2004).

Liam insisted on having testosterone treatment, and a male puberty unfolded almost immediately, during which his voice broke and he developed facial hair, although his hips remained large and his shoulders narrow. In his own mind, Liam decided that he was male. He did have doubts, but he didn't discuss them. He did think 'what if?' and 'what are you meant to be?', but he closed that down and got on with being a male. He continues to receive male hormone treatment to this day.

After his puberty settled down, an endocrinologist was appointed to Liam because there was evidence that the ovarian tissue inside was having an endocrine effect and secreting oestrogen. Liam's hormone receptors were not working well and were having difficulty accepting his testosterone treatment. Consequently, he was not virilizing as well as would have been expected. A full hysterectomy was offered, but Liam declined this, as he was keen to avoid major surgery. Events overtook him, however, because a build-up of internal fluid was diagnosed, and this was when further tests revealed that Liam had a partial uterus, a cervix and the top part of a vagina, but the opening, which was covered by his fused labia, had sealed up. Surgery was done to create a small opening through Liam's pelvic floor to allow the passage of the fluid, which was found to be menstrual. The surgery was carried out when Liam was twenty-three, and he reports that he still expels small quantities of menstrual blood irregularly. Subsequent genetic testing has shown Liam to have a 47,XXY karyotype, which he defines as 'partly female, with a male Y'. He describes his life now as 'living as a male, but with complications' (interview 2 May 2004).

The surgery had provided Liam with an opportunity to reconsider changing sex, and he did seriously think about doing so, but had decided that it all would have been too complicated. That being said, he states that he has often wondered about what his life would have been like if he had gone ahead with that: 'I often think "what if" ... [but] ... it has been a taboo subject for so long!' (Liam, interview 2 May 2004).

Liam has coped by being stoical: it just was the way it was, he had nothing to compare it to, and he 'just had to get on with it' (interview 2 May 2004). But Liam's story is extraordinary. He continued to live as a man, but to menstruate infrequently. He married, and he had children who were conceived naturally (indicating that his one testis is functional and the reproductive apparatus linking testis to penis is intact). The marriage broke down, and his children now live with him. There is not necessarily a direct comparison here with the case earlier of a 47,XXY *woman* who was a *mother* (Röttger et al. 2000), and clearly, the physiology in Liam's case is entirely different, with a mixture of anatomy inside which testifies to some more complex form of intersex than a singular 'genetic intersex'. Nevertheless, again we see the symbolic converse of the 'phallic female' operational in the 'menstruating man', and again can consider intersex as a potent challenge to binary 'norms' of sex and to cultural icons of 'the male' or 'the female'.

Liam admits that he has had difficulties with what he calls 'the female bit' (interview 2 May 2004) of himself, and yet he has wanted to keep his ovary working in spite of those difficulties. He believes that has been best for his healthy development, but he does not know what will happen if he experiences a menopause. Emotionally, the 'female bit' has always been at the back of his mind. He blames 'Nature' for these difficulties, but at the same time accepts what was 'Nature's intent'. He believes he was 'probably going to be a woman but kicked in as a man' (interview 2 May 2004) at some point in his development. Liam describes his life as a mix of turmoil and calm, and he admits that he ponders a great deal on how gender-divided society is. In his own mind, he does not assign himself to one or other gender, but he lives and presents as a man and a father. He would not wish to be called 'intersexed' on his birth certificate, and his main objection is how it gets mixed up with 'transsexual', which he has difficulty with.

Does he make a good 'bloke'? Liam suggests that he is 'more understanding and compassionate than most guys' (interview 2 May 2004) but he tends not to mix socially with many men. His condition is known by a very small number of close family members, and he receives their support. He is 'all for people understanding it more' (interview 2 May 2004), although he knows that he tends to conform to a stereotype of maleness in order to help people feel comfortable in his company.

Testosterone

Parental insistence that their child is essentially *masculine* was reiterated by a number of correspondents and interviewees, and frequently couched in gender stereotypical language: 'S's never been inclined to play with girl's toys' (Nic, interview 23 May 2004). Parental insistence is frequently that their child is also essentially *male*: 'we have been told it only takes one y to make him male' (K, correspondence 21 May 2004). Nevertheless, boys whose karyotypes are known to be XXY or variant are carefully monitored for indicators of how much personal testosterone their bodies begin to secrete as they approach puberty.

Boys with the XY karyotype typically experience testicular enlargement and then the growth of pubic hair between ages nine and fourteen, with development of underarm and facial hair, and deepening of the voice, most frequently occurring between the ages thirteen and sixteen (Hambley 1999). Generally, children with XXY and variant karyotypes enter puberty straightforwardly, without delay of physical maturity – underarm hair can develop, the voice can deepen and the penis can begin to grow (Ratcliffe 1982). Marie's son, for example, developed pubic hair at age ten, but then failed to carry through with his pubescent changes (interview 11 May 2004), and this falling off of pubescent change is typical (Klinefelter Syndrome and Associates 2004). The usual clinical approach is to provide the individual with synthetic testosterone at and beyond puberty (Ratcliffe and Paul 1986; Bock 1993) via intra-muscular injections, skin patch delivery, gels, implanted pellets or oral pills. Indeed such treatment can avoid or reverse some of the features associated with the pubescent development of Klinefelter's Syndrome (Sørensen *et al.* 1981). For example, breast development is minimized; growth of the penis and scrotum is promoted; face and body hair develops (Nielsen undated); lean body mass and muscle formation are noticeable with reduced 'female-form' body fat (Wayne and Hellstrom undated); the voice deepens. Testes almost always remain small, however, with no increase of personal testosterone secretion (Klinefelter's Syndrome Association 2004), and their diminished size is one of the diagnostic signs related to XXY karyotype. With testosterone therapy there can also be improvement of mood in relation to anger, confusion, depression, lack of confidence and fatigue, which are frequently reported as part of the experiences of these individuals (Bock 1993):

> I was a paranoid kinda guy before I was put onto hormone therapy ... I was anxious and panicky all the time. I was weak and didn't have any energy. Just kept sleeping ... so depressed I did think I should just end it ...
>
> When they took me into hospital cos I was so ill the doctors realised I had Klinefelters and that I had not been given hormones before ... this was a big breakthrough and with the hormones things really began to change for the better. I got energy, stopped panicking and worrying and being afraid of life. It made just this really big difference to me. (Steven, correspondence 12 June 2003)

Reported other benefits include clarity of thought, better retention of details, higher degree of endurance, lessening of hand tremors, better self-control, greater sexual drive, improved verbal fluency and an easier time in school and work settings (Wayne and Hellstrom undated; Sørensen *et al.* 1981):

> I find the treatment to be good and have found that it has made me feel like a different person. This is a good thing. My learning and thought processes have become stronger. I am a much more outgoing person and I have become more of a leader. (Stefan, correspondence 17 May 2004)

Improvements in bone density, and lowering of the risk of osteoporosis associated with poor bone mass, have also been realized with testosterone therapy (Wayne and Hellstrom undated), and there are indications that the varicose veins and ulceration on the legs which are more frequent than expected in elderly persons with Klinefelter's Syndrome may be prevented by continuous testosterone treatment from puberty (Nielsen undated).

It is important to note here that testosterone therapy also presents some health issues. These include potential liver damage especially with the high doses associated with oral administration, as well as heart problems, hypertension and the build-up of salt and fluid in the body. There can be an increased risk of narrowing of the walls of the arteries through fat built-up, which then increases the risk of a stroke, and there is also the possibility of higher than normal concentration of red blood cells in the blood and slight risk of problems for individuals undergoing anti-coagulant treatment. It is thought that testosterone therapy *may* also result in prostate enlargement or BHP (as experienced by David – who has had two prostate reduction surgeries in the last three years), which is also common in typical XY karyotype males, affecting more than 50 per cent of men in their sixties (Wayne and Hellstrom undated; Bock 1993; David, correspondence 11 February 2007). There can also be short-term problems including aggression, psychosis and mania associated with getting the dosage exactly correct since the amount of testosterone produced in the testes by adult males with Klinefelter's Syndrome varies between individuals. There can be a tendency to mood swings involving temper 'spikes' and cyclical depression, and sex drive fluctuations can also be related to the method of administration of the hormone.

Apart from these negative health implications of testosterone therapy, some advocates of the therapy indicate that testosterone is not a 'universal panacea' even for those identifying as male, and that its use is problematic for those individuals with XXY and variant karyotypes who do not identify as male (Hambley 1999). Bock (1993) writes that there must be a positive decision on the part of the subject to stick to the regular routine of self-administration, and suggests that most physicians are now sensitive enough not to *insist* on testosterone treatment use for adolescents. However, in parent interviewees there was no questioning of the benefits of the treatment, either in terms of health implications or in relation to the virilizing effects of the hormone. In fact, there was a sense of absolute trust in the rightness of the treatment: 'His body will probably not produce enough testosterone once he reaches puberty and into adulthood. So we will be visiting an endocrinologist soon to work on assistance with that' (Debra, correspondence 25 May 2004).

Admittedly, for those children and adolescents who are not diagnosed as having a chromosomal variation, and who are not given testosterone as treatment, there can be many difficulties. Tony recounts that at that time for him in his development 'life was hell' (interview 1 May 2004). When puberty should have precipitated his voice deepening, his physical maturation, testicular enlargement, beard and body hair growth, Tony remained physically immature, with unbroken voice and no hair growth change. On top of this, he experienced what felt like daily hormone fluctuations, swinging from anger to upset, and now relates those to the kinds of hormonal mood fluctuations many women experience. Arguably these difficulties are as much to do with not knowing what is causing them, as with the absence of synthetic testosterone as an option for treatment. That being the case, the distress caused to undiagnosed and untreated individuals with these chromosome variations must not be underestimated.

Jonathan self-diagnosed at age forty-six when his testicles, which had previously been described by his doctor as 'especially small', were found to be atrophying or shrinking. He recalls 'panicing [sic] a lot over whether this ment [sic] my penis would be smaller' (correspondence 3 May 2001). Jonathan had been experiencing very low libido and erectile dysfunction for some years – 'I didn't want sex and I didn't even want to want it' (correspondence 5 May 2001) – and had never had a full sexual relationship. For a person like Jonathan, who identifies as a man, but who has experienced difficulty operating successfully as 'sufficiently male', testosterone treatment would most probably have helped immensely. In fact, Jonathan emigrated and contact was terminated. For someone whose sense of self was less assuredly male, or who had not been conditioned and nurtured through male-bias, testosterone treatment would arguably represent a grossly incorrect assignment of sex.

Tony's Story

Tony left school just before his sixteenth birthday, and began to work in the company of men who were slightly older than him. Their reassurances that he 'still had a couple of years' to start shaving and for his voice to break ran out in his early twenties, when he was beginning to feel that 'something was seriously wrong' (correspondence 1 May 2004). Nielson (undated) clearly states that it is still often the case that young people with XXY karyotypes and variations are often provided with poor information too late, and that this causes unnecessary anxiety and suffering for many people in this position.

At twenty-three, in spite of his difficulties, Tony married a woman who already had two children. After a year of marriage, he went for a routine sperm test since they had not managed to conceive. The results of this test indicated that the comparatively few sperm Tony did produce were dead, and, shortly afterwards, his marriage ended. This was a very bleak time for a young person who was not developing physically as typical, whose sperm was insufficient and of poor quality and whose marriage had fallen apart ostensibly as a result of his lack of 'maleness'.

The main route for *adult* diagnosis of the XXY and variant karyotype is when men who otherwise may have few or no Klinefelter's Syndrome symptoms (such as significant breast growth) experience problems when trying to conceive a child (Bojeson 2003). While adults like Tony are capable of completely normal sexual function including erection and ejaculation, they are almost universally unable to conceive children due to failure to produce enough sperm or sperm of sufficient quality (Ratcliffe and Paul 1986). Before puberty the testes will have a lower than average number of sperm-producing cells, but during puberty a process of shrinkage, scarring and damage occurs which results in sterility (Klinefelter Organisation 2004). Usually only a few thousand sperms per ejaculation are present compared with the 200 million sperms per ejaculation in males with typical XY chromosomes (Nielsen undated). Inability to conceive cannot be resolved by testosterone therapy. While some of those with XY/XXY mosaics may have enough typically functioning cells in the testes to be *potentially fertile*, the majority who are non-mosaic are sterile. Nielsen (undated) documents six genetically verified cases of 46,XY/47,XXY mosaic fathers, and it is notable that sophisticated, though costly, methods of innovative reproductive technology, such as sperm extraction for *in vitro* fertilization, are beginning to allow some persons with XXY karyotype to biologically conceive a child:

> We were trying for a baby in the late 1990s … and we had no idea that my partner was a 47 XXY until then when it was diagnosed because we could not get pregnant … we were lucky to find a private physician to try out this testicular sperm extraction and ovum injection procedure …
>
> We had also considered sperm donation but we had two rounds of this treatment and our natural son was born in 2001! (Michelle, correspondence 13 June 2005)

Others have less happy outcomes in respect of their adult diagnosis and fertility. Having learned that he was sterile at age twenty-four, but as yet uninformed of his karyotype anomaly, Tony received a subsequent medical examination during which he was told that he would require to be 'castrated' (interview 1 May 2004). It was some time before he was given a karyotype test, which indicated that he was an 'XX male' (interview 1 May 2004), and during the interval he had a nervous breakdown. No support was offered other than an endocrinology appointment at Hope Hospital, Manchester, which he has attended every year since he began testosterone therapy. Tony's greatest sadness is that he has not had children and he still finds that hard although he has come to terms with his karyotype. He is currently receiving counselling to help him deal with his infertility. For a male-identified person, infertility, threatened castration, an XX karyotype with a 'bit of y chromosome in there somewhere' all present tremendous challenges to one's sense of maleness. Relating back to the strong assertions of male potency by many Klinefelter Syndrome support organizations, and many within the 'Klinefelter's Syndrome community', one can see how these assertions become a way of coping with those challenges. Problematically, they also serve to normalize

how those with Klinefelter's Syndrome and sex chromosome variations are
allowed to look and act.

Concluding Comments

What do variations in sex chromosomes mean for the sexing of human bodies?

Just as *anatomical* sex is signalled genitally and internally, as well as through
particular secondary bodily characteristics, and has been shown to be sometimes ambiguous, so too can be *genetic* sex. It is apparent that a number of signifiers of sex are in operation, and they are either in tandem (usually), out of
alignment or in some way 'atypical'. Clearly, genetic sex is not always exclusively binary, and there are sex chromosome anomalies that effectively challenge normative configurations of male and female karyotypes.

In XXY karyotype and its variants, infants generally look like XY infants
(that is, they have male-pattern genitalia, which may be small, and testes may
on occasion be undescended). These infants are named and raised as boys
whether their chromosomal composition has been diagnosed or not (and in
childhood it is generally the learning and behavioural issues associated with
the karyotype which leads to pre-puberty diagnosis). Adults with Klinefelter's
Syndrome variously exhibit all, some or none of the following physical characteristics: enlarged breasts with pear-shaped body, low muscle mass, low
levels of testosterone secretion, sparse facial and body hair, male-patterned
genitalia, small testes. Most of these individuals begin testosterone therapy on
diagnosis and have their breasts – if these develop – surgically removed. The
vast majority of them, almost universally, are unable to produce sufficient or
healthy sperm, and are infertile. Most adults with XXY or variant/mosaic
karyotypes and/or Klinefelter's Syndrome identify as male, and live in the
world contentedly and assuredly as men. However, there are individuals with
XXY karyotypes who do not have a male phenotype; who do not have internal
male reproductive organs; and/or who do not identify themselves as essentially
male.

Sex chromosome variations present difficult issues for parents bringing up
children. Little boys are often expected, even subconsciously, to be 'little
men': active, confident, sporty and increasingly independent. Moreover, little
boys (as potential 'little men') can receive societal signals that thinness or tendency to fat, coupled with poor strength or lack of sportiness are less than masculine. Parents have embedded expectations of their children, which may be
fundamentally shaken by a sex chromosome variation diagnosis.

In respect of the question as to why 47,XXY, its variations and its associated syndrome are being discussed in a book concerned with intersex, there is
undoubtedly an issue of sexual development here regarding the achievement
of 'adult maleness', and this warrants some discussion. If maleness is an

anatomical state of the newborn, then *some* newborns with 47,XXY karyotypes are called male and raised as male, have internal testes and undervirilized genitalia. Consequently, it is reasonable to at least consider that their anatomy is atypical for a boy (as is their karyotype atypical). What that (sometimes) anatomical and (always) chromosomal variation means for maleness (whatever that slippery term means) or for intersex (whatever that less known term means) is open for discussion. If maleness is a developmental state, which includes 'satisfactory' transition through puberty into a particular state of physical maturity, then those with 47,XXY and/or Klinefelter's Syndrome do not universally achieve that state without testosterone assistance. What that incomplete, variable and challenging pubescent transition means for maleness (that slippery term again) or for intersex (that unknown again) is once again open for discussion. Finally, if maleness is a condition of how the individual feels or chooses to understand their body, then, again, that is another matter ...

Final wise words go to Belle, mother of a then thirteen months old child with a 47,XXY karyotype diagnosed *in utero*:

> I am the mom of a tiny xxy boy ... I was blown away when I found out there are people who consider themselves not males or females. That was a real surprise, a real shock to me ...
>
> I was half scared to death that my baby would be in the middle like them ... I did not know what to do about that and I'm supposed to fix it all?
>
> Now I guess I'm ok whatever he turns out to be. I cannot do anything about that whatever, so I just keep focused on making him happy. Best ways for a mom, right??
> (correspondence 2 September 2003)

CHAPTER 13

Sex Chromosome Variations: Turner Syndrome

An Intersex Condition?

On 27 April 2004, Arlene Smyth, Executive Officer of the Turner Syndrome Support Society (UK), responded to a general research enquiry sent out by this author to support groups for Turner (or Turner's) Syndrome. Her query was direct: why were *women* who have Turner Syndrome being included in a book about *intersex*? She asserted that, in her experience of working with *women* who have Turner Syndrome, she had never met anybody expressing themselves as anything other than *female*, and she objected to Turner Syndrome being included with intersex conditions like Androgen Insensitivity Syndrome and Congenital Adrenal Hyperplasia:

> girls who have Turner Syndrome are girls, and they grow up to be women … our members do not like to be grouped as 'Intersex' as this is just not the case. Only women can have Turner Syndrome so there is no question of their sex. (Smyth, correspondence 28 April 2004)

US American endocrinologist Dr Henry Turner gave his name to Turner Syndrome when, in 1938, he defined a syndrome physically manifesting in apparent women as short stature, lack of certain female sexual characteristics, neck-webbing and wide carrying angle of the arms. These characteristics had also been noted in 1930 by German paediatrician Otto Ullrich. When, in 1959, it became possible to analyse human chromosomes, it was discovered that these physical conditions were accompanied by the absence of all or part of one of the X chromosomes from some or all of the cells of the body.

Arlene Smyth acknowledged that some women who have Turner Syndrome don't feel as 'feminine' as they might, but this, she urged, was due to their non-functioning ovaries and resultant lack of oestrogen, the hormone that stimulates the development of female sexual characteristics and controls the female reproductive cycle. Smyth defended her organization's members against claims in press articles and television programmes that women who have Turner Syndrome are merely 'flat-chested with no periods', or even not women at all, and she indicated that hormone replacement therapy was most successful as a treatment. Smyth concluded that she 'deeply objected to being lumped in' with intersex (interview 27 April 2004). Fausto-Sterling, however, defines Turner Syndrome as both a 'common [type] of intersexuality' and an 'unusual chromosome composition' with 'females lacking a second X chromosome' (2000: 51–52). She configures it as a sex chromosome anomaly in the same vein as Klinefelter's Syndrome: where typical male and female karyotypes are XY and XX respectively, females who have Turner Syndrome – *and Fausto-Sterling names them as female* – have one intact X chromosome, with the other being lost or damaged somewhere in the cell division that follows conception (Turner Syndrome Society of the United States).

Karyotype, Symptoms and Frequency

Both the Turner Syndrome Support Society (UK) and the Turner Syndrome Society of the United States maintain that the syndrome occurs approximately once in every 2,000 live *female* births. The Magic Foundation suggests that occurrence is less frequent, proposing a rate of 1 in 3,000 live *female* births, and noting that approximately 98 per cent of pregnancies with Turner Syndrome abort spontaneously, while approximately 10 per cent of spontaneously aborted foetuses are found to have Turner Syndrome (Robinson 1990). Since there are about 29 million girls/women in Britain, Nielsen (1991) infers that there will be about 14,000 in Britain with Turner Syndrome.

The karyotype for classic Turner Syndrome is 45,X (or XO). That is, the second X chromosome – which would be present in a typical female – is simply absent. Classic Turner Syndrome is experienced by about 50 per cent of girls/women who have the syndrome, and they tend to exhibit the more noticeable features of the syndrome that allow diagnosis by scan *in utero* or by visible inspection after birth (for example, fluid around the neck or in the extremities). Chorionic villus sampling of the placental tissue or amniocentesis testing of the amniotic fluid around the foetus during pregnancy will also reveal a Turner Syndrome karyotype in a foetus. A second X chromosome appears in 20–30 per cent of those who have Turner Syndrome, but it is altered or incomplete (Turner Syndrome Society of the United States), while around 30 per cent have Turner Syndrome mosaic in which the second X chromosome is absent from only *some* of the cells, with other cells containing regular female XX chromosomes (46,XX/45,X). Turner Syndrome mosaics are more difficult to diagnose as these individuals have fewer Turner Syndrome features (since only some body cells are affected) than those who have non-mosaic Turner Syndrome. Finally, a very small percentage of those who have a 45,XO mosaic have some Y chromosome material in their cells (karyotype 46,XY/45,XO). This is otherwise known as one manifestation of Mixed Gonadal Dysgenesis (Fausto-Sterling 2000; Kim *et al.* 2002), and can, in some cases, indicate the presence of an internal gonadal structure, for example, a testis on one side and a streak gonad on the other (Kim *et al.* 2002). There is evidence that in these very rare cases there is a risk of malignant cell change if dysgenetic or streak gonads are present, and in such cases, these are generally removed on diagnosis (Statement of the British Association of Paediatric Surgeons Working Party on the Surgical Management of Children Born with Ambiguous Genitalia 2001; Elsheikh *et al.* 2002). Importantly, however, while these instances might share a 45,XO-type mosaic, they are not directly associated with Turner Syndrome.

The cause(s) of the chromosomal anomaly of Turner Syndrome are unknown, and no maternal risk factors are indicated. Notably, Turner Syndrome has a highly variable collection of characteristics, which may be present in the individual infant, girl or woman. Those that may be detected or diagnosed in infancy include extra folds of skin around the neck; puffiness of hands and feet; broad chest and widely spaced and sometimes inverted nipples; droopy eyelids; low hairline and low-set ears; nails that are narrow and curve upwards; short fourth toe and short fingers; curvature of the spine; and an increased risk of congenital hip displacement. A high arched palate or a small lower jaw, leading sometimes to feeding problems, often provides a diagnostic route in infancy, as do angled arms where it is difficult to straighten the elbow, narrowed or constricted aortal blood vessel in the heart and heart structure problems (Sybert undated). Girls and women who have Turner Syndrome can tend to have middle ear infections; hearing problems in adulthood; tendency towards short-sightedness, congenital glaucoma, wandering or crossed eye, red/green colour-blindness; slightly higher risk of diabetes and thyroid disorders; and moles. Approximately 10 per cent have high blood pressure (Sybert undated), and 33–50 per cent have renal anomalies such as a horseshoe-shaped kidney and urinary tract problems (The Magic Foundation). With the exception of a small group of individuals with a Turner Syndrome mosaic including a particular ring-formed chromosome, who can suffer severe intellectual impairment, people who have Turner Syndrome exhibit the normal range of intelligence. Children who have Turner Syndrome, however, can experience behavioural problems; non-verbal learning difficulties, spatial awareness problems; temporal processing and attention difficulties (Tecosky-Feldmane undated); gross and fine motor dysfunction (The Magic Foundation); and social cognition problems. *However, none of these is an intersex issue.*

The two *main* clinical features of Turner Syndrome (which are almost always present) are shorter than average stature (from birth onwards) and non-functioning ovaries. Girls who undergo hormone treatment for growth have a good chance of reaching the lower ranges of normal height for an adult female. Turner Syndrome is often formally diagnosed in early childhood when an individual's growth slows down, or at puberty when pubertal growth spurt, breast growth and/or menstruation fail to occur. In 10–15 per cent of girls with classic Turner Syndrome, and about 30 per cent of girls with Turner Syndrome mosaic, breast development and/or menstruation *do* occur (Nielsen 1993), but subsequently, at some early point, the ovaries fail, hormone production ceases, menstruation stops and an early menopause is experienced. This pattern of development allows another, less common, route for adult diagnosis.

Non-functioning Ovaries

While 90 per cent of women with Turner Syndrome have non-functioning ovaries, their Fallopian tubes, vagina and uterus are usually typical, although Preves (2003) maintains that the uterus and vagina can also be underdeveloped. The ovaries produce eggs and the hormones necessary for the development of secondary sexual characteristics, and oestrogen therapy is used strategically to induce breast and feminine body development, to ensure proper mineralization of bones, to help prevent early onset osteoporosis and – with progesterone – to cause periods to start. The great majority of girls who have Turner Syndrome do not start periods spontaneously. Oestrogen is also used to support satisfactory sexual activity as its absence can cause dryness and irritation in the vagina. Oestrogen therapy is normally continued until around age fifty when menopause would typically take place in a woman without Turner Syndrome.

Generally, contemporary treatments are successful in allowing many girls who have Turner Syndrome to begin puberty at the same time as their peers. Sexual function is normal in women with Turner Syndrome who receive hormone treatment, and they can be expected to have a healthy and satisfying sexual life. Fertility, however, is around 1–2 per cent, with the few pregnancies that do occur tending to be in women with 45,X and 45,X/46,XX karyotypes (Swapp *et al.* 1989; Nielsen 1993). There is a high risk of genetic problems and of miscarriage in cases of spontaneous pregnancy for mothers with Turner Syndrome, and – as for women without Turner Syndrome – pregnancy is possible using donor egg and IVF treatment.

Intersex Issues

The Turner Syndrome Support Society (UK) emphasize that 'the majority of girls and women with Turner Syndrome are healthy, happy and lead normal lives'. But, they also acknowledge that some girls with Turner Syndrome are bullied, feel isolated and suffer from low self-esteem as a result of the syndrome. Girls with Turner Syndrome can tend to behave more immaturely, have difficulty concentrating and problems with overactivity, all of which can affect their relationships with other children. Teenagers with Turner Syndrome tend, moreover, towards immaturity, anxiety, depression and social withdrawal, beginning dating and sexual activity later than other girls. There is a noted tendency for health care of girls with Turner Syndrome to drop away on reaching adulthood (Conway *et al.* 2000a). Undoubtedly, the problems of sexual maturation and infertility which are part of Turner Syndrome, the increased risk of malignancy associated with hormone replacement therapies, and the societal tendency to misunderstand or wilfully misread this complex syndrome, provide particular challenges for girls and women with Turner Syndrome. *However, none of these is an intersex issue.*

Arguably, Turner Syndrome gets included with intersex for a combination of reasons. First, the very small percentage of those with Turner Syndrome who have some Y chromosome material in their cells threaten the neat culturally acceptable binary of XX and XY sex in the same way that Klinefelter's 'extra X' does. The tiny whisper of Y that *might* be in all or some of the cells of a woman with Turner Syndrome is enough to destabilize a social-cultural understanding of her (in *some* registers) as a 'pure female'. Because 'female impurity' is culturally intolerable, women with Turner Syndrome are then shifted collectively (*by some commentators*) into the category of intersex. Where there is loss or damage to the second X chromosome of some women with Turner Syndrome, the charge alters from 'impure female' to 'incomplete female'. The same cultural shift then arguably applies. This, of course, is highly problematic from the viewpoint of intersexed people, for whom the notion of being either 'lesser' – as is implied by the resistance in Turner Syndrome support groups to any intersex labelling – or 'impure' – as is implied by the idea of a 'tainting' Y chromosome – is offensive. Nevertheless, there is an argument that women who have Turner Syndrome are labelled intersexed for these reasons. Further, where women are still valued via their fertility, women with Turner Syndrome present a female that is resolutely, if not uniformly, different to that norm. Women with Turner Syndrome require hormone treatment intervention to start and maintain the complex developments associated with female maturation, and, even with that, fail almost totally to achieve the 'ultimate social-culturally perceived goal' of 'whole women' – motherhood. But so do women without Turner Syndrome.

In combination, these factors help nudge women with Turner Syndrome nominally into the intersex categorization proposed by Fausto-Sterling (2000). Sarah Creighton was, however, more circumspect (interview 9 February 2006). She acknowledged that Turner Syndrome exhibits an issue of sex differentiation, but she does not include the syndrome as intersex. Arlene Smyth insisted that women with Turner Syndrome are exactly that, *women* (interview 27 April 2004), and this author is inclined to agree ...

CHAPTER 14

Conclusion

> Because variation occurs independently at many ... levels, the total number of biolog-
> ical/psychological possibilities will be very large indeed. The study of intersexuality
> forces us far from the view that humanity comes in two mutually exclusive sexes, readily
> distinguishable at birth by the presence or absence of external genitalia.
>
> Kipnis and Diamond, *Pediatric Ethics and the Surgical Assignment of Sex*

While the activities of intersexuals, advocacy groups and interested health-care professionals over the past decade have raised the profile of intersex, it is still not much discussed. The secrecy and stigma surrounding it tend to suggest that it is extremely rare. While exact definitions of intersex vary, clinical knowledge of some conditions remains significantly incomplete, long-term data collection is in disarray and frequencies fluctuate in different populations, general statistical evidence proposes that intersex in its various forms may affect a significant 1 in 2,000 people.

The term 'intersex' covers a complex range of manifestations in individuals, with genital ambiguity being the most obvious. Ambiguous genitalia are less common, however, than intersex at genetic level, in the gonads, in hormonal influences and balances and/or in the internal reproductive apparatus. In this text, a variety of intersex presentations and combinations have been described, and they are literally extra-ordinary. For example, there are genetic females with an underdeveloped or atypically formed uterus, oviducts, sometimes without a vagina, who have an enlarged clitoris resembling a hypospadic penis, and whose labia have so fused that they appear like a split scrotum. This is the archetypal 'phallic female'. Or there are poorly virilized genetic males with soft or undescended testes, a microphallus, a divided scrotum that resembles labia, and a hypospadic urethra exiting in the scrotum or perineum. This is the 'failed male' archetype. Moreover, there are apparent males who grow breasts at puberty, have no facial or body hair, who combine curvaceous hips with a very small penis, undescended testes and an inability to produce sperm ('boys with breasts'). And there are apparent females who progressively virilize through childhood and adolescence, developing a phallus and facial hair at puberty, but failing to menstruate or grow breasts ('girls with male gonads').

There are those who have wildly disarranged genitalia with urinary and ejacu-latory openings that are multiple and misplaced in the anus and rectum (the 'monstrous-feminine', the 'monstrous-masculine') or there are apparent males who menstruate at puberty through a vaginal introitus hidden by fused labia resembling a scrotum ('menstruating men'). There are individuals who combine one testis and one ovary, or who have various combinations of ovary, testis, ovotestis/ovotestes and/or streak gonads ('gonadal intersexuals'), and there are those who have an unusual karyotype or a sex chromosome mosaic ('genetic intersexuals').

These are indeed bodies extra to the ordinary, and their biodiverse configu-rations of anatomy contradict a Western conservative cultural belief in sex as a mutually distinctive, complementary and naturalized binary, and bodies as stable and essentially absolute. One can see why the complex manifestations of intersex described above trouble and affront, seeming 'queer' and disre-spectful to 'the hegemonic natural order'.

But the challenge of such bodies has arguably simultaneously relegated them to the position of chaotic deviants, biological abnormalities, cultural horrors, dysfunctional monsters and unclean sub-humans. This relegation in turn allows the articulation of intersexuals as the symbolic 'other', and permits their (actual) erasure by silence, secrecy, shame and stigma, and their (actual and symbolic) destruction by the 'normalizing' act of surgical/hormonal sex assignment as and when they manifest. In the symbolic order, there is no place for the archetypes named above, and culture – symbolically but undoubtedly – demands their radical exclusion.

Without long-term evaluative consideration, the kinds of actions taken to 'normalize' and 'correct' intersex bodies remain substantially unchallenged (although there are slow movements towards non-surgical management, or more considered approaches even within the interventionist camp). But the anecdotal evidence of adult intersexuals in the medical West confirms that pro-cedures causing permanent alteration of the body are used with impunity, and without subject reflection or consent. This has caused (for at least some) a range of substantial and fundamental physical, sexual, emotional and psycho-logical traumas. Treatments continue to be focused on infant genitalia, the outward signage of sex, and consequently there is a tendency to understand intersex as equalling ambiguous genitalia only, whereas symptoms of intersex emerge inside and outside the body and at anatomical, gonadal, endocrinal and genetic sites. Adult choices for intersexed individuals are limited by treat-ments provided in infancy and childhood, and there are growing numbers of intersexuals who are testifying in adulthood to their dissatisfaction with treat-ment and their inability to recover their 'body of origin'.

If altering intersex was necessary for the maintenance of infant health or preservation of life, it could not be argued against. Medical decisions are after all taken daily for interventionist treatment of health-threatening conditions in infants and children. What arguably colours the treatment protocols applied to intersexed babies is their bodies' perceived disregard for culture's neat sex binary. Why is intersex so shocking? Children with cleft lips challenge collective appreciation of facial configurations, as do children with Down Syndrome. Children with physical disabilities challenge collective understanding of the body's form. While culture may not always respond with sympathy and understanding to such children, arguably the intersexed child horrifies culture in a much more fundamental and powerful way than these others. The haste with which cosmetic surgeries are carried out on ambiguous genitalia, the rapidity with which only slightly risky gonads are whisked away when they are not in tandem with the child's apparent sex, the speed with which hormones are used to thwart or encourage sex signifiers at puberty to correlate with determined sex, all support a theory that this is emergency, reactive terror at work.

Human culture, for all our technological wizardry, microsurgical magic and social sophistication, is only a short evolutionary step away from the superstition and fear of darker days. Freud's uncanny works by reminding us through the familiar but long forgotten mechanism of the ancient terrors we encountered in our caves. Monsters, ghouls, creatures conceived of two distinct species, the fright and the freak. The 'phallic female', for example, is a little girl with Congenital Adrenal Hyperplasia on the one hand and a terrible symbol representing abjection, loss and horror on the other. We – lay-people, parents, physicians and surgeons – dance between the little girl and the terrible symbol, translating gibbering ranting terror into rational authoritative medical decisions 'for the good of the child'.

That child loses her sexual sensitivity, her erotic capability, her larger than typical phallus, because we – collectively – cannot cope with her virilized clitoris and its challenge to what a girl should be (and by default what a boy should be). Concern for the social embarrassment of the child is miniscule compared to this. The taboo of intersex dehumanizes her by temporarily erasing her humanity – she becomes configured as an archetypal monstrosity, a pathological bastardized mixture of male and female, and is dealt with accordingly. We know her parents love her, and her clinician cares for her as a good health professional, but in archetypal and symbolic terms, this girl is 'not proper', and in the currency of the Victorian sexual mores that continue to inform our culture, she is impure and coarse (characteristics not deemed appropriate to the feminine gender). Moreover, she hints – even as an infant – at the lesbian grotesque (still enormously marginalized) by seemingly privileging her immature protruding phallus over her ('appropriately heterosexual') vaginal receipt of a penis when she matures. She overtly represents the heady raw pleasure of a mega-clitoris in a culture still not comfortable with excessive female sexuality. She – even as a baby – is a symbolic castrator (whose phallus has she taken?). And she is unnatural (where nature is not all that manifests, but all that is deemed to be 'naturally' manifesting). The anxiety engendered by the 'phallic female' is mythic in meaning and proportion, and there is mythic symmetry in the culturally condoned and medically sanctioned castration by surgery, which is her most usual treatment.

This is the *clitoris*, a part of the human body – including the intersexed human body – with the sole purpose of sexual pleasure, an organ of great erotic sensitivity, erectile capability and nervous complexity. A larger than typical clitoris is not hazardous to health, and its removal – by whichever surgical technique – is predicated on cultural contempt for the little girl with genital virilization. How else could it be acceptable to perpetuate practices that can cause pain on engorgement, can minimize or eradicate erotic sensitivity and orgasmic function, can diminish libido and sexual confidence, and which have no guarantee of aesthetic satisfaction?

We know that to be a small girl with a visibly different genital configuration is not straightforward, that children and adults can be cruel and that genitals are charged like no other body part (although an incomplete or absent vagina is much more easily hidden from these critics than is a virilized clitoris). We know that parents suffer terribly on behalf of children whom they wish to preserve from the cruelties they may encounter, and we also know that parents struggle – sometimes unsuccessfully – with anxiety, shame, guilt and revulsion in the face of their child's intersexuality. We know that clinicians believe the technological advances medical science has made enable them to make radical alterations to bodies in the belief that these changes are a positive improvement for a child. But we also know that there are growing numbers of adult women whose clitorises were excised, recessed, shaved or removed, whose psychosexual and psychosocial development have been dramatically affected and who mourn in fury and despair at their loss.

The acceptable phallus, culture dictates, is not an enlarged clitoris on a girl, but is the absolutist and exclusive symbol of the essential male. The penis must be cosmetically acceptable and of appropriate dimension, its various functions – separate carriage of semen and urine exiting at the tip, erectile capability and ability to be flaccid, sexual sensitivity and penetrative ability – must be wholly intact, and urination while standing should be possible. This is what characterizes maleness, but it does not always characterize males. The genetic male with Complete Androgen Insensitivity Syndrome will appear so essentially female at birth that 'she' will be raised as the girl she resembles, while her Partial AIS 'genetic brother' will be incompletely virilized and therefore be deemed not sufficiently endowed to pursue his genetic sex. 'His' testes and penis will be surgically removed because 'he' is a 'failed male', and because – as a girl – 'she' must not have testes.

We know that incomplete virilization is terribly difficult for a boy when the 'big penis' is a formidable cultural icon, but males with damaged, small or even absent penises (or small or poorly developed testes) have lived sexually active, and sexually fulfilled, lives without being sex assigned as female. While a micropenis may not be culture's icon, its erectile and orgasmic function, and the subject's potential fertility, is likely to be as good as with a larger penis. Phalloplasty, while not ideal, is an option in adulthood, as is feminizing genital surgery.

The challenges to the 'iconic male' in the spectrum of intersex are many – there are many opportunities to be a 'failed male'. Yet, the man who menstruates occasionally is also a father and his infrequent bleeds remind him alone of his intersexed status. Symbolically, he is a failure, a horrific and disturbing sexual anomaly, and an aberrant man. Actually, he successfully aligns his gender identification as male with chromosomal and anatomical atypicality. Symbolically too, the 'boy with breasts', victimized for his male failure, has survived his personal threat to the hegemony of binary sex. Internal testes and undervirilized genitalia, non-XY karyotype, even breasts and menstruation, will not erase maleness if the subject's gender identification is male. Nor will feminizing surgery, oestrogen treatment or gonadectomy. Rather, they will mutilate, hurt and confuse that subject in a fundamental and irreversible way.

The argument is not for the ultimate preservation of enlarged clitorises and micropenises – because the issues of intersex treatment are complicated and need individual assessment. Rather, the argument is for dispassionate, prudent, cautious management when a child is born visibly intersexed, with ambiguous genitalia; where a child is found to be intersexed via karyotyping, ultrasound internal investigation or endocrine exploration; or where he or she develops symptoms of intersex during childhood or adolescence. If the child's gender identity or predisposition is at least partially formed *in utero* as seems to be the case, then the infant is not psychosexually neutral when born, but in fact has a fixed psychosexual bias. That infant, however, is incapable of expressing its bias until sometime into childhood, through social and environmental influence, and through the additional physical and hormonal changes of puberty (which will have been predetermined *in utero*). The appearance of the infant's genitalia, its internal anatomy, its hormone responses, its gonadal configuration or even its karyotype cannot give a full picture of the gender identification of the child (as it cannot for non-intersexed infants either). The child will know its gender and will grow to articulate it.

Consequently, to permanently alter that child where there is no threat to health is to wrongly close down its possibilities to somatically illustrate its own essential gender identification when it is capable of doing so. Surgery and hormonal treatment will alter the somatic presentation but will not adjust the gender identification of the subject, and because for the intersexed harmony between gender identity and the sex assigned is the desired conclusion, a non-surgical, non-endocrinal approach must be preferred, at least until adolescence. This approach leaves open the possibility that the person can express his/her gender identity, and that can inform subsequent sex assignment.

This then in turn requires a family, a physician and a community to deal with the difficult challenge of intersex in real terms and not run screaming towards the cave. That is, while we acknowledge that Western culture operates in a binary *gender* system of males and females, men and women, feminine and masculine, *sex* does not align exactly to that. Intersex evidences that *sex* is constructed of multiple variations on binary themes. Where all characteristics are in alignment, male or female is indicated. Where characteristics are not aligned, the extra-ordinary – but nevertheless real – variations of intersex are present and that subject, *gender* identifying as male or female, *gender* role playing as masculine or feminine, is not capable of inclusion in a binary *sex* framework.

Let's stop non-consensual cosmetic sex assignment until comprehensive, qualitative research on past treatments reveals that its benefits outweigh the pain currently being reported. Let's consider ways by which to make amends for deceitful practices and secrecy, however well intentioned. Let's evaluate humans not as monsters, symbols or archetypes, nor as 'phallic females' or 'failed males' but as people capable of love, intimacy in relationships, sexual function and mutual pleasure.

First do no harm: Primum non nocere

Appendix 1: Correspondence and Interviews

It should be noted that interviews were conducted either in person or via telephone conversations.

Alison: UK – correspondence 6 August 2003

Anja: Germany – correspondence 22 January 2004, 2 March 2004, 15 September 2005, 2 February 2007; interview 10 September 2005

Anon: Netherlands – correspondence 17 May 2003

Anon: Canada – correspondence 2 September 2006

Avril: Germany – correspondence 30 November 2002

Belinda: South Africa – correspondence 6 October 2004

Belle: Canada – correspondence 2 September 2003

Beth: Australia – correspondence 7 August 2004

Briffa, Tony (President of the AIS Support Group Australia): Australia – correspondence 3 April 2002

Carina: USA – correspondence 3 August 2004, 17 September 2004

Chase, Cheryl (Intersex Society of North America): USA – correspondence 27 July 2006

Chris Somers XXY: Australia – correspondence 15 May 2004, 19 May 2004, 21 May 2004, 6 February 2007, 19 February 2007; interview 21 May 2004, 22 May 2004

Claire: UK – correspondence 29 March 2002, 17 January 2007

Creighton, Sarah (Elizabeth Garrett Anderson Hospital, University College London Hospitals): UK – interview 9 February 2006

David: USA – correspondence 11 February 2007; interview 19 June 2004

Debra: USA – correspondence 25 May 2004

Derek: Ireland – correspondence 3 March 2005

Diamond, Milton (John A. Burns School of Medicine, University of Hawaii and the Pacific Center for Sex and Society, Hawaii): USA – correspondence 2 April 2002, 2 December 2005, 6 January 2006, 13 January 2007

Diane: USA – correspondence 20 March 2004

Donal: Ireland – interview 17 September 2004

Edele: Canada – correspondence 8 November 2005

Ellen: location undisclosed – interview 3 March 2004

Elizabeth: USA – correspondence 11 February 2004

Eoin: Ireland – correspondence 3 September 2004

Esther: USA – correspondence 28 December 2006; interview 19 August 2004

Guy: UK – correspondence 13 November 2004

Holmes, Morgan: USA – correspondence 2 February 2007

Hugh: USA – correspondence 17 January 2003

Jacob: USA – correspondence 2 April 2004, 4 April 2004; interview 23 April 2004

Jane: location undisclosed – interview 9 June 2004

Jean: Canada – correspondence 18 January 2004; interview 13 March 2004

Jennifer: USA – correspondence 2 October 2004

Joanne: Australia – interview 3 October 2003

Jonathan: UK – correspondence 3 May 2001, 5 May 2001

K: USA – correspondence 21 May 2004

Keith: USA – correspondence 19 May 2004, 25 May 2004, 3 January 2007

Klinefelter's Syndrome Association: UK – correspondence 27 April 2004, 8 May 2004, 11 January 2007

Laura: UK – correspondence 22 March 2003; interview 3 August 2004

Liam: UK – interview 2 May 2004

Lorna: USA – correspondence 3 March 2005; interview 17 March 2005

Louise: UK – correspondence 28 November 2005; interview 27 September 2005

Mark: UK – interview 11 May 2005

McCabe, Tony (Klinefelter Organisation): UK – correspondence 2 May 2004; interview 29 April 2004

Malcolm: UK – correspondence 3 March 2005

Marie: Ireland – correspondence 9 May 2004, 18 May 2004; interview 11 May 2004

Martha: USA – correspondence 2 January 2007

Mental Health Advocate on behalf of Sarah-Jane, UK – correspondence 16 May 2005

Meyer-Bahlburg, Heinz F.L. (Department of Psychiatry, Columbia University, New York): USA – correspondence 3 April 2002

Michelle: USA – correspondence 13 June 2005

Money, John (Johns Hopkins Hospital, Baltimore): USA – correspondence 2 April 2002

Nic: UK – correspondence 9 February 2007; interview 23 May 2004

Oluyemi – correspondence 7 May 2004, 9 June 2004

Oluyemi's mother – correspondence 7 May 2004, 8 June 2004

Peggy: USA – correspondence 5 January 2007, 7 January 2007, 12 January 2007, 2 March 2007, 18 March 2007

Rachel: Canada – correspondence 17 July 2003

Ransley, Philip (Consultant Paediatric Urologist, Great Portland Street, London): UK – interview 6 September 2005

Ray: USA – correspondence 27 March 2003

Reid, Russell (Consultant Psychiatrist, London): UK – correspondence 24 January 2007; interview 2 May 2004

Sal: USA – correspondence 2 April 2002

Sarah-Jane: UK – correspondence 17 January 2007, 19 January 2007; interview 9 June 2004

Simmonds, Margaret (Androgen Insensitivity Syndrome Support Group): UK – correspondence 28 March 2002, 28 April 2004

Smyth, Arlene (Turner Syndrome Support Society): UK – correspondence 28 April 2004, 4 January 2007; interview 27 April 2004

Stefan: USA – correspondence 5 May 2004, 17 May 2004; interview 10 May 2004

Steven: USA – correspondence 12 June 2003

Tony: UK – correspondence 1 May 2004; interview 1 May 2004

Woodhouse, Christopher (University College London Hospitals) – correspondence 10 January 2007

Appendix 2: Societies and Advocacy Groups

The Adrenal Hyperplasia Network, www.ahn.org.uk

The Androgen Insensitivity Syndrome Support Group, www.aissg.org

The Androgen Insensitivity Syndrome Support Group Australia Inc., home.vicnet.
net.au/~aissg/

Bodies Like Ours, www.bodieslikeours.org.

Cancer Research (UK), www.cancerresearchuk.org

The CARES Foundation Inc., www.caresfoundation.org

The Congenital Adrenal Hyperplasia UK Support Group, www.cah.org.uk

The Endocrine Society, www.endo-society.org

The Gender Identity Research and Education Society, www.gires.org.uk

The Gender Public Advocacy Coalition, www.gpac.org

Gender Talk, www.gendertalk.com

The Gender Trust, www.gendertrust.org.uk

The Harry Benjamin International Gender Dysphoria Association, Inc.,
www.hbigda.org

The Hypospadias and Epispadias Association, www.hypospadias.org

The International Foundation for Gender Education, www.ifge.org

The International Foundation of Androgynous Studies, www.ifas.org.au

Intersex Awareness Day, www.intersex-awareness-day.org

The Intersex Initiative, www.intersexinitiative.org

Intersex People, www.intersexuelle-menschen.net

The Intersex Society of North America, www.isna.org

The Johns Hopkins University School of Medicine (USA), www.hopkinsmedicine.
org/pediatricendocrinology/patient.html

A Kindred Spirit, www.kindredspiritlakeside.homestead.com

The Klinefelter Organisation (UK), www.klinefelter.org.uk

Klinefelter Syndrome and Associates (USA), www.genetic.org

The Klinefelter's Syndrome Association (UK), www.ksa-uk.co.uk

The Klinefelter Syndrome Support Group, www.klinefeltersyndrome.org

The Magic Foundation, www.magicfoundation.org

MRKH.org, www.mrkh.org

NotJustSkin, www.notjustskin.org

Press for Change, www.pfc.org.uk

The Rosa Group (MRKH – Mayer-Rokitansky-Kuster-Hauser Syndrome),
email rosagroup@yahoo.co.uk

The Survivor Project, www.survivorproject.org

Tayside Hospital (UK) re. Congenital Adrenal Hyperplasia (CAH), www.dundee.ac.uk/medther/tayendoweb/congenital_adrenal_hyperplasia. htm

The Transgender Education Association, www.tgea.net

Transsexual, Transgender and Intersex History, www.transhistory.org

The Turner Syndrome Society of the United States, www.turner-syndrome-us.org

The Turner Syndrome Support Society, www.tsss.org.uk

The UK Intersex Association, www.ukia.co.uk

XY Turners, www.xyxo.org

XY-Women, www.xy-frauen.de

Bibliography

Ahmed, S.F., Cheng, A., Dovey, L., Hawkins, J.R., Martin, H., Rowland, J. (2000) Phenotypic Features, Androgen Receptor Binding, and Mutational Analysis in 278 Clinical Cases Reported as Androgen Insensitivity Syndrome. *Journal of Clinical Endocrinology and Metabolism* 85: 2: 658–665.

Ahmed, S.F., Morrison, S., Hughes, I.A. (2004) Intersex and Gender Assignment: The Third Way? *Archives of Disease in Childhood* 89: 847–850.

Ahuja, A. (2004) Unnatural Selection. *The Times T2* (UK) (2 February): 9.

AIS Support Group UK (2005) Media Guidelines 2005. www.medhelp.org/www/ais/PDFs/aissg-media-info.pdf (accessed 27 December 2006).

Alexander, T. (1997) The Medical Management of Intersexed Children: An Analogue for Childhood Sexual Abuse. www.isna.org/articles/analog (accessed 2 January 2005).

Alizai, N.K., Thomas, D.F., Lilford, R.J., Batchelor, A.G., Johnson, N. (1999) Feminising Genitoplasty for Congenital Adrenal Hyperplasia. What Happens at Puberty? *Journal of Urology* 161: 1,588.

Alvarez-Nava, F., Gonzalez, S., Soto, M., Martinez, C., Prieto, M. (1997) Complete Androgen Insensitivity Syndrome: Clinical and Anatomopathological Findings in 23 Patients. *Genetic Counselling* 8: 7–12.

Alvarez-Nava, F., Soto, M., Temponi, A., Lanes, R., Alvarez, Z. (2004) Female Pseudohermaphroditism with Phallic Urethra in the Offspring of a Mother with an Adrenal Tumor. *Journal of Pediatric Endocrinology and Metabolism* 17: November: 1,571–1,574.

American Academy of Pediatrics Policy Statement (1996): Timing of Elective Surgery on the Genitalia of Male Children with Particular Reference to the Risks, Benefits, and Psychological Effects of Surgery and Anesthesia (RE9610). *Pediatrics* 97: 4(April): 590–594.

American Academy of Pediatrics Policy Statement (2000): Evaluation of the Newborn With Developmental Anomalies of the External Genitalia (RE9958). *Pediatrics* 106: 1(July): 138–142.

Angier, N. (1996) Intersexual Healing: An Anomaly Finds a Group. *The New York Times* (4 February): 14.

Anon (1834) Hermaphrodite. *The Lancet* 22: 567(12 July): 558.

Anon (1994) Welcome, Readers! *Hermaphrodites with Attitude* 1: 1(Winter): 6.

Anon (2002) Letter. *The Link*, Klinefelter Organisation (UK).

Anton, L.H. (1995) The Taboo on Talking. *ALIAS: Newsletter of the AIS Support Group* 1: 1: 6–7.

Bailez, M.M., Gearhart, J.P., Migeon, C., Rock, J. (1992) Vaginal Reconstruction after Initial Construction of the External Genitalia in Girls with Salt-Wasting Adrenal Hyperplasia. *Journal of Urology* 148: 680–684.

Bangsboll, S., Qvist, I., Lebech, P.E., Lewinsky, M. (1992) Testicular feminization syndrome and associated gonadal tumours in Denmark. *Acta Obstetricia et Gynecologica Scandinavica* 71: 63–66.

Baskin, L.S., Erol, A., Li, Y.W., Liu, W.H., Kurzrock, E., Cunha, G.R. (1999) Anatomical Studies of the Human Clitoris. *Journal of Urology* 162: 1,015–1,020.

Baskin, L. (2001) Hypospadias: A Critical Analysis of Cosmetic Outcomes Using Photography. *British Journal of Urology* 87: 534–539.

Batch, J., Patterson, M., Hughes, I. (1992) Androgen Insensitivity Syndrome. *Reproductive Medicine Review* 1: 131–150.

Beh, H.G., Diamond, M. (2000) An Emerging Ethical and Medical Dilemma: Should Physicians Perform Sex Assignment on Infants with Ambiguous Genitalia? Prepublication version prepared for the Internet. www.hawaii.edu/PCSS/online_artcls/intersex/intersex00_00.html (accessed 13 May 2005) (published in the *Michigan Journal of Gender & Law* 7: 1: 1–63).

Beh, H.G., Diamond, M. (2005) David Reimer's Legacy: Limiting Parental Discretion. *Cardozo Journal of Law & Gender* 12: 5–30.

Benjamin, H. (1966) *The Transsexual Phenomenon*. New York: Julian Press.

Bin-Abbas, B., Conte, F.A., Grumbach, M.M., Kaplan, S.L. (1999) Congenital Hypogonadotropic Hypogonadism and Micropenis: Effect of Testosterone Treatment on Adult Penile Size – Why Sex Reversal is Not Indicated. *Journal of Pediatrics* 134: 579–583.

Birnbacher, R., Marberger, M., Weissenbacher, G., Schober, E., Frisch, H. (1999) Gender Identity Reversal in an Adolescent with Mixed Gonadal Dysgenesis. *Journal of Pediatric Endocrinology and Metabolism* 12: 687–690.

Black, D. (2004) Sex, Lies and a Quest for Identity. *Toronto Star* (11 May): A.03.

Blackless, M., Charuvastra, A., Derryck, A., Fausto-Sterling, A., Lauzanne, K., Lee, E. (2000) How Sexually Dimorphic Are We? Review and Synthesis. *American Journal of Human Biology* 12: 2: 151–166.

Bock, R. (1993) *Understanding Klinefelter Syndrome: A Guide for XXY Males and Their Families*. Office of Research Reporting, National Institute of Child Health and Development, USA. NIH 93: August: 3,202. www.nichd.nih.gov/publications/pubs/klinefelter (accessed 17 May 2004).

Bojeson, A. (2003) *The Link*, Klinefelter Organisation (UK): 2.

Bradley, S.J., Oliver, G.D., Chernick, A.B., Zucker, K.J. (1998) Experiment of Nurture: Ablatio Penis at 2 Months, Sex Reassignment at 7 Months, and a Psychosexual Follow-up in Young Adulthood. *Pediatrics* 102: July: 132–133.

Bragge, L. (2005) Choosing the Right Gender. *The Age* 1: 1 February. www.theage.com.au/articles/2005/01/31/1107020318710.html (accessed 1 May 2006).

Burns, C. (2000) Campaign Issues. www.pfc.org.uk/campaign/pfcissue.htm (accessed 10 August 2000).

Butler, J. (1990) *Gender Trouble: Feminism and the Subversion of Identity*. New York: Routledge.

Butler, J. (1993) *Bodies that Matter: On the Discursive Limits of 'Sex'*. New York: Routledge.

Cannon, N. (2004) Sophie Was Just a Baby When She had Drastic Surgery. *Woman* (5 April): 22–23.

Centers for Disease Control (USA) (undated) Hypospadias Trends in Two US Surveillance Systems. www.cdc.gov/od/oc/media/pressrel/hypospad.htm (accessed 8 August 2006).

Chang, H.J., Clark, R.D., Bachman, H. (1990) The Phenotype of 45,X/46,XY Mosaicism: An Analysis of 92 Prenatally Diagnosed Cases. *American Journal of Human Genetics* 46: 156–157.

Chase, C. (1994) Dr. Money and The Five Sexes. *Hermaphrodites with Attitude* 1: 1(Winter): 5.

Chase, C. (1998a) Perpetuating the Silence?, www.pfc.org.uk/node/907 (unpaginated) (accessed 20 February 2007).

Chase, C. (1998b) Affronting Reason. In Atkins, D. ed. *Looking Queer: Body Image and Identity in Lesbian, Bisexual, Gay and Transgender Communities*. London: Harrington Park Press, 205–219.

Clayton, P.E., Miller, W.L., Oberfield, S.E., Ritzén, E.M., Sippell, W.G., Speiser, P.W. (2002) Joint LWPES/ESPE CAH Working Group – Consensus Statement on 21-hydroxylase deficiency from The Lawson Wilkins Pediatric Endocrine Society and The European Society for Paediatric Endocrinology. *Journal of Clinical Endocrinology and Metabolism* 87: 4,048–4,053.

Cohen-Kettenis, P. (2003) *Transgenderism and Intersexuality in Childhood and Adolescence. Making Choices.* Thousand Oaks, CA: Sage.

Colapinto, J. (2000) *As Nature Made Him: The Boy Who Was Raised a Girl.* New York: HarperCollins.

Colapinto, J. (2004) Gender Gap: What Were the Real Reasons Behind David Reimer's Suicide? (3 June). slate.msn.com/id/2101678 (accessed 3 January 2006).

Conway, G.S., Elsheikh, M., Cadge, B., Ostberg, J. (2000a) Adult Turner Follow-up: The Middlesex Experience. In Saenger, P., Pasquino, A.M., eds. *Proceedings of the 5th International Turner Symposium – Optimising Health*

Care for Turner Patients in the 21st Century. Amsterdam: Elsevier: 295–306.

Conway, G. (2000b) *Congenital Adrenal Hyperplasia: Information for Adults.* London: Department of Endocrinology, The Middlesex Hospital.

Cossey, C. (1991) *My Story.* London: Faber and Faber.

Costa, E.M., Mendonca, B.B., Inácio, M., Arnhold, I.J., Silva, F.A., Lodovici, O. (1997) Management of Ambiguous Genitalia in Pseudohermaphrodites: New Perspectives on Vaginal Dilation. *Fertility and Sterility* 67: 2: 229–232.

Coventry, M. (1998) The Tyranny of the Esthetic: Surgery's Most Intimate Violation. *On the Issues* 7: 3(Summer). www.ontheissuesmagazine.com/su98coventry.html (unpaginated) (accessed 25 July 2006).

Crawford, J.D. (1970) Syndromes of Testicular Feminization. *Clinical Pediatrics* 9: 3: 165–178.

Creed, B. (1993) *The Monstrous-Feminine: Film, Feminism and Psychoanalysis.* London: Routledge.

Creighton S.M., Minto, C.L., Steele, S.J. (2001a) Objective Cosmetic and Anatomical Outcomes at Adolescence of Feminising Surgery for Ambiguous Genitalia Done in Childhood. *The Lancet* 358: 9,276(14 July): 124–125.

Creighton, S., Minto, C. (2001b) Managing Intersex. *British Medical Journal* 323: 1,264–1,265.

Creighton, S., Minto, C. (2001c) Appendix: Clitoral Surgery. Statement of the British Association of Paediatric Surgeons Working Party on the Surgical Management of Children Born with Ambiguous Genitalia. www.baps.org.uk/documents/intersex%20statement.htm (accessed 21 December 2005).

Creighton, S., Alderson, J., Brown, S., Minto, C.L. (2002) Medical Photography: Ethics, Consent and the Intersex Patient. *British Journal of Urology International* 89: 67–72.

Creighton, S.M., Liao, L.-M. (2004a) Changing Attitudes to Sex Assignment in Intersex. *British Journal of Urology International* 93: 659–664.

Creighton, S.M. (2004b) Long-term Outcome of Feminisation Surgery: The London Experience. *British Journal of Urology International* 93: (Supplement 3): 44–46.

Crouch, N.S., Creighton, S.M., Woodhouse, C.R.J. (2003) Changing Attitudes to Intersex Management. *European Urology Today* 14: 2(June): 1,5.

Cull, M.L. (2005) A Support Group's Perspective. *British Medical Journal* 330(12 February): 341.

Daaboul, J. (2000) Does the Study of History Affect Clinical Practice? Intersex as a Case Study: The Physician's View. *American Association for the History of Medicine Annual Conference*, Bethesda, USA (May). www.isna.org/articles/daaboul_history (accessed 15 July 2006).

Daaboul, J. (2003) Management of the Patient with Intersex: A Middle Way.

Endocrinology Newsletter American Academy of Pediatrics (Winter/Spring): 13–14.

David (1995–6) Clinicians: Look to Intersexual Adults for Guidance. *Hermaphrodites with Attitude* (7 October).

Davis, K. (2004) Scientists in Touch With Feminine Side. *New Scientist* 13: (21 October): 48. www.newscientist.com/article.ns?id=dn6564 (accessed 30 November 2005).

Diamond, M., Sigmundson, H.K. (1997a) Management of Intersexuality: Guidelines for Dealing with Individuals with Ambiguous Genitalia. *Archives of Pediatrics and Adolescent Medicine* 151: October: 1,046–1,050.

Diamond, M., Sigmundson, H.K. (1997b) Sex Reassignment at Birth: A Long Term Review and Clinical Implications. *Archives of Pediatrics and Adolescent Medicine* 151: March: 298–304.

Diamond, M. (1999) Pediatric Management of Ambiguous and Traumatised Genitalia. *Journal of Urology* 162: 1,021–1,028.

Diamond, M. (2004a) Pediatric Management of Ambiguous and Traumatized Genitalia. *Contemporary Sexuality* 38: 9: i–viii.

Diamond, M., Watson, L.A. (2004b) Androgen Insensitivity Syndrome and Klinefelter's Syndrome: Sex and Gender Considerations. *Child and Adolescent Psychiatric Clinics of North America* 13: 623–640.

Diamond, M. (2004c) Sex, Gender, and Identity Over the Years: A Changing Perspective. *Child and Adolescent Psychiatric Clinics of North America* 13: 591–607.

Diamond, M., Beh, H.G. (2006) The Right to be Wrong: Sex and Gender Decisions. In Sytsma, S. ed. *Ethics and Intersex*. Netherlands: Springer, 103–114.

Dittman, R.W., Kappes, M.E., Kappes, M.H. (1992) Sexual Behaviour in Adolescent and Adult Females with Congenital Adrenal Hyperplasia. *Psychoneuroendocrinology* 17: 2/3: 153–170.

Dolk, H., Vrijheid, M., Scott, J.E.S., Addor, M-C., Botting, B., de Vigan, C., de Walle, H., Garne, E., Loane, M., Pierini, A., Garcia-Minaur, S., Physick, N., Tenconi, R., Wiesel, A., Calzolari, E., Stone, D. (2004) Toward the Effective Surveillance of Hypospadias. *Environmental Health Perspectives* 112: 3: March: 398–402.

Donahoe, P.K., Hendren, W.H.I. (1976) Evaluation of the Newborn with Ambiguous Genitalia. *Pediatric Clinics of North America* 23: 361–370.

Donahoe, P.K. (1987) The Diagnosis and Treatment of Infants with Intersex Abnormalities. *Pediatric Clinics of North America* 34: 1,333–1,348.

Donahoe, P.K. (1991) Clinical Management of Intersex Abnormalities. *Current Problems in Surgery* 28: 519–579.

Dreger, A. (1995) Doubtful Sex: The Fate of the Hermaphrodite in Victorian Medicine. *Victorian Studies* 38: 3(Spring): 335–370.

Dreger, A.D. (1998a) *Hermaphrodites and the Medical Invention of Sex.* Cambridge, MA: Harvard University Press.

Dreger, A.D. (1998b) 'Ambiguous Sex' – or Ambivalent Medicine? Ethical Issues in the Treatment of Intersexuality. *The Hastings Center Report* 28: 3(May/June): 24–35. www.isna.org/articles/dregerart.html (unpaginated) (accessed 25 July 2003).

Dreger, A. (1999) ed. *Intersex in the Age of Ethics.* Hagerstown, MD: University Publishing Group.

Driver, B. (2004) Bodies Like Ours Mourns David Reimer's Death (quoting E. Koyama). E-mail list bodieslikeours@lists.bodieslikeours.org (accessed 11 May 2004).

Duckett, J.W., Baskin, L. (1993) Genitoplasty for Intersex Anomalies. *European Journal of Pediatrics* 152: Supplement 2: 580–584.

Edgerton, R.B. (1964) Poket Intersexuality: An East African Example of the Resolution of Sexual Incongruity. *American Anthropologist* 66: 1,288–1,299.

Edman, C.D., Winters, A.J., Porter, J.C., Wilson, J., MacDonald, P.C. (1977) Embryonic Testicular Regression – Clinical Spectrum of XY Agonadal Individuals. *Obstetrics and Gynecology* 49: 208–217.

Ehrhardt, A.A., Meyer-Bahlburg, H.F. (1981) Effects of Prenatal Sex Hormones on Gender Related Behavior. *Science* 211: 1,312–1,318.

Elsheikh, M., Dunger, D.B., Conway, G.S., Wass, J.A.H. (2002) Turner's Syndrome in Adulthood. *Endocrine Reviews* 23: 120–140.

Eugenides, J. (2002) *Middlesex.* London: Bloomsbury Publishing.

Farhat, W.A. (2005) Early Intervention of CAH Surgical Management. *Journal of Pediatric and Adolescent Gynecology* 18: January: 66–69.

Fausto-Sterling, A. (1993) The Five Sexes. Why Male and Female Are Not Enough. *The Sciences* 33: March/April: 20–25.

Fausto-Sterling, A. (1999) Sexing the Body: How Biologists Construct Sexuality. *The International Journal of Transgenderism.* www.symposion. com/ijt/gilbert/sterling.htm (accessed 26 March 2006).

Fausto-Sterling, A. (2000) *Sexing the Body: Gender Politics and the Construction of Sexuality.* New York: Basic Books.

Foucault, M. (1980) trans. R. McDougall *Herculine Barbin: Being the Recently Discovered Memoirs of a Nineteenth-Century French Hermaphrodite.* New York: Pantheon.

Fraker, D. (1996) Hermaphrodites Come out Fighting: New 'Intersex' Movement Challenging Need for Corrective Surgery. *Southern Voice* 19 September: 14–16.

Freud, S. (1919) The Uncanny. In Strachey, J. ed. and trans. *Standard Edition of the Complete Psychological Works of Sigmund Freud (Vol.17).* London: The Hogarth Press (1955), 218–252.

Freud, S. (1925) Some Psychical Consequences of the Anatomical Distinction between the Sexes. In Strachey, J. ed. and trans. *Standard Edition of the Complete Psychological Works of Sigmund Freud (Vol.19)*. London: The Hogarth Press (1961), 243–258.

Freud, S. (1931) Female Sexuality. In Strachey, J. ed. and trans. *Standard Edition of the Complete Psychological Works of Sigmund Freud (Vol.21)*. London: The Hogarth Press (1961), 223–243.

Freud, S. (1933) Femininity. In Strachey, J. ed. and trans. *Standard Edition of the Complete Psychological Works of Sigmund Freud (Vol.22)*. London: The Hogarth Press (1960), 112–135.

Freyd, J.J. (1996) *Betrayal Trauma: The Logic of Forgetting Childhood Abuse.* Cambridge, MA: Harvard University Press.

Gearhart, J. (1993) It's Easier to Make a Hole than Build a Pole. *Johns Hopkins Magazine* November: 15, referenced in Holmes, M. (1994b) Remembering a Queer Body. *Undercurrents.* Faculty of Environmental Studies, York University, Ontario, Canada (May): 11–13 www.medhelp.org/www/ais/articles/HOLMES.HTM (accessed 25 July 2003).

Gearhart, J.P., Burnett, A., Owen, J.H. (1995) Measurement of Pudendal Evoked Potentials During Feminizing Genitoplasty: Technique and Applications. *Journal of Urology* 153: 486–487.

Glaser, K. (2000) I Just Want to be Normal. *Jewish Chronicle* (4 August): 25.

Gooren M.D., Cohen-Kettenis, P.T. (1991) Development of Male Gender Identity/role and a Sexual Orientation Toward Women in a 46, XY Subject with an Incomplete Form of the Androgen Insensitivity Syndrome. *Archives of Sexual Behavior* 20: 459–470.

Goujon, E. (1869) Etude d'un cas d'hermaphrodisme bisexuel imparfait chez l'homme. *Journal de l'anatomie et de la physiologie normales et pathologiques de l'homme et des animaux* 6: 599–616.

Greenberg, J.A., Chase, C. (1999) Columbia High Court limits Surgery on Intersexed Infants. www.isna.org/node/21 (unpaginated) (accessed 24 March 2006).

Grino, P.B., Isidro-Gutierrez, R.F., Griffin, J.E. (1989) Androgen Resistance Associated with a Qualitative Abnormality of the Androgen Receptor and Responsive to High-dose Androgen Therapy. *Journal of Clinical Endocrinology and Metabolism* 68: 578–584.

Gruppuso, P.A. (1999) Should Cosmetic Surgery be Performed on the Genitals of Children Born with Ambiguous Genitals? (Point/Counterpoint) *Physician's Weekly* XVI: 31(16 August). www.physiciansweekly.com/archive/99/08_16_99/pc.html (unpaginated) (accessed 2 December 2005).

Hambley, V. (1999) Klinefelter Syndrome 47XXY. 47xxy.org/PrintXXY.htm (accessed 15 February 2006); 47xxy.org/Gloss/male.htm (accessed 25 March 2006).

Hampton Young, H. (1937) *Genital Abnormalities: Hermaphroditism and*

Related Adrenal Diseases. Baltimore, MD: The Williams and Wilkins Company.

Hatch, D.A. (2003) Abnormal Development of the Penis and Male Urethra in Genitourinary Development: A Tutorial Correlating Embrology with Congenital Anomalies. www.meddean.luc.edu/lumen/MedEd/urology/hrmphdt.htm (unpaginated) (accessed 25 July 2003).

Hendren, W.H., Atala, A. (1995) Repair of High Vagina in Girls with Severely Masculinised Anatomy from Adrenogenital Syndrome. *Journal of Pediatric Surgery* 30: 91–94.

Hendricks, M. (2000) Into the Hands of Babes. *Johns Hopkins Magazine* (September). www.jhu.edu/~jhumag/0900web/babes.html (accessed 5 December 2005).

Hensle, T.W., Tennenbaum, S.Y., Reiley, E.A., Pollard, J. (2001) Hypospadias Repair in Adults: Adventures and Misadventures. *Journal of Urology* 165: 77–79.

Herdt, G. (1996) Mistaken Sex: Culture, Biology and Third Sex in New Guinea. In Herdt, G. ed. *Third Sex, Third Gender: Beyond Sexual Dimorphism in Culture and History*. New York: Zone Books, 419–445.

Hester, J.D. (undated) Intersex(es) and the Rhetorics of Healing. *InterFakultäres Zentrum für Ethik in den Wissenschaften, Uni-Tuebingen* (reference provided in hard copy by a correspondent, 2004).

Hines, M., Ahmed, S.F., Hughes, I.A. (2003) Psychological Outcomes and Gender-Related Development in Complete Androgen Insensitivity Syndrome. *Archives of Sexual Behavior* 32: 2: (April): 93–101.

Hines, M., Ahmed, S.F., Hughes, I.A. (2004) Neuroscience and Intersex. *The Psychologist* 17: 8: (August): 455–458.

Holmes, M. (1994a) I'm Still Intersexual. *Hermaphrodites with Attitude* 1: 1: (Winter): 5–6.

Holmes, M. (1994b) Re-membering a Queer Body. *Undercurrents*. Faculty of Environmental Studies, York University, Ontario, Canada (May): 11–13. www.medhelp.org/www/ais/articles/HOLMES.HTM (unpaginated) (accessed 25 July 2003).

Holmes, M.M. (1995) Queer Cut Bodies: Intersexuality and Homophobia in Medical Practice (Concordia University). www.usc.edu/isd/archives/queer-frontiers/queer/papers/holmes.long.html (unpaginated) (accessed 25 July 2000).

Holmes, M. (1998) In(to)Visibility: Intersexuality in the Field of Queer. In Atkins, D. ed. *Looking Queer: Body Image and Identity in Lesbian, Bisexual, Gay and Transgender Communities*. London: Harrington Park Press, 221–232.

Holmes, M. (2002) Rethinking the Meaning and Management of Intersexuality. *Sexualities* 5: 2: 159–180.

Holt, L.E. (1897) *The Diseases of Infancy and Childhood.* New York: D. Appleton and Co.

Holt, W.M. (1861) Acephalous Hermaphrodite Monster. *The Lancet* 77: 1,961: (30 March): 328.

Hughes, I.A., Houk, C., Ahmed, S.F., Lee, P.A. (2006) Consensus Statement on Management of Intersex Disorders. *Archives of Disease in Childhood* 91: 7: (July): 554–563.

Hugill, B. (1998) She'd Have Been a God in Ancient Greece. In Wales, They Spit on Her. *The Observer* (UK) 24 May: 7.

Hurtig, A.L., Radhakrishnan, J., Reyes, H.M., Rosenthal, I.M. (1983) Psychological Evaluation of Treated Females with Virilizing Congenital Adrenal Hyperplasia. *Journal of Pediatric Surgery* 18: 6: 887–893.

Imperato-McGinley, J., Peterson, R.E., Gautier, T., Sturla, E. (1979a) Male Pseudohermaphroditism Secondary to 5 alpha-reductase Deficiency: A Model for the Role of Androgens in both the Development of the Male Phenotype and the Evolution of a Male Gender Identity. *Journal of Steroid Biochemistry and Molecular Biology* 11(1B): 637–645.

Imperato-McGinley, J., Peterson, R.E., Stoller, R. (1979b) Male Pseudo-hermaphroditism Secondary to 17B-hydroxysteroid Dehydrogenase Deficiency: Gender Role Change with Puberty. *Journal of Clinical Endocrinology and Metabolism* 49: 391–395.

Imperato-McGinley, J., Miller, M., Wilson, J.D., Peterson, R.E., Shackleton, C., Gajdusek, D.C. (1991) A Cluster of Male Pseudohermaphrodites with 5-a Reductase Deficiency in Papua New Guinea. *Clinical Endocrinology* 34: 4: 293–298.

Jha, A. (undated) Intersex (Genital Ambiguity): Bristol Urological Institute. www.bui.ac.uk/Tutorials/intersex.htm (unpaginated) (accessed 1 December 2005).

Josso, N., Briard, M.L. (1980) Embryonic Testicular Regression Syndrome: Variable Phenotypic Expression in Siblings. *Journal of Pediatrics* 97: 200–204.

Katz, M.D., Kligman, I., Cai, L.Q., Zhu, Y.S., Fratianni, C.M., Zervoudakis, I., Rosenwaks, Z., Imperato-McGinley, J. (1997) Paternity by Intrauterine Insemination with Sperm from a Man with 5-alpha Reductase 2 Deficiency. *New England Journal of Medicine* 336: 994–998.

Kerr, S.-L. (2005) The Hidden Gender. *Sunday Times* (W. Australia) 18 September: 10–13.

Kessler, S. (1990) The Medical Construction of Gender: Case Management of Intersexed Infants. *Signs: The Journal of Women in Culture and Society* 16: 3–26.

Kessler, S.J. (1998) *Lessons from the Intersexed.* New Brunswick, NJ: Rutgers University Press.

Kim, K.R., Kwon, Y., Joung, J.Y., Kim, K.S., Ayala, A.G., Ro, J.Y. (2002) True Hermaphroditism and Mixed Gonadal Dysgenesis in Young Children: A Clinicopathologic Study of 10 Cases. *Modern Pathology* 15: 10: 1,013–1,019.

Kipnis, K., Diamond, M. (1998) Pediatric Ethics and the Surgical Assignment of Sex. *Journal of Clinical Ethics* 9: 4(Winter): 398–410.

Kitzinger, C. (2000) Women with Androgen Insensitivity Syndrome. In Ussher, J.M. ed. *Women's Health*. Leicester: British Psychological Society, 387–394.

Kitzinger, C. (2004) The Myth of the Two Biological Sexes. *The Psychologist* 17: 8(August): 451–454.

Kristeva, J. (1982) trans. L.S. Roudiez *Powers of Horror: An Essay on Abjection*. New York: Columbia University Press.

Latou Dickinson, R. (1949) *Human Sex Anatomy*. Baltimore, MD: The Williams and Wilkins Company.

Lee, E.H. (1994) Producing Sex: an Interdisciplinary Perspective on Sex Assignment Decisions for Intersexuals. Senior Thesis, Brown University, USA.

Lee, V. (2002) She Shoots, She Scores. *The Observer Review: Screen* (UK) 15 December: 8.

Lehrman, S. (1999) Sex Police. *Salon.com* (5 April). www.pfc.org. uk/news/1999/sex-pol.htm (unpaginated) (accessed 10 May 2004).

Letellier, P. (2004) San Francisco Probes Intersex Issues. www.gay.com/news/ article.html?2004/05/28/3, 28 May: 3 (accessed 29 May 2005).

Liao, L.-M. (2003) Learning to Assist Women with Atypical Genitalia. Journey through Ignorance, Taboo and Dilemma. *Journal of Reproductive and Infant Psychology* 21: 229–238.

Liao, L.-M., Boyle, M. (2004) Surgical Feminising: The Right Approach? *The Psychologist* 17: 8(August): 459–462.

Lomax, R. (1996) The Dilemma of a Double Life. *Watford Observer* (UK) 29 March: 17.

McCabe, T. (2003) Intersex and KS. *The Link*, Klinefelter Organisation (UK) February: 2: 2.

McGillivray, B.C. (1991) The Newborn with Ambiguous Genitalia. *Seminars in Perinatology* 16: 365–368.

Marshall, Y. (2000) Review of Alice Domurat Dreger ed. *Intersex in the Age of Ethics*. *The New England Journal of Medicine* 342: 19: 1457.

Masters, W., Johnston, V. (1966) *Human Sexual Response*. Boston: Little, Brown.

May B., Boyle, M., Grant, D. (1996) A Comparative Study of Sexual Experiences. Women with Diabetes and Women with Congenital Adrenal Hyperplasia due to 21-hydroxylase Deficiency. *Journal of Health Psychology* 1: April: 479–492.

May, L. (2005) *Transgenders and Intersexuals*. Bowden, Australia: East Street Publications.

Mayer, Prof. (1836) Description of An Hermaphrodite, Known under the Respective Names of 'Marie Dorothee Derier,' and 'Charles Durge'. *The Lancet* 27: 685(15 October): 140–142.

Meyers-Seifer, C.H., Charest, N.J. (1992) Diagnosis and Management of Patients with Ambiguous Genitalia. *Seminars in Perinatology* 16: 332–339.

Migeon, C.J., Wisniewski, A.B., Gearhart, J.P. (2001) *Syndromes of Abnormal Sex Differentiation: A Guide for Parents and their Families*. Baltimore, MD: The Johns Hopkins Children's Center.

Migeon, C.J., Wisniewski, A., Brown, T.R., Rock, J.A., Meyer-Bahlburg, H.F.L., Money, J., Berkovitz, G.D. (2002a) 46,XY Intersex Individuals: Phenotypic and Etiologic Classification, Knowledge of Condition, and Satisfaction with Knowledge. *Adulthood Pediatrics* (September): 110: 3: e32: 1–8.

Migeon, C.J., Wisniewski, A.B., Gearhart, J.P., Meyer-Bahlburg, H.F.L., Rock, J.A., Brown, T.R., Casella, S.J., Maret, A., Ngai, K.M., Money, J., Berkowitz, G.D. (2002b) Ambiguous Genitalia with Perineoscrotal Hypospadias in 46,XY Individuals: Long-term Medical, Surgical, and Psychosexual Outcome. *Pediatrics* (September): 110: 3: e31: 1–10.

Miller, W.L. (2003) Letter to the Editor: Authors' Response: Regarding the Consensus Statement on 21-hydroxylase Deficiency from the Lawson Wilkins Pediatric Endocrine Society and The European Society for Paediatric Endocrinology. *The Journal of Clinical Endocrinology and Metabolism* 88: 7: 3,456.

Minto, C.L., Liao, L.-M., Conway, G.S., Creighton, S.M. (2003a) Sexual Function in Women with Complete Androgen Insensitivity Syndrome. *Fertility and Sterility* (July): 80: 1: 157–164.

Minto, C.L., Liao, L.-M., Woodhouse, C.R.J., Ransley, P.G., Creighton, S.M. (2003b) Effects of Clitoral Surgery on Sexual Outcome in Individuals who have Intersex Conditions with Ambiguous Genitalia: A Cross Sectional Study. *The Lancet* 361: 1,252.

Money, J. (1952) Hermaphroditism: An Inquiry into the Nature of a Human Paradox. Doctoral Thesis, Harvard University, USA.

Money, J., Hampson, J.G., Hampson, J.L. (1955) Hermaphroditism. Recommendations Concerning Assignment of Sex, Change of Sex and Psychologic Management. *Bulletin of the Johns Hopkins Hospital* 97: 284–300.

Money, J., Hampson, J.G., Hampson, J.L. (1957) Imprinting and the Establishment of Gender Role. *Archives of Neural Psychiatry* 77: 333–336.

Money J. (1961) Sex Hormones and Other Variables in Human Eroticism. In Young, W.C. ed. *Sex and Internal Secretions*. 3rd edition. Baltimore, MD: Williams & Wilkins, 1,383–1,400.

Money, J. (1965) Psychological Evaluation of the Child with Intersex Problems. *Pediatrics* 36: 1: 51–55.

Money, J. (1968) *Sex Errors of the Body. Dilemmas, Education and Counselling.* Baltimore, MD: Johns Hopkins University Press.

Money, J., Ehrhardt, A.A. (1972) *Man & Woman, Boy & Girl: Differentiation and Dimorphism of Gender Identity from Conception to Maturity.* Baltimore, MD: Johns Hopkins University Press.

Money, J. (1974) Psychologic Consideration of Sex Assignment in Intersexuality. *Clinics in Plastic Surgery* 1: April: 215–222.

Money, J., Tucker, P. (1975) *Sexual Signatures: On Being a Man or Woman.* Boston, MA: Little Brown & Co, Inc.

Money, J., Devore, H., Norman, B.F. (1986) Gender Identity and Gender Transposition: Longitudinal Outcome Study of 32 Male Hermaphrodites Assigned as Girls. *Journal of Sex and Marital Therapy* 12: 3: 165–181.

Money, J., Lamacz, M. (1987) Genital Examination and Exposure Experienced as Nosocomial Sexual Abuse in Childhood. *The Journal of Nervous and Mental Disease* 175: 713–721.

Money, J., Musaph, H. (1991) eds. *Biographies of Gender and Hermaphroditism in Paired Comparisons.* New York: Elsevier Publishing Company.

Money, J. (1994) The Concept of Gender Identity Disorder in Childhood and Adolescence After 39 Years. *Journal of Sex and Marital Therapy* 20: 3(Fall): 163–177.

Money, J. (1995) *Gendermaps: Social Constructionism, Feminism, and Sexosophical History.* New York: Continuum Publishing Company.

Morgan, J.F., Murphy, H., Hubert Lacey, J., Conway, G. (2005) Long Term Psychological Outcome for Women with Congenital Adrenal Hyperplasia: Cross Sectional Survey. *British Medical Journal* 330: 340–341.

Mortimer, R. (2002) Director's Statement. *Gender Trouble.* www.wonder-dog. co.uk/gender2.html (accessed 30 June 2006).

Mosley, M., Bidder, R., Hughes, I. (1989) Sex Role Behaviour and Self-image in Young Patients with Congenital Adrenal Hyperplasia. *British Journal of Sexual Medicine* 16: 72–75.

Natarajan, A. (1996) Medical Ethics and Truth-telling in the Case of Androgen Insensitivity Syndrome. *Canadian Medical Journal* 154: 568–570.

Navarro, M. (2004) When Gender isn't a Given. *New York Times* 19 September: 9: 1, 6.

Newman, K. (1992a) The Surgical Management of Infants and Children with Ambiguous Genitalia. *Annals of Surgery* 215: 644–653.

Newman, K. (1992b) Functional Results in Young Women Having Clitoral Reconstruction as Infants. *Journal of Pediatric Surgery* 27: 180–183.

Nielsen, J. (undated) *Klinefelter's Syndrome AN ORIENTATION.* National Society of Turner Contact Groups, Denmark; Turner Centre of the

Psychiatric   Hospital,   Aarhus,   Denmark.   www.aaa.dk/TURNER/ ENGELSK (accessed 9 May 2004).

Nielsen, J. (1991) *Follow-Up of 25 Unselected Children With Sex Chromosome Abnormalities to Age 12.* March of Dimes, Birth Defects Foundation, USA: Original Article Series 26: 201–207.

Nielsen, J. (1993) *What More Can be Done for Girls and Women with Turner Syndrome?* Risskov,   Denmark: Elsevier   Science   Publishers   B.V. www.aaa.dk/TURNER/ENGELSK/INDEX.HTM   (accessed   16   May 2005).

Noble,   A.M.   (1996)   The   Conceptualisation   of   Transsexualism   In Matrimonial   Proceedings.   www.pfc.org.uk/cgi/printit.pl?/gendrpol/ anoble.htm (unpaginated) (accessed 14 March 2001).

Ogilvy-Stuart, A.L., Brain, C.E. (2004) Early Assessment of Ambiguous Genitalia. *Archives of Disease in Childhood* 89: 401–407.

Palmero, G., Joris, H., Devroey, P., Van Steirteghem, A.C. (1992) Pregnancies after Intracytoplasmic Injection of a Single Spermatozoon into an Oocyte. *The Lancet* 340: 12–18.

Pang, S. (undated) The Magic Foundation: Congenital Adrenal Hyper-plasia.   www.magicfoundation.org/www/docs/100/congenital_adrenal_ hyperplasia.html (accessed 4 December 2005).

Phornphutkul, C., Fausto-Sterling, A., Gruppuso, P.A. (2000) Gender Self-Reassignment   in   an   XY   Adolescent   Female   Born   with   Ambiguous Genitalia. *Pediatrics* 106: 1: (July): 135–137.

Preves, S.E. (2000) Negotiating the Constraints of Sex Binarism: Intersexuals' Challenge to Gender Categorization. *Current Society* 48: (3): 27–50.

Preves, S.E. (2003) *Intersex and Identity: The Contested Self.* New Brunswick, NJ: Rutgers University Press.

Quigley, C.A., de Bellis, A., Marschke, K.B., El-Awady, M.K., Wilson, E.M., French, F.S. (1995) Androgen Receptor Defects: Historical, Clinical and Molecular Perspectives. *Endocrine Reviews* 16: 3: 271-321.

Ralph, D. (2004) Op Can Boost Size of Micro-penis. *BBC News online* 6 December.   news.bbc.co.uk/1/hi/health/4071657.stm   (unpaginated) (accessed 13 July 2005).

Ratcliffe,   S.G.   (1982)   The   Sexual   Development   of   Boys   with   the Chromosome   Constitution   47,XXY   (Klinefelter   Syndrome).   *Clinical Endocrinology and Metabolism* 11: 703–716.

Ratcliffe, S.G., Paul, N. (1986) eds. *Prospective Studies on Children with Sex Chromosome Aneuploidy.* March of Dimes, Birth Defects Foundation, USA: Original Article Series 22: 23–71.

Reilly, J.M., Woodhouse, C.R.J. (1989) Small Penis and the Male Sexual Role. *Journal of Urology* 142: August: 569–571.

Reiner, W.G., Gearhart, J., Jeffs, R. (1996a) Psychosexual Dysfunction in

Adolescent Males with Bladder Exstrophy. *Pediatrics: Abstracts of Scientific Presentations Presented at the 1996 Annual meeting of the American Academy of Pediatrics* (October): 88: 3.

Reiner W.G. (1996b) Case Study: Sex Reassignment in a Teenage Girl. *Journal of the American Academy of Child and Adolescent Psychiatry* 35: 799–803.

Reiner, W., Kropp, B.P. (2004a) A 7-year Experience of Genetic Males with Severe Phallic Inadequacy Assigned Female. *The Journal of Urology* 172: 6(December – Part 1 of 2): 2,395–2,398.

Reiner, W.G. (2004b) Psychosexual Development in Genetic Males Assigned Female: The Cloacal Exstrophy Experience. *Child and Adolescent Clinics of North America (Sex and Gender)* 13: 3: 657–674.

Rink, R.C., Adams, R.C. (1998) Feminizing Genitoplasty. State of the Art. *World Journal of Urology* 16: 212–218.

Robinson, A. (1990) Demographic and Prevalence of Turner Syndrome. In Rosenfield, R.G., Grumbach, M.M. eds. *Turner Syndrome.* New York: Marcel Dekker, 93–100.

Rolla, A. (1999) XXY+ADULTS Support Mailing List XXY+ADULTS@ HOME.EASE.LSOFT.COM (accessed 28 February 1999).

Rolla, A. (2004) KS&A XXY+ADULTS e-list www.genetic.org/ks/scvs at 47xxy.org/PrintXXY.htm (accessed 17 May 2004).

Rosario, V. (2004) From Hermaphrodites to SOX9: The Molecular Deconstruction of Sex. *Presentations in the History of Medicine.* Royal Australian College of Physicians. www.usyd.edu.au/su/hps/racp.html (accessed 12 February 2006).

Rosenberg, C., Mustacchi, Z., Braz, A., Arnhold, I.J., Chu, T.H., Carnevale, J., Frota-Pessoa, O. (1984) Testicular Regression in a Patient with Virilized Female Phenotype. *American Journal of Medical Genetics* 19: 183–188.

Röttger, S., Schiebel, K., Senger, G., Ebner, S., Schempp, W., Scherer, G. (2000) An SRY-negative 47,XXY Mother and Daughter. *Cytogenetics and Cell Genetics* 91: 204–207.

Saavedra-Castillo, E., Cortes-Gutierrez, E.I., Davila-Rodriguez, M.I., Reyes-Martinez, M.E., Oliveros-Rodriguez, A. (2005) 47,XXY Female with Testicular Feminization and Positive SRY: A Case Report. *Journal of Reproductive Medicine* 50: February: 138–140.

Samango-Sprouse, C. (1999) *The Hidden Disability: Sex Chromosome Variations (SCV).* American Association for Home-Based Early Interventionists, USA, NEWS EXCHANGE Parent and Providers Working Together 4: (Fall): 4.

Sandberg, D.E., Meyer-Bahlburg, H.F.L., Aranoff, G.S., Sconzo, J.M., Hensle, T.W. (1989) Boys with Hypospadias: A Survey of Behavioral Difficulties. *Journal of Pediatric Psychology* 14: 4: 491–514.

Sarto, G.E., Opitz, J.M. (1973) The XY Gonadal Agenesis Syndrome.

American Journal of Medical Genetics 10: 288–293.

Schmid, M., Guttenbach, M., Enders, H., Terruhn, V. (1992) A 47,XXY Female with Unusual Genitalia. *Human Genetics* 90: December: 4: 346–349.

Schober, J.M. (1998a) Feminizing Genitoplasty for Intersex. In Stringer, M.D., Oldham, K.T., Mouriquand, P.D.E., Howard, E. eds. *Pediatric Surgery and Urology: Longterm Outcomes.* Philadelphia: W.B. Saunders Company Ltd, 549–558.

Schober, J.M. (1998b) Early Feminizing Genitoplasty or Watchful Waiting. *The Journal of Paediatric and Adolescent Gynecology* 11: 3: 154–156.

Schober, J.M. (1999) Longterm Outcomes and Changing Attitudes to Intersexuality. *British Journal of Urology International* 83: (Supplement 3): 39–50.

Schober, J.M. (2001) Sexual Behaviors, Sexual Orientation and Gender Identity in Adult Intersexuals: A Pilot Study. *Journal of Urology* 165: 6: 2,350–2,353.

Sheehan, E.A. (1997) Victorian Clitoridectomy: Isaac Baker Brown and His Harmless Operation. In Lancaster, R.N., di Leonardo, M. eds. *The Gender/Sexuality Reader: Culture, History, Political Economy.* London: Routledge, 325–334.

Shibley Hyde, J. (1986) *Understanding Human Sexuality.* 3rd edition. New York: McGraw-Hill Book Company.

Singer, J. (1997) *Androgyny: Towards a New Theory of Sexuality.* London: Routledge & Kegan Paul Ltd.

Slocum, V. (1995) Letter. *Hermaphrodites with Attitude* (Summer): 6–7.

Solomon, M.L. (undated) Rabbinic Curiosities – Real Lives (unreferenced and unpaginated text sent to the author by interviewee, 2004).

Somers, C. (undated) Ultra-Sounds: XXY Perspectives. www.47xxy.org/Chris.htm (unpaginated) (accessed 21 May 2004).

Somers, C. (1999) Sexing the Difference in Gender and the Anomalies of Interpretation. *14th Annual Conference of the Australian and New Zealand Society of Criminology.* The University of Western Australia (27–30 September).

Sørensen, K., Sorensen, A.M., Nielsen, J. (1981) Social and Psychological Development of Adolescents with Klinefelter's Syndrome. In Schid, W. and Nielsen, J. eds. *Human Behaviour and Genetics.* Amsterdam: Elsevier/North-Holland Biomedical Press, 45–63.

Statement of the British Association of Paediatric Surgeons Working Party on the Surgical Management of Children Born with Ambiguous Genitalia (2001). www.baps.org.uk/documents/intersex%20statement.htm (accessed 21 December 2005).

Swapp, G.H., Johnston, J.L.W., Couzin, D.A. (1989) A Fertile Woman with

Non-mosaic Turner's Syndrome: Case Review and Review of the Literature. *British Journal of Obstetrics and Gynaecology* 96: 876–880.

Sybert, V. (undated) *Aortic Dissection and You.* Turner Syndrome Society of the United States, USA. www.turner-syndrome-us.org (accessed 1 May 2004).

Tanna, A. (1999) Ms Sarah Jane Brookes: I Just Want to be Accepted as a Woman. *The Watford Observer* 26 November: 17.

Tecosky-Feldmane, A. (undated) *Turner's Syndrome and Learning Disability.* Turner Syndrome Society of the United States, USA. www.turner-syndrome-us.org (accessed 1 May 2004).

Thangaraj, K., Gupta, N.J., Chakravarty, B., Singh, L. (1998) A 47,XXY Female. *The Lancet* 3: October: 352(9,134): 1,121.

Verp, M.S., Simpson, J.L. (1987) Abnormal Sexual Differentiation and Neoplasia. *Cancer Genetics and Cytogenetics* 25: 191–218.

Warne, G. (1998) Advances and Challenges with Intersex Disorders. *Reproduction, Fertility and Development* 10: 79–85.

Warne, G.L. (undated) *Complete Androgen Insensitivity Syndrome.* Victoria, Australia: Department of Endocrinology and Diabetes, Royal Children's Hospital.

Wayne, J.G., Hellstrom, M.D. (undated) Testosterone Replacement Therapy. *Digital Urology Journal.* www.duj.com/Article/Hellstrom2/Hellstrom2.html (accessed 26 March 2006).

Williamson, S. (1998) The Truth about Women. *New Scientist* 1: 2,145: (August): 34–35.

Wilson, B.E., Reiner, W.G. (1998) Management of Intersex: A Shifting Paradigm. *Journal of Clinical Ethics* 9: 360–369.

Yronwode, A. (1999) Human Rights for Intersexuals: Intersex Individuals Dispute Wisdom of Surgery on Infants. *Synapse – Campus Newspaper of University of California at San Francisco Medical School* (11 March). www.luckymojo.com/tkintersex.html (unpaginated) (accessed 25 July 2004).

Zhou, J.N., Hofman, M.A., Gooren, L.J.G., Swaab, D.F. (1995) A Sex Difference in the Human Brain and its Relation to Transsexuality. *Nature* 378: 68–70.

Zucker, K.J., Bradley, S.J., Hughes, H.E. (1987) Gender Dysphoria in a Child with True Hermaphroditism. *Canadian Journal of Psychiatry* 32: 10: 602–609.

Zucker, K.J., Bradley, S.J., Oliver, G., Blake, J., Fleming, S., Hood, J. (1996) Psychosexual Development of Women with Congenital Adrenal Hyperplasia. *Hormones and Behavior* 30: 300–318.

Zucker, K.J. (2002a) Evaluation of Sex- and Gender-Assignment Decisions in Patients with Physical Intersex Conditions: A Methodological and

Statistical Note. *Journal of Sex and Marital Therapy* 28: 269–274.

Zucker, K.J. (2002b) Mini-Review: Intersexuality and Gender Identity Differentiation. *Journal of Pediatric Adolescent Gynecology* 15: 3–13.

Zucker, K.J. (2004) Self-reported Sexual Arousability in Women with Congenital Adrenal Hyperplasia. *Journal of Sex and Marital Therapy* 30: 5(October/December): 343–355.

Television Drama, Documentary, Film

Dark Secret: XY Women (1996) BBC, BBC2, 29 August.

Footballers' Wives: Series 2, Episode 5 (2003) Shed Productions, ITV1, 5 February.

Gender Trouble (2002) (Director/Producer: Roz Mortimer, Great Britain), Wonderdog Productions in association with the Wellcome Trust.

Heart of the Matter: More Sexes Please (1997) BBC, BBC1, 15 June.

Horizon: The Boy Who Was Turned into a Girl (2000) BBC, BBC2, 7 December.

Secret Intersex: Part 1 and 2 (2004) Wag TV, Channel 4, 5–6 April.

Ted and Alice, Episode 1 (2002) Granada TV, BBC1, 4 April.

Woman's Hour: Intersex Conditions (2001) BBC, BBC Radio 4, 11 December.

Index

DATE DUE